LIVE HIGH ON LOW FAT

Live High
On Low Fat

BY SYLVIA ROSENTHAL

REVISED EDITION

WITH A FOREWORD BY
JEREMIAH STAMLER, M.D.

J. B. Lippincott Company
PHILADELPHIA
& NEW YORK

Copyright © 1962, 1968 by Sylvia Rosenthal
Printed in the United States of America
Library of Congress Catalog Card Number 68-54036

Paperbound: ISBN-0-397-00533-4
Clothbound: ISBN-0-397-00532-6

Fifth Printing

To My Husband

Acknowledgments

IT is with a profound sense of affection and gratitude that I acknowledge the help and encouragement given me by Dr. Norman Jolliffe in this venture. He enriched the lives of all who were privileged to know him, and remained a tower of strength to his friends and colleagues until the last moments of his distinguished and productive career.

As a housewife concerned with my family's well-being, I should like to express my appreciation to the scientists all over the world whose nutritional investigations and clinical research are showing us the way to achieve better health for all.

A word of thanks also to Dr. George J. Christakis, former acting director of the Bureau of Nutrition of New York City's Health Department, and Miss Ethel Maslansky, supervising nutritionist of the Anti-Coronary Club, for their many helpful suggestions.

My sincere appreciation goes to my many friends who, over the years, patiently shared with me the formulae for their kitchen triumphs.

I am especially grateful to Gerry Platt, Annette Tulipan and Mae Fineberg for their interest and faithful assistance with the tedious details of preparing and checking the manuscript.

Contents

We may live without poetry, music and art;
We may live without conscience, and live without heart;
We may live without friends, we may live without books;
But civilized man cannot live without cooks.

He may live without books—what is knowledge but grieving?
He may live without hope—what is hope but deceiving?
He may live without love—what is passion but pining?
But where is the man that can live without dining?

from Lucile, by Owen Meredith

Foreword

By JEREMIAH STAMLER, M.D.

Director, Heart Disease Control Program and Chronic Disease Control Division, Chicago Board of Health; Assistant Professor, Department of Medicine, Northwestern University Medical School

---

This book is a fitting sign of the times. It betokens the urgency of the coronary heart disease problem in the United States today, and the necessity for large-scale efforts to grapple with it.

This book is unique, in that its author is neither nutritionist nor physician. She is an intelligent, gifted woman whose husband, a physician, was stricken by a heart attack. Stimulated by this harsh circumstance, she learned that it may be possible to prevent repeat attacks—and first attacks as well—by dietary means. As this book eloquently testifies, she proceeded to become a past master of the science and fine art required to "Live High on Low Fat." In this labor of love, she had the good fortune to be aided by the late Dr. Norman Jolliffe and his colleagues of the Anti-Coronary Club, New York City Department of Health.

Books like this are urgently needed. Atherosclerotic coronary heart disease is the mid-twentieth-century epidemic afflicting Americans. As everyone knows from personal experience, it strikes down persons in the prime of life, as well as the elderly. The average healthy middle-aged American man—women are much less susceptible—has about one chance in five of developing this disease before age sixty-five, and about one chance in fifteen of dying from it before age sixty-five. Over one third of all deaths in men aged forty-five to fifty-four—a grand total of 36,825 deaths in 1965—are due to this one disease. In

9

about thirty-five per cent of cases, the first attack is acutely fatal within four to six weeks of onset. Many of the deaths occur suddenly; people drop dead. Of those surviving the first attack, twenty to forty per cent (depending upon the circumstances of the acute attack) are destined to die in the next five years, if reliance is placed solely upon the older approaches to treatment.

These few statistics alone are enough to emphasize the need for more effective measures, particularly to achieve primary prevention—that is, the prevention of the disease from ever occurring clinically. A few additional facts further highlight this need. A large group of middle-aged American men—more than twenty per cent in fact—have a very high risk of developing coronary disease in the prime of life, much higher than the average man. These men are susceptible or coronary-prone because of such abnormalities as hypercholesterolemia (a high level of the fatty material, cholesterol, in their blood), high blood pressure, overweight, diabetes, excessive cigaret smoking, sedentary living habits, and other abnormalities. Men with two or more of these abnormalities in combination have a very high risk of premature heart attacks, as high as one chance in two, or two chances in three—or worse. These men, numbering in the millions in the United States today, are particularly in need of timely preventive measures.

Fortunately, it is now possible, thanks to the research successes of recent years, to offer hope in the face of these dire statistics. It is now possible to treat the abnormalities associated with increased risk of atherosclerotic coronary heart disease. They can be corrected in whole or part, and controlled, by modern medical means. This is true for high blood cholesterol, high blood pressure, overweight, diabetes, excessive cigaret smoking, lack of exercise, etc. Therefore, a mood of restrained cautious optimism has become widespread among the expert researchers in this field. It may be possible, as the recent Statement by the American Heart Association emphasized, to prevent heart attacks—and strokes as well.

Modern nutritional science is one cornerstone of this new preventive approach. For it has been shown that high blood cholesterol, overweight and (to a limited degree) high blood pressure and diabetes can be brought under control by dietary means. High blood cholesterol, for example, can be readily lowered at least fifteen to twenty per cent in most cases. And the available statistics warrant the prediction that this change alone might lead to a twenty-five to fifty per cent fall in the rate of heart attacks in middle-aged men. Encouraging data are already available on the salutary effects of controlling overweight, high blood pressure, diabetes and heavy cigaret smoking.

A cardinal consideration is the need for a *permanent change* in habits. Short-lived efforts—the frequent American pattern of going on a diet, and then going off—are futile. A *sustained correction*—for years—of high blood cholesterol, overweight, etc., must be achieved, if anything is to be accomplished in the way of preventing heart attacks.

The dietary approaches required to attain these goals have been worked out in great detail, as this book amply illustrates. In the language of nutrition, they involve diets moderate in total calories, total fats, polyunsaturated fatty acids, monounsaturated fatty acids and carbohydrates; *low in saturated fatty acids and cholesterol*; and high in all essential nutrients (proteins, amino acids, vitamins, minerals). In terms of foodstuffs this means:

Emphasizing the low-fat dairy products (skim milk, buttermilk, cottage cheese), and de-emphasizing the high-fat (sweet cream, sour cream, ice cream, whipped cream, cheeses, butter).

Emphasizing the lean cuts of meat and poultry, and de-emphasizing the fat cuts, with trimming off fat before cooking, cooking so as to get rid of fat (broiling, rotisserieing, roasting with discarding of drippings, letting stews and soups stand in the refrigerator overnight with skimming off congealed fat); use of vegetable oils in braising meats, etc.; moderation of meat portion size (four to six ounces, not twelve to sixteen!).

Emphasizing fish and sea food; de-emphasizing eggs.

Emphasizing vegetable oils, and de-emphasizing solid table spreads (butter, margarines) and solid shortenings (lard, suet, hydrogenated vegetable fats).

Emphasizing fruit desserts (citrus and non-citrus), and de-emphasizing commercial cakes, pastries, shortcakes, cookies and pies.

Emphasizing green and yellow vegetables and legumes (peas, beans).

Emphasizing moderation in use of starches (potatoes, rice, spaghetti, breads, cereals), carbohydrate-rich spreads (jellies, jams, honey, marmalade), alcoholic beverages.

Mrs. Rosenthal's book spells out in rich detail precisely what this means in terms of day-to-day eating. It should therefore receive a hearty welcome in millions of American homes where a desire exists to take the simple reasonable steps needed to change dietary patterns in an attempt to prevent heart attacks. Anyone scanning the pages and pages of delightful and tempting recipes in *Live High on Low Fat* must be convinced that pleasure lies ahead along this way of good hope for the prevention of heart attacks. Indeed, one of the major merits of this book is its demonstration that one of the pleasures of the good life—the pleasure of good eating—can and should remain with us as we make the effort to end the contemporary epidemic of premature heart attacks.

1

Speaking of Cholesterol . . .

ONCE upon a time, the word "cholesterol" and I shared less than a nodding acquaintance. I had heard it, of course. One can't be a doctor's wife for more than a quarter of a century without some exposure to bits and pieces of scientific jargon and medical terminology. However, it was part of my conversation and thoughts about as often as exotica like schistosomiasis or diverticulosis. I did not, as the psychiatrists say, relate.

Then, one bleak day more than a dozen years ago, my husband suffered a coronary occlusion. A whole new world of words and concepts presented themselves . . . and I began to relate.

Since it is less fascinating to read about other people's illnesses than to talk about our own, I will draw a quick curtain over the coronary episode. Except for one wifely comment: of all the various kinds of patients in the world—good, bad, cooperative and otherwise, sick doctors are in a class by themselves. They are the worst kind. In their defense, though, we must admit that their firsthand knowledge of assorted complications must be of questionable comfort when the symptoms absorbing their attention are their own.

The enforced leisure of the long convalescence gave my favorite cardiac patient plenty of time to visit with his friends and colleagues, and to catch up on his reading in the reams of medical literature that flood doctors' offices and spill over into their homes. Thus it was that "cholesterol," or more accurately, "serum cholesterol level," became as familiar to me as the cracks in the ceiling of our upstairs study.

Just at that time, a series of reports of investigations by scientists from various parts of the world were beginning to trickle into the medical literature. They called attention to an interesting and revealing corollary between diet and the incidence of heart disease. Our national diet in the United States is high in fat—from forty to fifty per cent of total calories—a large part of them from meat and dairy fats. It is also high in cholesterol. Some populations in Asia, Africa and Latin America have barely a third as much fat and cholesterol intake and a correspondingly lower coronary disease rate. Suspect items like tobacco, heredity and environmental factors seemed to play a less important part in the statistics than the character of the fats used in the diet.

As an example, in the last war, the coronary disease mortality in Norway dropped greatly during the German occupation. This was associated not only with the decreased consumption of cholesterol and saturated fats which those stringent times made difficult to obtain, but also with bomb damage to the plants which manufactured the hard or saturated fats.

There were obvious inferences to be drawn from studies done on Japanese living in Japan, Hawaii and California in relation to coronary heart disease. In each case, the death rate of this ethnic group paralleled that of the community in which it lived. The coronary death rate was lowest in Japan, where little dairy fat is consumed, and highest in California, where the usual American dietary, high in saturated fat, prevailed.

This was but a small part of the data which made an impressive case for a change in our cooking routines, although I must confess to a few misgivings about abandoning a recipe file bulging with goodies. On the other hand, how can a roux made with country-fresh butter stand up against such dismal reports as those showing that forty-seven per cent of all American men over thirty-five are killed by heart attacks and strokes, and that in the United States today coronary heart disease has the macabre distinction of being the leading cause of death —if there is the slightest possibility that the ingredients in the roux may be a contributing factor? With my concern selfishly centered on the one cardiac patient whose well-being obscured all else, I resolved to be unimpressed by what Escoffier might have done if he were handed some nonfat milk solids instead of heavy cream. Particularly since Escoffier is dead and we aren't.

Atherosclerosis, or hardening of the arteries, is a disease in which arteries are narrowed and hardened by deposits of minute globules containing a waxy substance called cholesterol which is ingested in the diet and manufactured by the body. When the blood vessels become clogged with deposits of this, the flow of blood to the heart and brain is restricted, resulting in heart attacks and strokes. The best scientific information at this time indicates that among the factors which predispose toward atherosclerosis is a high cholesterol content in the blood.

To attempt to reduce the tremendously complicated disease process of atherosclerosis to a few well-rounded phrases is an impossible task, even for doctors' wives, who are an intrepid lot, medically. Unhampered by formal training and proper degrees, we are walking repositories of a long string of diagnoses and folklore which we can unleash at the drop of a symptom. Whereas our husbands, cautious, inhibited souls that they are, require a history, clinical examination and laboratory tests before hazarding an opinion, we are restrained by no such technicalities. Fortunately, nobody listens to doctors' wives except other doctors' wives, who are automatically safeguarded by the doctors.

Mindful of the failings of the ladies who dwell on the fringes of legitimate medicine and properly humble (for the moment), I will not attempt to distill the physiological principles of serum cholesterol levels in relation to body metabolism and fat intake in twenty-five words or less. This is not a scientific treatise and I am not a scientist. Readers interested in firsthand authoritative studies on this subject are referred to the bibliography at the end of the book.

For us, the cooks, it is enough to know what we are trying to do (reduce intake of cholesterol and saturated fats and increase polyunsaturated fats); why we are doing it (a high ratio of polyunsaturated fats over the saturated generally reduces the blood cholesterol); how to go about it (follow the diet pattern and the recipes).

It has been found that the serum cholesterol level will also be lowered when the cholesterol intake is reduced and the total fat intake is limited to from fifteen to twenty per cent, or less, of the total calories. However, this stringent limitation imposes a considerable hardship and deprivation on a dieter (except for a confirmed vegetarian, perhaps), and thus is less desirable from a practical and realistic standpoint than the method of increasing the polyunsaturated fatty acids over the saturated.

While the concept of introducing polyunsaturated vegetable oils into the diet has recently become popular, the essential consideration for success in using them is not so widely understood. Unless they are used to replace a large portion of the saturated fat, with an accompanying alteration in the diet that will reduce the total fat intake, they cannot bring about the desired effect. Substituting margarine for butter won't do it. Neither will adding an ounce of corn oil daily to an already too-abundant diet. This will result only in the usual consequences of increased caloric intake, similar to those encountered by the misguided soul who discovered he could finish the ten-day reducing diet in six days by eating five meals a day.

Fats are composed of three types of fatty acids, depending upon their chemical composition—the saturated, polyunsaturated, and monounsaturated fatty acids. Saturated fatty acids have the effect of raising the cholesterol level in the blood, the polyunsaturated tend to lower it, and the monounsaturated are neutral in their effect, neither raising nor lowering it to any extent. Olive oil is a good example of this last.

All three types of fatty acids are usually present in any single food, but in varying proportions. For practical purposes, foods containing large amounts of saturated fatty acids are called saturated and those containing large amounts of polyunsaturated acids are referred to as polyunsaturated.

Polyunsaturated fats are usually liquid oils of vegetable origin such as corn, cottonseed, soybean, and safflower (see table, page 306). They contain large quantities of linoleic acid, an essential nutrient that must be supplied by food because the body cannot make it. Fish, grains, and some nuts—particularly walnuts—are high in polyunsaturates.

Saturated fats are usually solid and of animal origin—the fats in meat, whole milk, sour cream, sweet cream, cheeses made from whole milk, butter, solid shortenings such as ordinary margarines, lard, and hydrogenated vegetable shortenings such as Crisco and Spry. Coconut oil and chocolate are also saturated. These are the items we seek to limit.

The process of hydrogenation that converts liquid vegetable oils into a solid state is, unfortunately, a double-edged sword. While this method converts the fat into a creamy solid that looks attractive and keeps well, it also changes the polyunsaturated qualities of the liquid oil into saturated ones, thereby removing it from our orbit.

Cholesterol is a fatlike substance found in all animal products. It is present in considerable quantities in egg yolks, animal organs (liver, brains, sweetbreads, etc.) and in shellfish (see table, page 307). It is not present in foods of plant origin, such as fruits, vegetables, cereal grains, legumes and nuts. However, the cholesterol content of the diet is just one of a number of factors that influence the amount of cholesterol in the blood.

Like most new medical concepts, the dietary theory that forms the basis of this book did not come into popular acceptance at once. It had its disciples and its detractors. But in 1962, the American Heart Association, after many years of scrupulous observation and carefully controlled studies in various parts of the world, issued a statement in relation to it. It declared, in part, "Reduction or control of fat consumption under medical supervision with reasonable substitution of polyunsaturated for saturated fat is recommended as a possible means of preventing atherosclerosis and decreasing the risk of heart attacks and strokes." The statement held out hope that a change of diet might reverse the possibility of recurrences in people who had had one or more arteriosclerotic heart attacks or strokes.

It would be irresponsible oversimplification to suggest that as a result of this diet, one could be assured of the usual fairy-tale ending, "and they lived happily ever after." The human organism is not as simple as that, and the ultimate answer to the complex problem of what causes heart disease has not yet been determined. However, among the factors known to influence incidence of the disease—diet, heredity, heavy cigarette smoking, psychological stress, sedentary living, hormone imbalance—diet is one of the most amenable to control. As long as these imperfect wrappings which cover our immortal souls are the only ones we'll ever be privileged to call our own, I for one am in favor of giving them every advantage that an enlightened medical science has developed.

You may have noticed that the males figure predominantly in most heart studies. The explanation for this may be found in the actuarial tables. For some not too clearly understood reason, the female sex hormones confer a degree of immunity on women up to the time of menopause. After the menopause they gain equality with the males— a Pyrrhic victory, to be sure—and the coronary rate between the sexes becomes the same.

Meanwhile, the battle being fought in the laboratories by dedicated researchers continues. The next decade will surely find many of our questions answered at the same time that new areas of doubt present themselves. And while no one would suggest that the final word on atherosclerosis has yet been written, neither would he deny that our present knowledge gives us good and sufficient justification for control of dietary fats.

Since we are not given the choice of selecting ancestors who could gift us with an inheritance of durable arteries and strong hearts along with substantial trust funds—all approved methods for reaching a rich old age—we must seek for ourselves, to the best of our abilities, a stronghold against the ever-growing threat of premature atherosclerosis. Which we now have reason to believe may be found in the kitchen with the friendly fat family.

"Friendly fat," by the way, is my private name for the polyunsaturated fatty acids. Medical nomenclature has always been remarkably unappealing, being above pandering to the public taste, but really, could anything sound more joyless than "unsaturated fatty acids"? The term grew out of my need for a quick answer to questions about our kitchen practices. I felt that a "no fat" explanation of the dietary was inaccurate, for obvious reasons. "Low fat," while partly descriptive, missed the scope and purpose, and "unsaturated fat" emitted a clinical aroma, hardly appetite-provoking. So "friendly fats" they've been ever since.

We have never considered our friendly fat program in the nature of a "diet." That word, particularly in a population like ours which is never out of earshot of a steady bombardment of nutritional propaganda and Cassandra-like pronouncements of the dire results of overweight (unfortunately substantiated by statistics), has an unpleasant connotation of deprivations, stringencies, omissions. Nothing could be further from the truth in this case. It is a method of cooking that can please the whole family. It can produce fascinating table fare in endless variety. It offers adventures in tastes and textures of food that might previously have been lost, drowned in blobs of whipped cream or some other unmentionable.

There are a few adjustments that the cook will have to make, of course—mostly in her viewpoint. She must be willing to emphasize certain foods and de-emphasize others. People now have the advantages of more knowledge and the availability of many excellent commercial products in which fats have been reduced. Consider the case of butter, for example. When we went off the hard-fat standard in 1956, doing without butter seemed a minor catastrophe. From my experience today, few people have a single qualm about eliminating it from their lives.

Many people mistakenly think that this dietary constitutes a reducing program. This could hardly be so, for fats are fats, with the same caloric values, whether they are manufactured by a cow or from corn. On the other hand, meal planning which consistently avoids the concentrated calories in cream, chocolate, rich desserts, fat meats and the like will automatically serve as a balance wheel to maintain weight at an even level. As Exhibit A, I offer my husband's waistline. The ten pounds he lost during his coronary illness—one of the few fringe benefits of that episode—have stayed lost. A praiseworthy record, in view of his enthusiasm about eating and his rather sedentary routine.

No volume concerned with diet and its effect on health would be complete without emphasis on the importance of keeping the weight within normal limits. With all media of communication constantly barraging the public to "watch its waistline in the interest of longer life and better health" it seems unlikely that there could be anyone still unaware of the dangers of overweight. The statistics peek out at us from practically every popular and medical publication.

Just as it is a rare man or woman who does not know that excessive body weight shortens life expectancy, it would be equally unusual to find someone similarly unacquainted with the concentrated calories lurking in starches, sugars, carbohydrates and fats. For most people who want to reduce, a simple modification of food intake, assiduously adhered to over a period of days, weeks or months, will bring about the desired result. An extensive weight loss should always be under-taken with medical supervision.

This is one situation where information is not enough, however, as evidenced by the oversize doctors one occasionally meets. Knowledge may be Power, but it is no substitute for the firm resolve to lessen food intake that constitutes the only successful weapon for victory over excess poundage.

In his book *Reduce and Stay Reduced*, Dr. Norman Jolliffe fash-ioned a wonderfully descriptive phrase, "empty calories." This sums up the goodies in the candy jar or the sweet nothings that pass for dessert. Lacking vitamins, proteins, minerals, guaranteed not to bring a sparkle to the eye, a glow to the skin, a spring to the step, these "empty calories" can bring a bump to the rump. If only the victims of overweight could decide once and for all that the momentary satis-faction derived from eating "empty calories" is too big a price to pay for the unpleasant consequences of excess weight, both physical and esthetic, they would be on their way to a trim, slim figure.

The friendly fat regime has a great deal to offer the young people in the family also, less from the standpoint of food restriction than the opportunity to educate them to sound habits of nutrition. Pres-ent-day medicine is concerned largely with prevention of disease. By setting the coming generation a better nutritional example and subtly trying to inculcate an awareness of its importance—sometimes con-cepts like this take hold in our young simply by the process of osmosis —we could significantly reduce its chances of developing clinical atherosclerosis.

Many parents make the mistake of forcing milk, meat and eggs on their young people because these foods are proteins. Unfortunately they are also high in saturated fat and cholesterol. The popular ham-burger eaten at the corner lunch counter frequently runs as high as seventy-five per cent of its calories in fat, and not the friendly kind. What most people consider plain cake, cookies and Danish pastry are chock-a-block with saturated fat. Small wonder that so many of our teen-agers are overfed and undernourished, considering the huge amount of "empty calories" in the snacks, sweets and carbonated beverages with which they ply themselves.

I don't believe my family was sharply aware of the moment of departure from our former cooking era with its unlimited use of saturated fats. If some items ceased coming to the table, others equally interesting and eye-appealing took their places. I improvised, adapted, experimented and produced a succession of dishes as varied and flavorful as I knew how.

This, I think, is the solution to the problem of successful meal planning that may be obliged to side-step some previously used ingredients which no longer fit into our eating program. Don't let any of the gaps show! Only a crusty curmudgeon would quibble about the lack of chocolate mousse when the apricot crepes make a flaming appearance. Fortunately, our cooking horizons under the friendly fat regime are practically unlimited.

2

Blueprint for a Prudent Diet

SHOULD any of the many participants and members of the Anti-Coronary Club conducted by the New York City Department of Health suspect that I've been copying from their book of rules, the Prudent Diet Pattern, they would be right. Their list of admonitions, precepts, foods allowable, and those forbidden, has provided the framework for our dietary. My contribution consists of translating these do's and don'ts into kitchen procedures, made practicable with measurements and ingredients.

Those not familiar with the Anti-Coronary Club, officially known as the Diet and Coronary Heart Disease Study, might be interested to learn something of its history and purpose. Planned as a research program to study the effect of the relationship between diet and coronary heart disease, it has been in operation since 1957 as a special project of New York City's dynamic Health Department. Dr. Norman Jolliffe, the distinguished authority on nutrition who was director of the Bureau of Nutrition at that time, was chiefly responsible for the study project.

His pioneer work in this area is being carried on by Dr. Seymour H. Rinzler, director of the Bureau of Nutrition. Since the inception of the study, 1,242 men aged 40 to 59 enlisted, but only those free of prior evidence of clinical heart disease were accepted. A team of doctors, nurses and nutritionists meet with the volunteers for a regular follow-up that includes blood tests to determine serum cholesterol levels. The men are pledged and willing to follow the Prudent Diet. In 1959 there was established a control group of volunteers who remained on their usual diet. The purpose was for comparison with the experimental group regarding serum cholesterol changes and incidence of coronary heart disease.

The 1967 findings on this study show that the Prudent Diet significantly lowered and sustained a drop in serum cholesterol levels when compared with the control group. More important, the experimental group with the lowered serum cholesterol experienced a significantly decreased incidence of coronary heart disease—about one-third less—when compared with the control group.

Recommended Foods

The Prudent Diet recommends the use of adequate amounts of protein at each meal in the form of cottage-type cheese, fat-free milk, chicken, turkey, egg whites, well-trimmed meats, legumes, and fish in all forms—fresh, canned, pickled, frozen, dried, or smoked.

Fish is high in polyunsaturates and may be eaten three times a day. Sea food is low in fat but high in cholesterol, which limits its use to not more than twice a month. Liver and other organs may be eaten once every three weeks, and veal and chicken four times a week. Young broilers, preferably skinned, may be used whenever the spirit or appetite moves.

Meats

Beef, pork, lamb and mutton are a different story. This whole family is restricted to a total maximum of four meals a week, with portions not to exceed four to six ounces. Plan your seven main courses at the beginning of each week to avoid being caught short with only a steak in your freezer when you've already reached your full quota with the pot roast you had for two meals, the leg of lamb and the pork loin. Taking a bird's-eye view of the week's rations is a simple procedure to which you can easily become accustomed. There is still a world of lovely choices for the main course, even if they don't revolve around twelve-ounce Delmonico steaks. In the chapter on meats you will find cooking techniques designed to eliminate as much of the fat from meat as is possible.

Eggs

Until such time as chickens learn to lay eggs with smaller yolks, the limit is four eggs a week for adults, and four to seven for children. The egg whites are pure protein, and you may have as much as you wish, but oh! the perfidious yolk.

The egg yolk prices itself out of our dietary reach because of the large amounts of *both* cholesterol and saturated fat it contains. It can claim the dubious honor of being higher in cholesterol than almost any other item of food, except brains. The daily two-egg breakfast is surely not for households which are interested in maintaining a lowered blood cholesterol level.

People with a deep and abiding passion for eggs will still be able to include a poached, boiled or fried egg a few times a week. However, to stay within the limit of four, they must take into account the fractions of eggs they eat in baked and cooked foods. While one portion of a two-egg layer cake may represent only a quarter or a fifth of an egg, these small segments have a way of adding up.

Powdered Egg White

Even though I have no sympathy with the unfriendly qualities of egg yolks, it does trouble my frugal soul to keep chucking them out. The answer to this dilemma is powdered egg white, which, when dissolved in water, performs the same as fresh egg white. The powder will last for years if kept in an airtight container in a cool dry place, away from moisture.

To put into solution, use 2 teaspoons of the egg white powder to 2 tablespoons of lukewarm water and allow to dissolve. This will take an hour or so and there isn't much you can do about it. Since the dissolving is such a slow business, I generally keep a container of egg white in solution in the refrigerator. It will keep for about a week, or as long as the fresh. Two tablespoons of the mixture are the equivalent of one egg white.

If there are any lumps in the solution when you're ready to whip it, rub them through a wire strainer. For maximum volume in the meringue, allow the solution to come to room temperature before whipping.

Powdered egg white is difficult to come by for retail users, since it is distributed to commercial baking concerns who probably buy it by the ton or hogshead. However, the following concern will accommodate private users like us with a pound, the equivalent of twelve dozen eggs. As an added attraction I'm told that the powdered egg white is sterilized—which is more than the chickens do for it. The cost is $2.50 a pound. Mail orders will be filled by:

Henningsen Foods, Inc.
2 Corporate Park Drive
White Plains, New York 10604

Substituting for Egg Yolks

Very often two egg whites may be used in place of one whole egg in baking and cooking. The white has about the same coating, binding and leavening properties as the yolk, but lacking the fat, flavor and some of the thickening properties of the yolk, it will not always satisfactorily substitute for it. Much depends on the function of the yolk in the recipe and no general rule for its substitution can be given that will assure good results. It is necessary to experiment with individual recipes to judge.

If you have been in the habit of baking cakes that use six or more eggs, abandon them. You can make excellent cakes with one or two eggs, as you will see.

Yolk-thickened sauces should likewise be abandoned, in favor of the cream sauces on page 208. These sauces may also be made with cornstarch—same method, same ingredients, but half as much cornstarch as flour is used.

Milk

Whole milk is permitted for coffee only. Otherwise, restrict milk to the nonfat varieties, such as fresh skim milk or the nonfat milk solids, fat-free buttermilk, or evaporated skim milk. Since the important vitamins, minerals and proteins are contained in the nonfat portions of the milk, you are giving up mainly the butterfat, which is high on the priority list of Good Things for Adults to Give Up. It would be well for teen-agers to limit their consumption of whole milk to two cups a day and confine the amounts over that to skim milk or fat-free buttermilk.

Since most of the commercial buttermilk we buy is artificially cultured, check with your dairy to find out if it is made with skim milk or whole milk. The dairy which supplies our buttermilk assured me that it was free of butterfat, and recently I noted it comes in a newly designed container which blazons the Fat Free in large blue letters. I assume there must have been a spate of similar inquiries.

The nonfat milk solids, or powdered skim milk, is a wonderfully satisfactory product. A box of it on your pantry shelf affords all the convenience of a lactating cow in your back yard, with none of the responsibilities. I use it almost exclusively in baking and cooking, for desserts, toppings and breading; and, well chilled, for drinking (see Vegetable-oil milk, page 313). When I liquefy the powdered skim milk, I generally fortify it with additional powder to give it more body. This is particularly effective for sauces, cream soups, custards, and breading meats or croquettes.

If your family is not enthusiastic about drinking milk, use more of it in cooking. They'll probably welcome it in the form of puddings, cream sauces and soups.

Skim Milk May Be Substituted for whole milk in any recipe, in the same proportions. Where a richer or creamier product is desired (sauces, soups, puddings), add 2 tablespoons of the nonfat milk solids to 1 cup of skim milk. Standard proportions for reconstituting the powder are ⅓ cup to ⅞ cup of water for one cup of skim milk.

Skim milk can be used in place of cream in almost all recipes. You may also use undiluted evaporated skim milk or the cream formula (page 313).

Whipped topping made from nonfat milk solids (page 274) may be substituted in the same amount for whipped cream in chiffon pies or frozen puddings.

Vegetable Oils and Table Spreads

The importance of vegetable oil in a diet dedicated to lowering serum cholesterol is frequently misunderstood or ignored. Disregard of the vegetable oil requirement is often a main reason for failure to obtain adequate serum cholesterol reduction. It is necessary for the cook to follow directions both for reducing hard fat and for using vegetable oil in planning and preparing the food.

Where an intensive course of weight reduction is not in progress, the daily requirement for liquid oil is 1½ ounces (3 tablespoons). It may be used in cooking, seasoning, and in salad dressings. People on a weight reduction program are advised to include 1 tablespoon of oil in their daily diet. Among the predominantly polyunsaturated vegetable oils are cottonseed, corn, soybean, or safflower. Safflower is the most highly unsaturated of all oils (see table, page 306).

In discussing the use of liquid vegetable oils, I find myself sounding like a television commercial. But there you are—the oils are easy to measure, require no creaming, are inexpensive, do not change the flavor of the foods, and give excellent results. But these are all bonuses, for it is essential to the success of a cholesterol reducing diet that liquid oils be included.

There are now a number of special margarines that can fulfill the housewife's need for a shortening and table spread. The new soft margarines, particularly, contain substantially higher levels of polyunsaturated fatty acids. However, no margarine can contain as much of the essential fatty acids as are present in liquid oil, which is why we cannot substitute one for the other. The process of hydrogenation, which converts the oil into a solid, also reduces the linoleic fatty acid content. Linoleic acid is one of the most prevalent polyunsaturated fatty acids in food fats and most valuable in lowering blood cholesterol. Do not be misled by the fact that a margarine is made from 100 per cent corn, soybean, or safflower oil. The statement may be true, but it is also meaningless.

Among the acceptable margarines are Chiffon, Fleischmann's, Mazola, and Saffola (see table, page 307). The diet or "imitation" margarines satisfy a need for a low-calorie table spread.

Adapting Your Own Recipes

In cooking, the liquid oils may be substituted in any recipe which calls for melted shortening, in lesser quantity than that required for the hard shortenings. If you have been in the habit of using a lightly salted butter, you might want to make up for the saltless quality of the oil by adding additional salt, but this is a matter of taste.

Standard baking recipes which call for hard fats will not give as good results when liquid oils are substituted. Use only recipes which have been designed for liquid shortening, unless you wish to experiment a bit with the balance of the other ingredients to achieve your usual results.

Use the following table as a guide to the amount of oil required to substitute for melted hard fats in cooking:

Melted Hard Fats	Oil
1 tablespoon	1 tablespoon
2 tablespoons	1½ tablespoons
¼ cup (4 tablespoons)	3 tablespoons
⅛ pound	3 tablespoons
⅓ cup	4 tablespoons
½ cup (¼ pound)	6 tablespoons
¾ cup	½ cup plus 2 tablespoons
1 cup	⅔ cup plus 1 tablespoon
2 cups (1 pound)	1½ cups

Cheese

The story of cheese for us low-fat dieters can be summed up in two words—cottage cheese. There are some ramifications, of course, but the high butterfat content of most cheeses, ranging from ten up to fifty per cent of total calories, serves as its own explanation.

Cottage cheese is made from skim milk and is an eminently desirable food, high in protein, low in fat and worthy of the overworked adjectives "delicious" and "nutritious." It can be used generously in our dietary, starting the day as a spread for the breakfast toast, and finishing as a salad accompaniment at dinner.

The dry-curd or uncreamed cottage cheese is better for our purposes than the creamed variety. If you have difficulty in obtaining this, you can treat the creamed cottage cheese by placing it in a colander and allowing cold water to run through it. This will wash away the cream which has been added. You may then "recream" it with skim milk and perhaps add the bit of salt which has also vanished in the washing process. Whenever cottage cheese is called for in the recipes that follow, it is always the dry-curd variety.

Farmer cheese is simply pressed cottage cheese and is an excellent substitute for cream cheese in canapés and sandwiches. (About four per cent of the total calories in farmer cheese are butterfat, whereas cream cheese may run as high as fifty per cent.) It can be mashed and softened with skim milk to make it creamier and easily spreadable. Hoop cheese is a completely skim milk pressed cheese which is, unfortunately, not widely available. It made an appearance for a time in our neighborhood stores, and then disappeared, in spite of my protestations. If you are able to get it in your area, by all means make its acquaintance.

For those who must have hard cheese occasionally, a dispensation is possible if they are willing to exchange half their beef, pork or lamb allowance for one ounce of cheese, or the entire serving of meat for two ounces of cheese. For a graphic picture of how much constitutes an ounce, consider the half-pound packages of sliced cheeses which contain eight one-ounce slices.

The cheeses made "partially from skim milk" must be viewed with skepticism, since we have no way of knowing how much is "partially." Some of these part skim milk cheeses have been laboratory tested for butterfat, and the results in many cases showed little, if any, difference between them and the regular cheeses. Unless you have more information than the "partly skim milk" stamped on the rind, these cheeses must be restricted with all the others.

For au gratin dishes and melted cheese toppings, we may use a Switzerland import called sapsago cheese. It is a combination of a skim milk cheese mixed with herbs and is suitable only for grating. It is available already grated and in a small, thimble-shaped cube form. It must be kept under refrigeration and should be allowed to come to room temperature before you grate it. For four or six servings, I sometimes combine the grated sapsago with a tablespoon or two of grated Parmesan for stronger flavor. In such dilution, the additional fat is negligible. The grocery department at B. Altman's, Fifth Avenue at Thirty-fourth Street, New York City, and Cheese Unlimited, Inc., 1263 Lexington Avenue, New York City, generally carry it. For information about where to obtain it in your area, write to the distributor, Otto Roth & Company, Inc., 177-179 Duane Street, New York 13, N.Y.

Out-of-Bounds

Actually, very little is forbidden in the Prudent Diet Pattern, as you can see. Certain foods are limited as to quantity, but the large choice of acceptable ones amply compensates.

The red flag with FORBIDDEN unequivocally waves over the following, however: butter, ordinary margarines and shortenings, lard, sweet cream, sour cream and ice cream, cream cheese, hard or dessert cheeses, and food containing any of these items in large quantities, such as commercially prepared cakes and pastries. Chocolate and coconut are both highly saturated and must be avoided.

The prohibition on commercial bakery pioducts does present a deprivation for some families, but where the housewife is willing to do her own baking, this is no problem. The assortment of breads, cakes, yeast doughs, and pastries that can come out of our kitchens can be a gratifying experience, giving satisfaction to the creator, to say nothing of the pleasure they bring to the people who eat them.

Of the prepared cake mixes, only the angel cake mix fulfills our requirements. A glance at the list of ingredients on the boxes will tell you why. The presence of butterfat, whole milk, hydrogenated shortening, is clearly indicated on all packaged foods, so please, please READ THE LABELS, including the fine print. I cannot stress too strongly the importance of this. For example, one of the whipped-cream substitutes in the markets heralds the news that it contains no milk or milk products. When you read further, you will see that it contains hydrogenated oil, which translates into saturated fat and will not do as well for our purposes as either skim milk whipped to stiff peaks or a meringue made of egg whites. The time you take for a careful glance at the information on the package will be well spent.

There have also appeared in the markets recently a number of coffee cream substitutes which make much of the fact that they are free of butter fat and contain only vegetable oil. Further investigation revealed the truth of this except that, unfortunately, the vegetable oil turned out to be coconut oil. Scarcely a friendly fat. If you are not sure of the composition of any product, do take the time to write to the manufacturer.

Planning the Family's Meals

The general outline for the family's meals must be based on its essential nutritional needs:

1. A source of protein at each meal, with emphasis on poultry and fish. Vegetable proteins found in dried peas, beans, nuts, potatoes and grain products can augment the proteins from animal sources—meat, fish, eggs and milk.
2. Four or more servings of vegetables, fruits and fruit juices a day. This includes citrus fruits, tomatoes, cabbage, strawberries, cantaloupe, and a dark green or yellow vegetable, such as broccoli, kale, spinach, pumpkin, sweet potato. Include potato and a variety of other vegetables for additional vitamins and minerals.
3. A pint of skim milk for adults and two to four cups for children, part of which may be used in cooking, or in the form of buttermilk made from skim milk. Skim milk cottage cheese often.
4. Whole grain and enriched breads ar'd cereals.

Cooking fats, sweets and nuts may be added according to the total calorie allowance.

Dining Out

This diet pattern presents no difficulties in restaurant dining. The most limited menu will offer acceptable choices—fish or vegetable dishes ordered without butter or cream sauces, sandwiches such as chicken, turkey, tuna fish, etc., clear soups or salads (the commercial mayonnaise is acceptable), fruits and gelatine desserts.

Speaking of restaurants reminds me that my husband wanted to be sure I mentioned the "lunch business," which apparently he considers as great a boon to ailing man as antibiotics. In order to carry out his doctor's order for a noontime rest period when he first returned to work after his coronary bout, we hit upon the expedient of his taking lunch from home. (What did you *think* doctors carried in their little black bags?)

In this way he avoided the midday restaurant rush, was assured a purely unsaturated sandwich, and found time for rest and meditation. The noontime siestas are a long-gone memory, but the sandwiches linger on. A number of our friends have instituted the same practice, for which their wives may or may not thank me, depending on how they feel about making a sandwich first thing in the morning.

To leave ourselves a margin for error and an unguarded, mad moment with, perhaps a miniature pizza at somebody's cocktail party, I keep our saturated fat consumption at home under even the minimum suggested by the Prudent Diet. After all, it is possible to control what happens in our own kitchens, whereas on the outside we may be victims of circumstance, to use a lame excuse.

We bypass most pork products and all beef so marbled with fat it cannot be trimmed. This includes rib roast beef. Goose, of course, is too unfriendly to merit a moment's thought. The presence of these foods at dinner parties need not be disconcerting, however. Angels with flaming swords are not likely to appear if you perform your guestly duties by eating. It would be worse, I think, to embarrass your hostess and yourself with a pointed refusal. Take small portions, no seconds, and leave the visible fat on your plate.

Hostesses generally don't mind substituting a simple fruit for a rich dessert. We have on occasion ended a dinner with a repeat of the fruit cup that began it. In these allergy-conscious days, I notice more and more hostesses asking about food preferences when they extend dinner invitations. I am never loath to suggest chicken, butterless vegetables, and anything for dessert as long as it's fruit.

Let us remember that success with this diet does not depend on following any one rule, such as "no cream" or "no butter" or "cooking with corn oil." Rather, it depends on the realization that both animal fat and vegetable oil must be controlled. Removing all visible fat from meat will not negate the effects of a richly marbled piece of meat, although it will help. The effect of frequently eaten overlarge servings of meat will not be counteracted by vegetable oil or special margarines. Close attention to the choice and preparation of foods will not insure complete success if the prescribed oil in the diet is neglected.

To sum up briefly, a diet that effectively lowers serum cholesterol contains all the usual food products. In addition to ordinary breads, cereals, fruits, vegetables, and fat-free beverages, there should be two servings a day of lean meat, poultry, or fish, with beef or lamb not exceeding four times a week. Polyunsaturated vegetable oils such as corn, cottonseed, soybean and safflower should replace hard fats in cooking. Special margarines may be used for table spreads. Up to four egg yolks a week are permitted. There is ample choice of food with few things prohibited.

This dietary or cooking program should not be considered as an interlude or a temporary expedient, later to be replaced by former habits of hard fats, cream, and the like. You may find, as we have, that your tastes have changed so that you couldn't go back to them if you would. It becomes a way of life, a permanent approach to the art of cooking and healthful eating. In our house, we have found the physical benefits and psychological satisfactions rewarding indeed.

3

The Battle of the Bulge

A slender and restricted diet is always dangerous in chronic diseases, and also in acute diseases, where it is not requisite. And again, a
diet brought to the extreme point of attenua-
tion is dangerous; and repletion, when in the
extreme, is also dangerous.*

THE last two lines of the above quotation might have been
borrowed from the Metropolitan Life Insurance Company's statement based on actuarial tables warning against the dangers of overweight. Actually, it was written by Hippocrates, the father of
medicine, who lived between 460 and 370 B.C.

This may remind us that there is nothing new about the concept
of dieting. It appears to have been receiving attention for the last
twenty-five hundred years, give or take a few centuries, although not
with the same obsessive interest it is accorded today.

As far as the ancient Greeks were concerned, my guess is that they
had an easier time of it than we do. For one thing, their togas were
kinder to bulges than our present fashions. And they weren't constantly being seduced by supermarkets with their diabolically be-
guiling food displays, by the wistful emptiness of their home freezer
compartments, by the honeyed tones of television announcers stim-
ulating their gastric juices with the lure of the Utopia awaiting them
with their first bite into the chocolate-marshmallow-coconut-triple-

* From *Source Book of Medical History*, compiled by Logan Clendening. New
York City: Dover Publications, Inc.

rich candy bar, and lastly, by the mechanics of television watching itself.

Of all the crimes of which television has been accused, including causing eyestrain and juvenile delinquency, perhaps the most valid is its contribution to the widespread (this is known as a descriptive adjective) overweight which prevails among teen-agers and adults. The incessant nibbling that so often accompanies the viewing can turn an hour-long program into a dangerous health hazard. However, blaming the television industry for self-inflicted paunches and jowls is neither a constructive approach nor a solution to the problem if it exists in our homes.

I claim no authority in the field of dieting except that born out of firsthand experience for lo, these many years. I have intimate knowledge of all the ruses used to duck the stringencies of self-denial, since at one time or another, I have availed myself of them: the artful dodge ("I'll start next Monday"); the rationalization ("I need the food energy"); the excuse ("My face gets haggard"); the self-delusion ("The cleaner shrunk the dress"); and the downright deceit ("I really don't eat much"). With all the righteous zeal of a reformed criminal, I now take a dim view of such proceedings.

Naturally, the first line of defense in the struggle against excess poundage is situated where the assault usually begins—at the dining table. Since we housewives are generally the persons responsible for meal planning and preparation, it falls to our lot to translate the usual weight-losing allowance of twelve hundred calories for women or sixteen hundred for men into as attractive fare as possible. It may be just as well that this job is relegated to the ladies, since statistics indicate less overweight among them than the men.

One of the obstacles to overcome in a restricted diet is an appearance of meagerness about a meal. This causes many people, particularly men, to feel put upon and deprived. Serve the meals with a full complement of courses that makes them look complete. Clear soups, vegetable juices, bulky salads dressed with lemon juice, generous portions of low-calorie vegetables to make up for limited portions of meat and starches; and for desserts, interesting arrangements of fresh fruit in preference to the more caloric canned varieties, impart a sense of lavishness not reflected in the total calories. If the main-course portions are a bit smaller than they used to be, serve them on a luncheon-size plate instead of the large dinner size so they won't look quite so frugal.

Acquaint yourself with calorie tables. Consider that 4 ounces of unsweetened pineapple juice is about 60 calories and a like amount of tomato juice is 25; 2 ounces of dry white wine is 45 and the same amount of scotch is 150; an average serving of apple pie is 375 and a small raw apple is 75. The inference is obvious.

Save a calorie wherever you can in your food preparation. Boiling, broiling, poaching, stewing and baking are preferable to frying in fat at a time when even the friendly fats are restricted, to expedite weight loss. The coated utensils such as Teflon, which require no grease, are satisfactory. Skip the thickenings in gravies. Stew fruits without sugar. Most grocery stores today stock a large variety of low-calorie, low-fat canned goods. Tuna fish and sardines are both available water-packed. Saccharin may be helpful to the reducer. It is inexpensive and safe in reasonable amounts. A ¼ grain tablet is equivalent in sweetening to about 1 teaspoonful of sugar.

An accurate bathroom scale is a must for a weight-watching family. Clothes may shrink or stretch, and waistlines fluctuate during the course of a day, but the arrow on the scale inexorably points to the truth. Weighing once or twice a week at the same time of day and under the same conditions can encourage a conscientious dieter, or mutely reprimand a miscreant.

I think the very real hardship that a restricted diet inflicts on some people is beyond the understanding of those who have small appetites or are uninterested in food. The doctors and nutritionists who come into contact with vast numbers of would-be and should-be dieters are softly sympathetic with these sufferers from medically imposed hunger. They are also aware that unless a person has great motivation and determination, he needs more than just a printed diet slip along with an encouraging slap on the back and a parting admonition.

He needs the help and encouragement of his family in addition to an understanding of himself. He must know whether the small piece of cake at which he's casting sheep's eyes will satisfy his "sweet hunger" or whether eating it will set off a chain reaction that will make him want to devour everything in sight.

Dieters should try to avoid coming to their dinner table in a ravenous state. A small cup of bouillon or coffee, or a few ounces of tomato juice with some celery stalks or carrot sticks, eaten half an hour before dinner, can take the edge off a hunger that might otherwise drive caution to the winds.

Provision must also be made for the evening hours (with or without TV) when idleness, boredom and frustration combine to produce a state of being hungry-in-the-head that drives wanderers in the direction of the refrigerator looking for something to do. They find it, too. This moment of madness during the quiet hours can keep a lass or laddie bulging at the seams forever. Those chronically addicted to the habit might find it helpful if they would save their dessert from dinner to eat at the time of night when food resistance is low.

Eating one's meals in low gear, waltz time, or however you would describe a slow tempo, is also helpful. Small bites, much chewing and lots of conversation between bites can save hundreds of calories each day. I've noticed that people who eat very slowly are rarely overweight.

No matter how helpful a family tries to be, the burden of a successful weight-reducing regime must rest with the dieter himself. No amount of cajoling, pampering, weighed and measured menus offered at home can atone for eating excesses indulged in at lunchtime or when no one is looking. The best we can do (outside of applying a muzzle and chaining the culprit to the bedpost—a procedure generally frowned upon) is to continue to provide proper meals, refrain from nagging, and pray that the light will dawn before it is too late. Sometimes it does.

Once the felicitous state of normal weight has been achieved, eternal vigilance must be the watchword. One eye on your scale, and the other on your conscience. This is not as formidable as it sounds because all habits, whether good or bad, become automatic after a while, and sound nutritional practices are no exception. Happily, our friendly fat dietary with its avoidance of the concentrated calories in dairy products and large meat portions is a great force for good in maintaining proper weight.

You may have to experiment a bit before you find the perfect formula for eating that keeps the pounds from creeping up. Perhaps it will be something as simple as avoiding bread and rolls at dinner, or limiting cake and pie desserts. In our own case, we have found that the cleaner never shrinks our clothes as long as we avoid eating between meals. With the exception of some fresh fruit or a drink, our rule is Never. It is with not the slightest sense of deprivation that we watch our friends guzzling blinis, hamburgers or cherry cheesecake at an after-theatre restaurant, because they won't be any happier in half an hour whether they ate it or not, and they'll probably hate themselves in the morning.

Crash diets, the widely publicized nine-hundred-calorie liquid formula, and appetite-depressant drugs are presently enjoying a great vogue. While they have their advantages in certain situations, medical men are profoundly concerned with their ineffectiveness in establishing sound eating habits that will maintain weight at a healthful level. None of these will take the place of self-discipline. And self-discipline doesn't come in bottles. Unfortunately.

4

Weight Tables *

DESIRABLE WEIGHTS FOR WOMEN AGED 25 AND OVER

Weight in Pounds According to Frame (in Indoor Clothing)

HEIGHT (with shoes on) 2-inch heels Feet Inches	SMALL FRAME	MEDIUM FRAME	LARGE FRAME
4 10	92– 98	96–107	104–119
4 11	94–101	98–110	106–122
5 0	96–104	101–113	109–125
5 1	99–107	104–116	112–128
5 2	102–110	107–119	115–131
5 3	105–113	110–122	118–134
5 4	108–116	113–126	121–138
5 5	111–119	116–130	125–142
5 6	114–123	120–135	129–146
5 7	118–127	124–139	133–150
5 8	122–131	128–143	137–154
5 9	126–135	132–147	141–158
5 10	130–140	136–151	145–163
5 11	134–144	140–155	149–168
6 0	138–148	144–159	153–173

For girls between 18 and 25, subtract 1 pound for each year under 25.

* Courtesy of Metropolitan Life Insurance Company

DESIRABLE WEIGHTS FOR MEN AGED 25 AND OVER

Weight in Pounds According to Frame (in Indoor Clothing)

HEIGHT (with shoes on) 1-inch heels		SMALL FRAME	MEDIUM FRAME	LARGE FRAME
Feet	Inches			
5	2	112–120	118–129	126–141
5	3	115–123	121–133	129–144
5	4	118–126	124–136	132–148
5	5	121–129	127–139	135–152
5	6	124–133	130–143	138–156
5	7	128–137	134–147	142–161
5	8	132–141	138–152	147–166
5	9	136–145	142–156	151–170
5	10	140–150	146–160	155–174
5	11	144–154	150–165	159–179
6	0	148–158	154–170	164–184
6	1	152–162	158–175	168–189
6	2	156–167	162–180	173–194
6	3	160–171	167–185	178–199
6	4	164–175	172–190	182–204

The approximate number of calories required to maintain weight may be calculated by multiplying the "ideal weight," as it appears above, by the following numbers:

Adults leading sedentary lives should multiply their ideal weight by 15.

Adults indulging in moderate physical activity should multiply their ideal weight by 17.

Adults whose work involves strenuous physical activity and fast-growing teen-agers should multiply their ideal weight by 20.

5

Seasonings

I DON'T believe that good cooks are born and not made. Not today, anyway. This may have been true years back, before the days of oven regulators, measuring cups and tested recipes, when a direction like "Add as much flour as you feel you need" really depended on how well you were feeling.

Bea Johnson (our gift from Heaven via Virginia a quarter of a century ago) is a graduate of the "feeling" school of cooking. "How much flour did you use?" I ask her. "That much," she says, throwing a mound of it into a bowl. I measured the amount a few times. Each time it came out *exactly* one cup. I couldn't duplicate that feat if my future depended on it. Bea is another story, however, and it is not for the likes of her that cookbook publishers stay in business. She never used a recipe or a measure in her life. She just copies the pictures.

For the rest of us simple mortals who come unequipped with built-in kitchen scales, I believe that cooking skills can be acquired, given an ability to read, willingness to make an effort, an adventuresome spirit—in the kitchen, that is—and some functioning taste buds. This last is of vital importance. Family preferences in degree of seasonings vary, and foods themselves are variable—some lemons are sourer than others, for example. No recipe can be all things to all people, and only the cook can determine if it's the soupçon of sugar or the dollop of spice or the extra sprinkling of salt that is needed to make the dish just right for her family. Taste while you're cooking, after you've seasoned, and just before serving. It won't make you fat. I promise. Chubby cooks got that way from eating, not tasting.

The condiment shelves of grocery markets and department stores offer a wide variety of salts and seasonings that will add interest and piquancy to your food. Lawry's seasoned salt and Beau Monde seasoning made by Spice Island are two of my favorites. From soups to stews, few dishes in our house get by without a dash of one or the other. You might experiment with some of the seasoned salts and the seasoned peppers now available until you find one to your liking.

I also recommend to your attention the G. Washington and MBT broth powders which I use extensively in place of water or stock. I find them less salty than bouillon cubes and they dissolve easily. The MBT chicken broth powder is particularly flavorful and the amount of fat it contains is so small as to be negligible. These powders sprinkled on uncooked poultry in place of salt provide excellent seasoning.

A reasonable facsimile of butter taste can be given foods, particularly sauces and baked goods, with Imitation Butter Flavoring. If it is not available in your markets, write to Durkee Famous Foods, 900 Union Commerce Building, Cleveland 14, Ohio, for information on where you can get it.

A little thought, effort and small expense will supply your pantry with adequate first-aid for ailing dishes. Often just a bit of meat glaze (Bovril, B-V), a teaspoon of Worcestershire sauce or Kitchen Bouquet, a pinch of dry mustard or a quarter-teaspoon of an herb are all you need to rescue a sauce from undistinguished mediocrity. With proper supplies on hand, observe the cardinal rule of good cookery: "Taste, judge and correct."

6

Breakfast

BASED on a modest and informal survey of breakfast habits (conducted one Saturday night at a large party), I have come to the conclusion that most people like change and variety in their food, but not when they first get up in the morning. On second thought, I don't know why I should be surprised by this. Judging by ourselves, our breakfasts are entirely predictable with a few minor variations, except for weekend mornings. Maybe we seek the familiar sight of the same old menu to give us the reassurance we need to face the rigors of another day, or perhaps we're not quite up to the unexpected in the first cold glare of the early morning light.

In any event, the reason is not important. Nothing is simpler than to vary a breakfast menu—pancakes instead of toast, waffles instead of pancakes, a whole orange in place of orange juice, Grape-Nuts substituting for oatmeal—and there you have it. The enormous variety of breakfast cereals that line the market shelves surely offer enough choice to please any palate. The essential consideration is that there be a breakfast; that it be adequate to provide enough energy and nourishment to carry through to lunch; that the choice of foods be consistent with the aims of our eating program.

The hastily gulped orange juice and coffee before going off to work, implemented at the ten-o'clock coffee break with a Danish pastry ("empty calories" and saturated fat!) is a poor substitute for a meal that should provide us with the nutrients and energy-producing foods we require. A proper breakfast includes fruit, fresh or stewed, or juice, a protein food such as cereal, cottage cheese, skim milk, and bread or toast plus a hot beverage.

You may still have an occasional ounce of well-cooked Canadian bacon with the occasional egg if you will remember to include it in the planning of your week's meat ration.

Pancakes are a simple matter to prepare, and made-in-advance batter keeps splendidly in the refrigerator. There are a number of acceptable ready-mixes for those who prefer to use them, such as Aunt Jemima's pancake mix and Duncan Hines Wild Blueberry mix, to mention just two. Your local stores probably have other brands also. Just be sure to take your bifocals when you market and READ THE LABELS on the boxes. The list of ingredients will tell you exactly what you need to know. If it includes hydrogenated oils, whole milk, butter, etc., replace it on the shelf and look further.

Whenever you bake muffins or scones, try to squirrel away a few for future breakfasts. They keep nicely in plastic bags in the freezer and take only a few minutes to warm up when needed.

Don't let your family be one of the group that saves its breakfast eating for weekends. This habit pays a poor dividend. Make sure that each member of the household starts the day with a well-balanced, nutritionally adequate meal.

French Toast

3 slices day-old bread	dash salt
2 egg whites	⅛ teaspoon cinnamon
2 tablespoons water	2 tablespoons oil
2 tablespoons skim milk	

With a fork, beat together egg whites, skim milk, water, salt and cinnamon. Heat oil in heavy skillet. Dip both sides of bread in egg white mixture and fry on each side until brown and crisp. Serve with jam or jelly, heated maple syrup, honey, or cinnamon and sugar.

Serves 2

Buttermilk Chiffon Pancakes

I make the pancakes quite small—no more than two inches in diameter. Five or six make an adequate portion. It is convenient to keep a jar of the batter without the egg white in the refrigerator. Then you have only to add the beaten egg white and the pancakes are ready to go. The batter keeps very well, and even improves with standing.

1⅓ cups all-purpose flour, sifted
½ teaspoon salt
1 tablespoon sugar
1½ cups skim milk buttermilk

¾ teaspoon soda
¼ cup oil
2 egg whites, stiffly beaten

Heat griddle over a low flame.

Stir soda into buttermilk. Add to sifted flour, sugar and salt, and stir just enough to dissolve flour. Overbeating makes pancakes tough. Stir in oil. Fold in stiffly beaten egg whites.

If a drop of water bounces off the griddle, it is hot enough to begin. Drop batter from tip of a spoon to ungreased griddle and cook until cakes puff up and bubbles begin to break. Turn just once and cook on the other side. Serve with warmed maple syrup or fruit preserves.

Serves 4

Delicious Buttermilk Waffles

Wrap the leftover waffles in aluminum foil or a plastic bag. They freeze beautifully and can be quickly heated in your toaster.

2 cups all-purpose flour
1 teaspoon baking powder
¾ teaspoon salt
2 cups skim milk buttermilk

2 teaspoons baking soda
3 egg whites, stiffly beaten
¼ cup oil

Sift together flour, baking powder and salt. Dissolve the baking soda in buttermilk. Add to flour mixture and mix well. Add oil and beat thoroughly until smooth. Strain into bowl or pitcher through wire strainer. Fold in stiffly beaten egg whites. Using about ½ cup of batter for each waffle, bake in hot waffle iron until golden brown. Serve with heated maple syrup or jam.

Makes 10 to 12 Waffles

Old-Fashioned Johnnycake

We like these also for lunch with creamed chipped beef.

1¼ cups yellow or white
    corn meal
½ teaspoon salt
1 tablespoon sugar

2 cups boiling water
¼ cup skim milk
oil for greasing griddle

Mix corn meal, salt and sugar together. Dribble boiling water over it gradually, stirring the whole time. The corn meal should be thoroughly moistened and thick but not runny, so stop when it reaches this point. Thin mixture with milk. It should be the consistency of thick gruel, so it will drop easily off the tip of a spoon.

Oil griddle and heat until it is sizzling. Drop small mounds of batter and flatten them with a spatula. Cook until brown and crisp, 3 or 4 minutes, turn and brown the other side. Serve hot.

Serves 4

Apple Pancakes

This is also suitable for a light supper or a substantial dessert after a feathery meal.

2 eggs (whole)
1 tablespoon sugar
3 tablespoons flour (heaping)
¼ teaspoon salt
⅓ cup skim milk

4 medium-sized tart apples
3 tablespoons sugar
cinnamon
1½ tablespoons oil
juice of ½ lemon

Preheat oven to 375 degrees.

Pour oil into 8-inch or 9-inch glass pie plate and slide into oven. Beat eggs until light in medium-sized bowl. Use an electric mixer, if you have one. Otherwise, a rotary beater will do. Add sugar, continue beating, and add flour and salt alternately with milk. Make it nice and creamy—you cannot overbeat this.

Slice peeled and cored apples very thin and mix thoroughly into batter. Pour this into the heated pie plate and spread out evenly. Bake for 40 to 45 minutes until the apples are soft. Take a look in the oven after the first 25 minutes—if the top is brown enough, cover with a sheet of aluminum foil.

When the pancake is done, remove from oven, sprinkle with lemon juice and spread liberally with cinnamon and sugar. Serve warm.

Serves 4

Baked Kippered Herring

I always try to keep a few cans of kippers on my pantry shelf. They're excellent for either breakfast or lunch. To heat them, place the can in a large flat skillet with a cover, add water about half the depth of the can, and boil, covered, for twenty minutes. Turn the can after ten minutes. Your kippers will come out of the can heated through and ready to eat.

For a more substantial kipper, get the large smoked ones at your fish store and bake them as follows:

Kippers are apt to be . . . redolent—for want of a more descriptive word—while cooking, but you'll find that wrapping them in aluminum foil helps somewhat (as does an air-freshener in the kitchen).

4 kippers	dash of Tabasco sauce
⅓ cup oil	dash of Worcestershire sauce
juice of ½ lemon	2 tablespoons chopped parsley

Soak kippers for 10 minutes in hot water. Drain well. Preheat oven to 400 degrees. Line baking dish with aluminum foil, leaving plenty of lap so that you can make a tight package. Arrange kippers in the dish, dribble half the oil over them and cover securely with the rest of the foil. Bake for 15 to 20 minutes, until they are completely heated through.

Meanwhile, heat the remaining oil in small saucepan, add Tabasco and Worcestershire sauce to taste, season with lemon juice and add chopped parsley. Remove kippers to a warm platter, pour the hot oil mixture over them and serve.

Serves 4

7

Hors d'Oeuvres, Appetizers

THE business of the hors d'oeuvres and appetizer course is to prickle the appetite and whet the palate, although sometimes its effect is to deaden one and dull the other. Too substantial, too starchy, too sweet or just plain too much can send diners to their main course in a state of narcosis. A sorry state, I might add, after we've been slaving over a hot stove for . . . well, that long.

A bowl of chilled, crisp celery stalks and carrot sticks, some spicy pickled mushrooms, olives, radishes, cherry tomatoes or perhaps some raw cauliflowerets with a garlic cream sauce to dunk them in can hold your most famished guests while they're sipping their drinks.

Happily for us followers of a low-fat regime, the fish and sea food family offer a made-to-order bounty of appetite-provokers. Paper-thin slices of smoked salmon or sturgeon; caviar; all kinds of herring except those in sour cream; tins of tiny smoked oysters, clams or mussels; cold broiled shrimp or lobster chunks with a simple dunk sauce of chili sauce, horse-radish and a squirt of lemon juice or some curried mayonnaise—any of these are guaranteed to keep guests content and unsated while waiting for the main event.

Out of the increasing informality that pervades our entertaining in these do-it-yourself days has emerged the American custom of Dunks and Dips. The day of the tortured sardine wearing a yellow cream-cheese rosette on its nose while lying on a soggy slab of bread has practically passed. Except for unwieldy gatherings so large that the canapés must circulate because the guests can't, or for the occasions when professional kitchen help is brought in, the order of the day seems to be a mound of some good-tasting mixture surrounded by toast or pumpernickel with which the guests can make their own canapés. Skim milk cottage cheese whipped creamy and smooth provides a wonderful base for this. In addition to the recipes for the cottage cheese spreads which follow, you might try improvising some of your own. Chopped smoked oysters, red caviar with a dollop of onion and a squeeze of lemon juice, minced garlic and chives, chopped smoked salmon etc., etc.—each lends its own distinction to the bland and pleasing texture of the whipped cottage cheese.

Cottage Cheese and Clam Spread

1½ cups skim milk cottage cheese
1 7½-ounce can minced clams, drained
½ teaspoon chopped chives

1 teaspoon chopped parsley
½ teaspoon Lawry's seasoned salt
freshly ground pepper
dash garlic powder (optional)

Whip, blend or sieve cheese to make it smooth and fluffy. Add minced clams, parsley, chives, salt, pepper and garlic powder, and mix well. Taste for seasoning. Refrigerate until ready to serve. Garnish with parsley sprigs and dust lightly with paprika. Serve with Melba toast or thin-sliced pumpernickel.

Yields 1¾ cups

Cottage Cheese Savory Spread

1½ cups skim milk cottage cheese
2 tablespoons oil
4 drained anchovy filets
1 tablespoon caraway seeds

1 tablespoon chopped capers
1 tablespoon chopped chives
1 teaspoon paprika
1 teaspoon prepared mustard

Whip cottage cheese until smooth and fluffy. Add oil and mix until completely blended. Mash anchovies and work into cheese. Add caraway seeds, capers, chives, paprika and mustard. Chill in small bowl until ready to serve. Unmold and garnish with parsley and slices of pimento-stuffed olives. Serve with Melba toast, crackers or thin pumpernickel.

Yields 1¾ cups

Stuffed Celery

This is a pleasing way of using any seasoned cottage cheese mixture.

2 large ribs Pascal celery
2 tablespoons seasoned cottage cheese mixture
pimento strip

Choose ribs of celery that match in size. Wash and dry them well. Stuff each stalk with cottage cheese mixture and fit them together to form a tube. Wrap tightly in waxed paper and refrigerate for two or three hours. When ready to serve, unwrap and slice in ½-inch slices. To serve lay circles flat. Garnish with a small cube of pimento in the center of each circle.

Garbanzo (Chick Pea) Dip

This is equally good as a dip for raw vegetables, a spread for cocktail crackers, or to add variety to a first-course antipasto.

1 1-pound 4-ounce can chick peas
¼ cup oil
½ teaspoon sesame seeds
½ teaspoon salt
freshly ground pepper
1 large clove garlic, minced
2 tablespoons lemon juice

Drain chick peas thoroughly. Whir in blender with oil, sesame seeds, salt, pepper, garlic and lemon juice until smooth and creamy. Chill in refrigerator. Serve in small bowl surrounded by celery and carrot sticks, or cocktail crackers.

Yields 1½ cups

Codfish Antipasto

This snowy white mound has an interesting and unusual flavor.

½ pound salt codfish
½ cup oil
½ cup (scant) skim milk
1 clove garlic, minced
2 teaspoons parsley, finely chopped
freshly ground pepper
¼ teaspoon basil
1 tablespoon lemon juice

Soak salt codfish overnight, changing the water a few times. Drain, cover with cold water, and slowly bring to a boil. Cook for 5 minutes and drain. If you have a blender, you can use it for the next operation. If not, grind fish through food grinder twice, and then mash it in wooden bowl with heavy fork or pestle. Add oil and milk alternately, a little at a time, working them in well. When completely mixed, add garlic, parsley, pepper, basil and lemon juice. Beat until fluffy. Place in small round bowl and refrigerate for 2 hours. Unmold on round plate, surround it with Melba toast or pumpernickel bread. Garnish with a few sprigs of parsley or watercress and serve.

Serves 4 to 6

Chopped Chicken Liver Pâté

I grew up in a household where chicken livers were chopped by hand in a wooden bowl. My mother would have been aghast at the suggestion of any mechanical device as a substitute for the clop-clop of the hand chopper as it struck against the hardwood bowl, pulverizing the chicken livers along the way. But then our Bea Johnson came along, up from the South, where she had never heard of the tradition of chopped liver, and was consequently free from the shackles of the folklore surrounding it. She puts the stuff through a food grinder and, if my memory serves me right, it's every bit as good as my mother's.

½ pound chicken livers
2 hard-boiled eggs
2 medium or 3 small onions, sliced
3 tablespoons oil

freshly ground pepper
½ teaspoon salt
1 tablespoon (or more) mayonnaise
paprika

In a heavy skillet with a cover, heat oil, add onions and cook until transparent. Add chicken livers and cook, turning frequently, until brown. Cover pan and cook over low heat for another 10 minutes, or until no blood runs out when pricked with a fork.

Grind livers, onion and hard-boiled eggs through food grinder. Add salt, pepper, paprika and enough mayonnaise to bind it together. The pâté will be quite loose at this point, but a few hours in the refrigerator will take care of that. Pack in small bowl and refrigerate. When ready to serve, unmold in the center of a round platter. Garnish with parsley, a dusting of paprika and a few slices of stuffed olives. Surround with thinly sliced pumpernickel, Melba toast or crackers.

Serves 8

Cocktail Nibbles

5 tablespoons oil
4 teaspoons Worcestershire sauce
1 teaspoon Lawry's seasoned salt
⅜ teaspoon garlic powder or onion powder (both optional)

1 cup walnut halves
2 cups each of:
   Wheat Chex
   Rice Chex
   Corn Chex

Heat oven to 250 degrees. In a large flat pan—I find a jelly-roll pan works very well—heat oil with Worcestershire sauce and seasonings over low flame. Add cereals and nuts and mix until all pieces are coated with the oil. Place in oven for 1 hour, stirring every 15 minutes. Spread on brown paper or absorbent towels to cool. Store in airtight containers.

These tidbits are convenient to have on your pantry shelf for unexpected callers.

Caponata
(Eggplant Appetizer)

This flavorful Italian antipasto, piled in a bowl flanked by crackers or Melba toast so that your guests can make their own hors d'oeuvres, is a splendid cocktail accompaniment. Or it may be served cold or hot as a first course, at the table.

1 medium-sized eggplant
6 tablespoons oil
1 clove garlic, minced
1 onion, coarsely chopped
4 tablespoons tomato sauce
½ cup celery, chopped
½ green pepper, diced

2 tablespoons capers
12 large stuffed green olives, sliced
2 tablespoons wine vinegar
1 tablespoon sugar
salt and freshly ground pepper to taste

Peel eggplant and cut into slices half an inch thick. Cut slices into half-inch cubes. In a large heavy skillet, heat 5 tablespoons of oil and sauté eggplant until brown. Remove eggplant with slotted spoon and set aside. Add the remaining tablespoon of oil and add minced garlic and chopped onion. Cook until golden.

Add tomato sauce, chopped celery and diced green pepper and simmer, covered, for 15 to 20 minutes, or until celery and pepper are tender. Add a little water if the sauce cooks down. Return eggplant to the skillet, and add capers and sliced olives. Heat vinegar and sugar together and add to eggplant. Add salt and pepper to taste. Simmer the mixture 15 minutes longer, stirring frequently so it doesn't stick.

Garnish with lemon wedges. If serving cold, place caponata on a bed of lettuce. This will keep well in the refrigerator in screwtop jars.

Serves 6 to 8

Smoked Salmon Canapés

A platter of these cold canapés is fixed quickly and easily and is standard equipment at our parties. I never like to serve the hot hors d'oeuvres until all the guests have arrived—and since many of our friends are doctors with unpredictable arrival hours, we keep the prompt guests from the brink of starvation with these.

4 slices thin pumpernickel
¼ pound farmer or hoop cheese
½ teaspoon white horse-radish
¼ pound smoked salmon, thinly sliced

lemon juice
2 black olives, sliced into crescents
chopped parsley

We prefer the Nova Scotia smoked salmon. It's bland and delicate, but you may like the saltier variety—purely a matter of taste.

Spread each slice of bread with farmer or hoop cheese mixed with horse-radish. (If the cheese seems too stiff, soften with a little skim milk and mix well to make it creamy.) Cover with slices of smoked salmon. Cut each slice into quarters. Sprinkle with lemon juice and garnish with a crescent of black olive and a sprinkling of chopped parsley.

Makes 16 canapés

Shrimp Canapés

jar of tiny cocktail shrimp
toast rounds

tartare sauce (see page 206)
garlic powder

Add garlic powder according to taste to the tartare sauce. Spread toast rounds with a layer of the seasoned tartare sauce and carefully place 3 or 4 tiny shrimp on top in a pleasing pattern.

Asparagus Rolled Sandwich

This hot cocktail bit is a great favorite. Apparently, few people recognize that it's just plain bread that forms the outer crust, since I'm so often asked for the recipe for it. A boneless and skinless sardine may be substituted for the asparagus.

10 slices thin white bread	1 tablespoon chili sauce
10 all-green small asparagus tips	pinch dry mustard
¼ pound farmer or hoop cheese	1 teaspoon Worcestershire sauce
½ teaspoon white horse-radish	1 teaspoon chopped parsley
oil for frying rolls	

In a small bowl, mash farmer or hoop cheese. If it seems a little dry—they vary in consistency—add a bit of skim milk, but don't make it watery. Add horse-radish, chili sauce, mustard, Worcestershire sauce and parsley, mixing well to make it smooth and fluffy.

Remove crusts from firm, thin white bread (like Arnold's) and roll out with rolling pin, making slices as flat as possible. Spread slices with the cheese mixture. Place an asparagus tip (cut the same length as the bread) along an outer edge. Roll up and press closed firmly—the cheese will make the end of the bread adhere. Roll in waxed paper and refrigerate until ready to fry.

Heat ¼ inch of oil in skillet over low flame. Fry just a few of the rolls at a time, so you can rotate them in the oil and brown them evenly. They cook quickly—3 or 4 minutes. As they are done, remove with slotted spoon and drain on absorbent paper. Add more oil as needed. Keep finished rolls warm in slow oven. Cut in half and serve.

Yields 20 rolls

Crab Meat Puffs

These are deceptively simple, delicious and impressive. You can make the puffs the day before you use them. Fill them later and pop them into the oven to warm as your company settles down with their before-dinner drink.

¼ cup oil	½ cup flour
½ cup boiling water	2 eggs
½ teaspoon salt	

Preheat oven to 375 degrees.

In a medium-sized saucepan, heat water and oil to the boiling point. Add salt and flour all at once, and stir vigorously until the flour is absorbed and mixture leaves sides of pan. Remove from fire and add unbeaten eggs, one at a time, beating vigorously after the addition of each egg. The mixture will become spongy and shiny and, with a little prodding from the beating spoon, form into a mound, leaving the sides of the pan.

Lightly oil flat cookie tin. Drop mounds of batter by the half teaspoonful about 1 inch apart. Make them as round as you can and keep them small. This amount should yield about 3½ dozen puffs. Bake in 375-degree oven for 30 minutes. Take one from oven for a test: if it does not fall, consider them done. When cool, cut open on one side near the top, and fill with crab meat mixture. Just before serving, heat in 350-degree oven for 5 or 6 minutes.

Crab Meat Filling

1 cup crab meat	¼ teaspoon dry mustard
2 tablespoons mayonnaise	1 tablespoon chopped parsley
1 tablespoon Worcestershire sauce	

Pick over crab meat and remove shells. Mix mayonnaise with the Worcestershire sauce, dry mustard, and chopped parsley. Add crab meat to mayonnaise. Taste for seasoning. Fill puffs with mixture and refrigerate until ready for use.

Variations: These puffs may also be filled with finely diced chicken which has been seasoned with mayonnaise and a spot of curry powder; finely chopped shrimp or lobster in place of the crab meat; or the chopped chicken liver pâté.

Hot Sardine Canapés

Half this recipe will do as a family first course with tomato juice.

2 3¾-ounce cans boneless and skinless sardines
1 teaspoon lemon juice
1 tablespoon mayonnaise
few drops of Tabasco sauce
¼ teaspoon dry mustard
freshly ground pepper
4 slices white bread
paprika
2 tablespoons oil

Remove crusts from bread and cut each slice in thirds. Heat oil in skillet and lightly brown both sides of bread oblongs. Drain on absorbent paper.

Mash sardines and moisten with mayonnaise. Add lemon juice, Tabasco sauce, dry mustard and pepper. Spread on toasted bread, dust with paprika and place in 350-degree oven for 6 to 8 minutes, or until the sardine mixture is heated through.

Makes 12 canapés

Broiled Artichoke Hearts

can of artichoke hearts
4 tablespoons oil
2 teaspoons lemon juice
½ teaspoon salt
freshly ground pepper
1 small clove garlic, minced
Lawry's seasoned salt
1 tablespoon sesame seeds
Melba toast rounds

Use water-packed artichoke hearts for this—not oil-packed. Wash and thoroughly drain the artichoke hearts and slice in half. Place each half, cut side up, on a toast round. Combine oil, lemon juice, salt, pepper and minced garlic and mix well. Pour this generously over artichokes, getting it into the crevices. Dust lightly with Lawry's seasoned salt. Sprinkle with sesame seeds. Bake for 10 minutes in 350-degree oven or until heated through. Place under broiler for a few minutes to brown the tops lightly.

Broiled Mushrooms Arturo

12 large mushrooms
½ teaspoon salt
freshly ground pepper
Lawry's seasoned salt
dash garlic powder

⅔ cup corn flake crumbs
⅓ cup almonds, coarsely chopped
2 tablespoons oil
2 teaspoons lemon juice

The mushrooms must be really large for this—the small or medium-sized ones have a way of shriveling up and disappearing and won't mean anything. Remove stems, wash well and wipe dry. Place caps, stem side up, in shallow baking pan. Sprinkle with salts, pepper, and garlic powder. Fill caps with coarsely chopped nuts and top with corn flake crumbs. Combine oil and lemon juice and mix well. Make a small depression in the middle of crumbs and carefully dribble in ⅔ teaspoon of oil mixture. Bake for 10 minutes in 350-degree oven and put under broiler for a few minutes to brown tops lightly.

Yields 12

Hot Clam Meringues

Simply superb and superbly simple. I usually put the ingredients together early in the day and add the beaten egg white at the last minute.

½ cup minced clams, well drained
1½ tablespoons mayonnaise
1 tablespoon bread crumbs
¼ teaspoon salt
⅛ teaspoon dry mustard

½ teaspoon minced green onions
    or chives (dried)
½ teaspoon horse-radish
1 egg white, stiffly beaten

Mix together minced clams, mayonnaise, bread crumbs, salt, mustard, dried green onions or chives and horse-radish. Taste and correct seasoning. Fold in stiffly beaten egg white. Mound on tiny squares of Melba toast (page 236). Place under broiler for 3 or 4 minutes, or until tops are nicely browned and puffy. Serve hot.

Makes 20 meringues

Scampi

Scampi are the Italian variety of the crustacean which we know as shrimp, generally prepared in a highly seasoned sauce. They make an excellent hot hors d'oeuvre or appetizer course that can be served in the living room. They are quickly and easily prepared and half an hour or more in the chafing dish before they're eaten won't hurt them a bit.

2 to 3 pounds large shrimp, uncooked
½ teaspoon Lawry's seasoned salt
freshly ground pepper
½ cup flour
1 cup oil

½ teaspoon salt
3 large cloves garlic, minced
1 teaspoon oregano
1 teaspoon dried basil
1 tablespoon minced parsley

Wash the shrimp. Remove shells, leaving tails, and devein. Pat dry with paper towels. Combine flour with Lawry's seasoned salt and pepper. Dredge shrimp with the seasoned flour lightly—we don't want a heavy coating of flour on them.

Place oil in large, heavy skillet. Add salt, minced garlic, oregano, basil and parsley and heat over low flame. I am not at all subtle about the garlic in this preparation. If the three cloves are a bit small, I might very well add another with a few dashes of garlic powder for good measure. Everyone seems to like these very garlic-y, but you taste it and decide for yourself.

When the oil is hot (3 to 4 minutes), add floured shrimp, as many as will make a single layer in the skillet. If you crowd them they won't cook properly. Cook them only until they turn pink—2 to 3 minutes on each side. When done, remove with slotted spoon, and continue until all are cooked. Place in chafing dish or casserole with a candle warmer, and pour a little of the seasoned oil in which they were cooked over them. Use small plates and forks for serving—they are too moist for finger food.

Serves 6 to 10

FRUITS AND FRUIT AND VEGETABLE JUICES

Fruits and juices serve admirably as an appetizer course. My only reservation, and this could be a personal thing, has to do with sweetened fruits and juices which have a tendency to sate the palate rather than tantalize it. For this reason, we save a fruit mélange for the close of dinner in preference to having it at the beginning. A half grapefruit, skillfully dissected between the membranes so you don't have to battle it with a dull teaspoon, is a fine start for a meal. For variety, you might like to dribble a bit of sherry over it, tuck a fresh strawberry in the center and brown it under the broiler. A slice of melon with a segment of fresh lime or lemon, or some assorted tiny melon balls in your prettiest compote dishes, will get your meal off to a good beginning.

Most fruit juices combine well with others. Unsweetened grapefruit juice mixed with pineapple, apricot or cranberry makes a refreshing drink. Experiment with a few mixtures of your own for variety. Chilled V-8 or tomato juice are prime favorites. We prefer the tomato juices which come from California. They are distinguished by a richness of texture and flavor that, in our opinion, make them superior to many others. The S & W and Sacramento are two California brands with which I am familiar; your grocer can probably tell you about others.

In addition to fruits and juices, here are some appetizer ideas which we like:

Oyster Cocktail

It would be sacrilege to embellish fresh, delicious oysters with anything except lemon juice and a dash of black pepper. Serve them on the half-shell on a bed of crushed ice. Figure six oysters, if they are decent size, to the portion.

Avocado-Shrimp Cocktail

1 pound shrimp
1 small avocado
watercress

1 teaspoon chopped chives
½ cup Russian dressing or garlic
    cream dressing (pages 205–6)

Boil shrimp according to recipe on page 149. Shell and devein. Scoop tiny balls out of avocado with your smallest-size scoop. Mix chopped chives with dressing and combine with shrimp and avocado balls. Chill in refrigerator for 2 hours. Serve in sherbet glasses or on your prettiest glass plates. Garnish with watercress.

Serves 4

Herring Salad

1 cup herring, diced
⅔ cup cooked beets, diced
1 cup raw apple, peeled, diced
¼ cup cucumber pickle, diced
⅔ cup cooked potato, diced
3 tablespoons vinegar
1 tablespoon sherry

freshly ground pepper
1 tablespoon sugar
1 tablespoon (or more)
    mayonnaise
white of hard-boiled egg and
    parsley for garnish

You may use either regular salt filet of herring, or a jar of herring tidbits in wine sauce, drained. The latter will make it less sharp. Dice herring, beets, apple, pickle and potato in quarter-inch cubes and mix together. Add seasonings, vinegar, sherry and mayonnaise and toss lightly. Taste to correct seasoning. Chill at least two hours in the refrigerator.

Serve on individual plates on crisp lettuce. Sprinkle with white of hard-boiled egg rubbed through a sieve and garnish with parsley. Accompany with thinly sliced pumpernickel.

Serves 4

Italian Antipasto

This can be served on a single large round platter and passed, but I prefer to arrange individual plates, thus ensuring fair and equal distribution.

1 7-ounce can tuna fish
1 tablespoon mayonnaise
1 teaspoon capers
2 tomatoes, thinly sliced
French dressing
¼ teaspoon basil
1 teaspoon chopped chives
8 sardines
artichoke hearts

4 celery hearts, split
4 halves sweet pimento
4 green olives
4 black olives
2 hard-boiled eggs
2 anchovy filets
3 tablespoons skim milk cottage cheese

Marinate thinly sliced tomatoes and artichoke hearts in French dressing, separately. Split hard-boiled eggs lengthwise and discard yolks. Mash anchovy filets into a paste and blend smoothly with whipped cottage cheese. Fill egg whites with this mixture and cut into quarters.

Place a quarter of a can of drained tuna fish, decorated with a dab of mayonnaise and a few capers, in the middle of each plate you will use for this appetizer course. Arrange around this in rows radiating from the center, the marinated tomatoes sprinkled with chives and basil, 2 sardines, celery hearts, pimento half, artichoke hearts, green and black olives, and two quarters of hard-boiled egg. Serve with thin Italian breadsticks.

Serves 4

Asparagus Appetizer

1 can small green asparagus
6 large choice tomato slices
½ cup French dressing
6 stuffed olives

½ teaspoon sweet basil (dried)
½ teaspoon oregano
watercress

Use 3 or 4 asparagus tips for each tomato slice. Trim asparagus the same size as tomato slices. Marinate tips in French dressing and let chill in refrigerator for an hour or so. When ready to serve, place a slice of tomato on each plate, sprinkle with basil and oregano, cover with asparagus tips and decorate with slices of stuffed olive. Garnish with watercress.

Serves 6

Salmon Cornucopias

6 slices smoked salmon
½ cup mayonnaise
1 tablespoon prepared horse-radish
    (or more, depending on taste)
freshly ground pepper

¼ teaspoon dry mustard
6 thin lemon slices
12 small asparagus tips
1 tablespoon chopped parsley

Combine mayonnaise, horse-radish, pepper and dry mustard. If you are using the less salty smoked salmon (Nova Scotia), you may want to add a bit of salt. The strength of the horse-radish is variable, so use your own judgment as to whether or not you need more.

Spread a heaping tablespoon of this mixture on each salmon slice and roll into a cornucopia shape. Place each cornucopia on a slice of lemon on individual plates. Arrange 2 asparagus tips in the open end of each cornucopia. Sprinkle with chopped parsley and chill well. Serve with thinly sliced pumpernickel bread.

Serves 6

Crab l'Aiglon

1 pound crab meat
6 scallions, chopped fine
1 small clove garlic, minced
1 small green pepper, chopped
4 tablespoons oil
½ cup white wine

½ teaspoon tarragon
½ teaspoon salt
white pepper
2 tablespoons chopped parsley
¼ cup brandy

Pick over crab meat carefully and set aside. In medium-sized skillet, heat oil. Sauté scallions, garlic and green pepper until scallions are golden, but do not brown. Add crab meat, wine, tarragon, salt and pepper and heat through thoroughly. All of this may be done in the chafing dish, or you may transfer it from the kitchen skillet at this point. Add parsley. Warm brandy, ignite it, and pour it over crab meat mixture. Serve on toast triangles when the flame dies out.

Serves 6

Crab Imperial

This well-seasoned crab, served in shells or the little ovenproof glass crab dishes, is simple enough to prepare for your family, even on a busy day—and elegant enough for guests.

1 pound fresh lump crab meat
½ teaspoon dry mustard
½ teaspoon salt
¼ teaspoon white pepper
1 teaspoon Worcestershire sauce

1 tablespoon fresh chopped dill
(or ½ teaspoon dill seed, but the first is better)
1 tablespoon chopped parsley
6 tablespoons mayonnaise

Pick over crab meat and remove any bits of shells. Mix together mustard, salt, pepper, Worcestershire sauce, dill and parsley with the mayonnaise. Toss crab meat lightly in this sauce. Pile into 4 or 5 crab shells or ramekins. Spread top with an additional thin layer of mayonnaise. Bake in 375-degree oven for 20 or 25 minutes, or until browned. Serve hot.

Serves 4 or 5

Coquilles St. Jacques

These may be baked in either shells or ramekins—the first preferred.

1½ pounds sea scallops
1 4-ounce can sliced mushrooms
2 tablespoons onion, minced
1 tablespoon oil
6 scallions, chopped
½ cup dry white wine
1 tablespoon parsley, chopped

½ teaspoon salt
¼ teaspoon Lawry's seasoned salt
freshly ground pepper
¼ cup bread crumbs
2 tablespoons grated sapsago cheese

Wash scallops and pat dry on absorbent paper. Cut into 2 or 4 pieces, depending on the size. The pieces should be small—about the size of bay scallops. In a medium-sized skillet, heat oil and cook minced onion until golden brown. Add white wine, scallops, chopped scallions and mushrooms. Bring to a boil over low flame, cover skillet and simmer gently for 6 to 8 minutes or until the scallops have lost their raw look. Add salts, pepper and parsley. Taste and correct seasoning. Divide scallops among the 4 shells. Sprinkle with bread crumbs and grated cheese. Bake for 20 minutes in 375-degree oven and serve piping hot.

Serves 4

Steamed Mussels in Wine Sauce

The comparatively lowly mussel reaches Lucullan heights when steamed in this luscious wine sauce.

3 pounds mussels	1 small clove garlic
½ cup dry white wine	freshly ground pepper
½ cup water	pinch thyme
2 tablespoons chopped parsley	2 tablespoons oil
2 or 3 shallots, chopped	French bread, sliced and toasted
1 small onion, chopped	

Use a stiff brush to scrub mussels thoroughly. Discard any with opened shells. (There always seem to be a goodly number of these, which is why we have to start with what may seem an inordinately large quantity.)

Heat 2 tablespoons of oil in large kettle with cover and brown clove of garlic. Discard garlic and add wine, water, thyme, chopped shallots, onions and pepper. Add mussels, cover pan and cook over brisk heat until the mussel shells open—7 or 8 minutes. Remove top shells from mussels. Place mussels on their half shells in a serving dish and keep warm.

Strain wine sauce through fine strainer and reduce it over high heat for a few minutes. Add chopped parsley. Pour over mussels and serve hot in soup bowls.

Serve the sauce generously. You'll want to drink every delicious drop of it, or sop it up with the hot, toasted French bread.

Serves 4

Cocktail Ribbon Sandwiches

These gay little sandwiches are made by putting together four slices of bread of different hues with various fillings, and slicing each sandwich square thus made into strips. Their professional look belies the small effort involved. Too substantial for a dinner hors d'oeuvre, they're lovely for cocktails or tea, or to add interest to a salad luncheon.

Use firm loaves like Arnold's or Pepperidge in assorted colors—white, rye, whole wheat, brown, etc.

These are some of the fillings we use:

Beat cottage cheese until it is smooth and fluffy and combine with any of these: a clove of minced garlic or a dollop of onion juice or grated onion plus chopped parsley (enough to make it green) and caraway seeds; enough minced smoked salmon to make the cheese pink; finely minced clams, seasoned with a pinch of dry mustard, salt and chopped chives.

Canned salmon, finely mashed and seasoned with mayonnaise, curry powder and lemon juice.

Tuna fish, finely minced, seasoned with lemon juice, mayonnaise and finely chopped green pepper.

Boneless and skinless sardines, mashed with a little oil from the can, lemon juice, dry mustard, Worcestershire sauce and mayonnaise.

Finely minced chicken, made into a paste and moistened with chili sauce and mayonnaise.

You can dream up any number of combinations, vary the tastes, colors and textures. When putting the sandwiches together, try to use a dark filling (like the sardine) on the light bread. Spread the slices that will take the fish mixtures with a little mayonnaise to make the filling adhere. Each sandwich square consists of 4 slices of bread put together with 3 fillings.

Wrap the sandwich squares in a damp towel, cover with waxed paper and refrigerate at least 5 or 6 hours. They will be perfectly fresh even after an overnight stay in the refrigerator.

When ready to serve, unwrap and let stand at room temperature for 20 minutes. With a sharp knife, remove the crusts and slice crosswise into 5 slices. Lay the sandwiches flat on your prettiest sandwich platter. Garnish with parsley sprigs.

8

Soups and Chowders

THE gastronomic virtues of a delicious bowl of soup are only a small part of all it has to offer in our low-fat scheme of things. For an eating program like ours where we wish to keep certain foods at a minimum, soup can do more than please our palates and make us warm on a cold day. It can lessen the need for excessive meat portions and give even a light meal a feeling of completeness.

I would prefer to allow the gustatory pleasures of soup to rest on their own laurels, but I am impelled to make the observation that it has so much to recommend it nutritionally we should serve it often. Cream soups can fulfill part of the one-pint-daily skim milk needs of adults, and as for vegetable soups—consider the additional advantages of serving the vitamin-laden liquid in which the vegetables have cooked, instead of consigning it to the kitchen sink!

We generally save the hearty fish stews and chowders for the leading role at lunch or supper. With some hot scones or muffins, followed by a fruit compote, they perform handsomely. Bouillabaisse is a wonderful main course for dinner and a great favorite for guests. Consommé, meat and vegetable broths, and cream soups do very well as an appetizer course. If you've had any reservations about the quality of cream soups possible within this dietary, I suspect you'll have some pleasant surprises in store.

Buy canned and dehydrated soups with caution, since many of them are made with hydrogenated shortenings and butter. This will include cream soups, but there are many other acceptable ones. The list of ingredients on the wrappers will tell you what you need to know.

Both canned consommé and chicken soup provide excellent bases for more elaborate soups in combination with vegetables and cream sauces. We use lots of both. Considering the ingredients and the time and effort needed to produce homemade consommé, I feel grateful to Mr. Campbell for his. Served hot and undiluted, with a spot of sherry and a thin slice of lemon or avocado floating on top, it makes an agreeable beginning for a meal. I prefer the canned chicken soup to the homemade also, but only because I am not then left with a soup chicken which takes second place to broilers for our purposes. Keeping the chicken broth refrigerated solidifies the blob of fat and makes the skimming simple.

The packaged soup mixtures consisting of a variety of dried peas and beans with mushrooms and barley are easily prepared also. They cook up to a substantial soup which you can vary with the addition of a veal knuckle or meat bone and fresh tomatoes or tomato sauce.

Cold jellied soups can be refreshing on a hot day. Three cups of tomato juice, beef bouillon or chicken broth seasoned to taste with salt, pepper and lemon juice, then mixed with one tablespoon gelatine which has been dissolved in half a cup of the hot liquid, will chill to a soft jelly consistency.

Serve the hot soups *hot*, the cold ones *chilled*, and all of them seasoned to the best of your ability.

Fresh Vegetable Soup

1½ pounds soup meat and bones	1 cup sliced carrots
1 veal knuckle bone	3 cups canned tomatoes
5 cups cold water	½ cup peas
1 tablespoon salt	½ cup cut-up green beans
6 peppercorns	1 cup sliced celery
2 onions, sliced	½ cup rice
1 bay leaf	3 tablespoons chopped parsley

In a large soup kettle, combine soup meat and bones, 5 cups cold water, bay leaf, salt, peppercorns and sliced onion. Cover and simmer slowly for 2 hours. Remove meat and strain. Chill soup stock overnight in refrigerator. The next day, skim fat from stock, return stock to soup kettle and add the remaining ingredients. Simmer 1 hour, or until vegetables are tender. Sprinkle chopped parsley on top of soup. (Leftover soup may be frozen.)

Serves 8 to 10

Minestrone

Minestrone is the generic term for Italian vegetable soup made with beans. Each district in Italy—Lombardy, Tuscany, Liguria, Latium, etc.—has its own variation and each is distinctive in its own way. This recipe is a compilation of a few, adapted with our own dietary aims in view.

The celery, zucchini and carrot may be substituted by, or used in combination with, other vegetables such as 1 pound of fresh peas, 1 cup of string beans, diced turnip, ½ pound sliced mushrooms or 4 or 5 leeks, thinly sliced.

This makes a large quantity of soup, but the leftover freezes very well.

1 cup white beans
1 veal knuckle
1½ tablespoons oil
1 large onion, thinly sliced
1 carrot, diced
2 stalks celery, diced
1 potato, diced
1 zucchini, diced
1 teaspoon parsley, chopped

2 medium-sized tomatoes, diced
3 teaspoons salt
white pepper
1 very small cabbage, thinly sliced
1 clove garlic, minced
½ teaspoon basil
¼ cup uncooked rice
2 tablespoons grated Parmesan
    or sapsago cheese

Soak beans overnight in 1½ quarts of cold water. Drain and place in large soup kettle with 2½ quarts of cold water, 2 teaspoons salt and the veal knuckle. Simmer over low heat, covered, for 1 hour.

In a large skillet, heat oil and cook sliced onion until golden. Add diced carrot, celery, potato, zucchini, tomatoes, chopped parsley, garlic, basil, 1 teaspoon salt, and pepper. Cook together for 5 minutes and add to the soup. Add sliced cabbage and rice and cook slowly for 2 hours or more, covered, until the beans and vegetables are soft. Remove veal bone and correct seasoning.

Just before serving, add grated cheese. Serve hot.

Serves 6 to 8 as a main dish;
10 to 12 as a first course

Cock-a-Leekie Soup

My first reason for making this soup was because of its enchanting name. (It loses some of its magic when translated into chicken and leeks, but no matter.) We have continued to make it because we like it. It is an excellent main course for luncheon or supper. In line with its Scottish origin, we are apt to follow it with some hot scones, fruit preserves and a cup of tea. I suppose a kilt and a bagpipe would also be appropriate.

1 3- to 3½-pound chicken, cut
    in eighths
2½ quarts of water
3 large onions, sliced
1 bay leaf
½ teaspoon marjoram
½ teaspoon ground sage
½ teaspoon ground allspice

1 tablespoon salt
20 whole peppercorns
8 or 10 large leeks
½ cup Uncle Ben's rice
1 10-ounce package frozen baby
    lima beans
1 tablespoon Worcestershire sauce
2 tablespoons chopped parsley

Fill large soup kettle with 2½ quarts of cold water. Add cut-up chicken with onions, bay leaf, marjoram, sage, allspice, salt and peppercorns. Cover kettle and bring to a boil slowly. Simmer until chicken is tender, about 1¼ hours. Discard bay leaf. Remove chicken from soup, cool and refrigerate overnight.

Skim broth thoroughly. Split leeks halfway down the stem and hold under running water to remove all traces of sand. Cut both the green and white portions of leeks into ½-inch lengths and add to chicken broth. Add rice, frozen lima beans and Worcestershire sauce and simmer for ½ hour.

Skin and bone chicken pieces and cut meat into generous bite-size pieces. Add these to soup and taste for seasoning. Serve in large soup bowls. Sprinkle with chopped parsley.

Serves 6

Sweet and Sour Cabbage Soup

This is one of those homely, homey soups I was brought up on. When we serve it to some of the sophisticated palates that occasionally sit at our table, it is greeted with as much enthusiasm as the news of a successful rocket launching.

2 pounds soup meat and bones
  (marrow bones, beef and
  veal)
1 large carrot, sliced
1 onion, coarsely chopped
3 stalks of celery and tops
1 tablespoon salt

freshly ground pepper
1 small head cabbage
½ cup brown sugar
2 cups canned tomatoes, strained
  (No. 1 can)
sour salt crystal (about the size
  of a green pea)

Place meat and bones in large soup kettle and cover with 2 quarts of cold water. Cook slowly to the boiling point and skim. Add onion, celery cut into 2-inch lengths, sliced carrot, salt and pepper. Cook, covered, over low flame for 1½ hours, or until the meat is tender. Strain broth, discarding the meat and vegetables, and refrigerate overnight.

The next day, skim the broth carefully of all fat. Add sour salt, shredded cabbage, brown sugar, and strained tomato pulp. Simmer slowly for 1 hour. Taste and correct seasoning—you may want it a little sweeter, or a little more sour—or perhaps both.

Serves 6 to 8

Lamb and Barley Broth

2 pounds of lean lamb and bones
  (neck of lamb is a convenient
  cut)
1 onion cut in quarters
6 peppercorns
1 teaspoon salt
1 large carrot

3 stalks celery
1 onion, chopped
1 small turnip
3 tablespoons barley
1 teaspoon salt
freshly ground pepper
1 tablespoon chopped parsley

Wipe meat and bones well. Place in kettle with 2 quarts of cold water. Add cut-up onion, peppercorns and salt. Bring to a boil slowly and simmer over low fire for 1 hour. Skim broth a number of times. Let cool. Strain broth and refrigerate, preferably overnight.

Skim fat from broth and return broth to soup kettle. Dice all vegetables and add to broth. Add barley, salt, and pepper. Cook slowly for 1½ hours, covered, or until the vegetables are tender. Taste and correct seasoning. Sprinkle each serving with chopped parsley.

Serves 6

Onion Soup

3 tablespoons oil
4 large onions, very thinly sliced
1 tablespoon flour
3 10½-ounce cans beef consommé
2 teaspoons lemon juice

4 tablespoons sherry (optional)
5 slices toasted French bread
2 tablespoons grated sapsago or Parmesan cheese (See note on cheese, pages 28-30)

Heat oil in heavy skillet and sauté the very thinly sliced onion rings until golden. Blend in flour thoroughly. Add consommé and simmer over low flame for 10 minutes. Add lemon juice and sherry. Taste to see if it needs any seasoning. Sprinkle toasted French bread with grated cheese and place under broiler until cheese is lightly browned. Serve hot with a slice of toast on top of each bowl of soup.

Serves 4 or 5

Clam Broth Consommé

1½ cups clam juice (bottled)
2 cans beef consommé

salt
¼ cup sherry

Combine undiluted consommé with clam juice in large saucepan. Add salt if you need it. Clam juices vary in degree of saltiness and it may be unnecessary to add any seasoning. Simmer for a few minutes over low flame. Just before serving, add sherry and heat through.

Serves 4

Chicken and Mushroom Broth

1 cup mushrooms
⅔ cup water
1 small onion, sliced

2 13½-ounce cans chicken broth
4 tablespoons sherry
1 tablespoon minced parsley

Refrigerate chicken broth and skim when cold.

Wash and clean mushrooms, removing stems. Cook stems and sliced onion in salted water for 15 minutes. Place skimmed chicken broth in saucepan and add mushroom liquid, discarding stems and onion. Add sliced mushroom caps and cook over low flame for 7 or 8 minutes. Add sherry and heat through. Sprinkle some parsley on top of each bowl of soup.

Serves 4

Purée Mongole

In the old days, I used to make this with canned soups and we thought it was very good. So it was—but not nearly as good as this.

A can of crab meat or lobster added to it turns it into an adequate luncheon dish.

1 medium onion, finely chopped	2 cups tomato juice
2 tablespoons oil	5 cups water
1 teaspoon salt	½ cup nonfat milk solids
freshly ground pepper	croutons
1 cup green split peas	

Cover green split peas with water and soak overnight. Drain the following day.

In 3-quart kettle, heat oil and cook onion for 10 minutes, or until limp and golden. Add drained peas, 5 cups of water, 2 cups of tomato juice, salt and pepper. The amount of salt you need depends on the tomato juice, so you'll have to use your own judgment, but don't oversalt. Bring to a boil, reduce heat and let simmer slowly for 45 minutes, or until the peas are soft and mushy. Force through sieve or food mill to purée the peas, return to kettle and add nonfat milk solids. You may thin the soup with some water or consommé if it seems too thick.

To make the croutons, remove crusts from 2 slices of white bread. Cut into ½-inch cubes, brown lightly in oil, drain on absorbent paper and dry out in oven.

Serves 6 to 8

Watercress and Pea Soup

This soup offers a lovely medley of flavors, beginning with the pleasantly astringent and distinctive watercress taste. It may be served either hot or cold, although we prefer the former. This is a must for the blender—no other way to make it.

1 bunch watercress (about 2 cups)
2 cups chicken broth
1 10-ounce package frozen green peas
½ teaspoon salt
freshly ground pepper
dash nutmeg
⅓ cup nonfat milk solids
white of hard-boiled egg

Wash and drain watercress. Strip blossoms from stems, discarding stems. Whir through blender with ½ cup of chicken broth until liquefied. Place frozen green peas in saucepan with ½ cup boiling, salted water and cook for 3 minutes, or until thawed. Whir drained peas through blender with ½ cup of broth. Combine liquefied watercress and pea purée in saucepan, add the remainder of the broth, pepper, nutmeg and nonfat milk solids and heat through. The amount of salt needed depends on the seasoning in the broth, so taste as you go.

Garnish with white of hard-boiled egg, forced through a ricer.

Serves 4

Lentil Soup

1 cup dried lentils
1½ quarts boiling water
1 small can Italian tomato paste
½ cup chopped celery
½ cup onion, chopped
2 carrots, thinly sliced
1 medium potato, cubed
1 tablespoon salt
freshly ground pepper
2 tablespoons oil

Soak lentils overnight in 2 cups of cold water. Transfer to 3-quart kettle. Add boiling water, tomato paste, vegetables, salt and pepper. Cover kettle and cook over low heat for 1 hour, or until lentils are completely soft. Purée through food mill, add oil and reheat. If too thick, you can dilute the soup with either boiling water or stock made with a broth powder. Taste to correct seasoning. Serve with crisp croutons.

Serves 6

Bouillabaisse

This classic French fish stew, like the Italian minestrone, varies with each province, restaurant and home in France. Basically, it is a highly seasoned mélange of fish and sea food in broth served in large soup bowls with more space allotted the fish than the liquid. A steaming bowl of bouillabaisse, some crusty, warm French bread, a mixed green salad and perhaps some fruit make a meal that can add a glow even to a dreary day.

You may use whiting, red snapper, sea bass, cod, haddock—or a combination of some of these.

3 pounds assorted fish, cleaned and boned (reserve heads and bones)
2 lobster tails
1 dozen mussels (in their shells)
½ pound raw shrimp, shelled and deveined
5 tablespoons oil
1 medium carrot, sliced
1 large onion, sliced
2 ripe tomatoes, peeled, seeded and chopped

¼ teaspoon dried thyme
1 bay leaf
1 clove garlic, minced
1 tablespoon parsley, chopped
½ cup dry white wine
⅛ teaspoon saffron
2 tablespoons lemon juice
freshly ground pepper
1 teaspoon salt
dash Tabasco sauce

Wash, shell and devein raw shrimp. Cook shells with heads and bones of fish in 3 cups of cold water for 10 minutes. Drain and reserve stock.

In a heavy soup kettle, heat oil. Add sliced onion, chopped tomato, sliced carrot and garlic and cook until they are soft. Add thyme, bay leaf, saffron, parsley and fish stock. Bring to a boil, reduce heat, and simmer 5 minutes longer. Strain stock and return to soup kettle. (This stock can be prepared in the morning and refrigerated when cooled. The bouillabaisse may then be completed in less than half an hour at dinnertime.)

Cut fish and lobster tails into portion-size pieces. Add fish to simmering stock in kettle and cook slowly for 15 minutes. Add lemon juice, white wine, Tabasco sauce, salt, pepper, raw shrimp, lobster and well-scrubbed mussels and cook, covered, another 6 or 7 minutes, or until the mussels are open. Taste and correct seasoning. Serve fish and sea food with some of the liquid in deep bowls with lots of French bread for dunking.

Serves 6

Fish Chowder

1 pound halibut	½ teaspoon ground allspice
3 pounds filets (sea bass or pike)	½ cup sherry (or more)
2 cups fish stock	2 tablespoons Worcestershire sauce
salt and pepper	juice of lime or lemon
4 potatoes, diced in ½-inch cubes	large Bermuda onion, sliced paper
4 cups canned peeled Italian tomatoes (No. 3 can)	thin (or 6 small yellow onions)

Have your fish man fillet and skin the sea bass or pike, whichever he decides you should use for the chowder, and give you the bones, skin and heads. These you will cook in 3 cups of cold water until it cooks down to 2 cups. Cut halibut and fish filets into 1½-inch pieces. Wash and drain fish, sprinkle with salt and freshly ground pepper and place them on the bottom of large heavy soup kettle. Layer potatoes on fish, then sliced onions—and I hope you get the Bermuda onion for this—it gives a better flavor than the other kind. Pour over it canned tomatoes and the spice. Add the 2 cups of fish stock which has been put through a wire strainer. Simmer slowly, covered, for 2 hours. Add sherry, Worcestershire sauce and juice of lime or lemon.

Mix gently but thoroughly and taste and correct seasoning. Soup's on!

Serves 6 to 8

Smoked Fish Chowder

If you have never eaten fish chowder made with smoked fish—the Down Easters will tell you you've never eaten fish chowder.

1 pound finnan haddie
1 medium-sized onion, chopped
2 tablespoons oil
2 cups fish stock
1 carrot, finely diced
1 stalk celery, finely diced
1 potato, finely diced

1 quart skim milk
white pepper
1 tablespoon flour
dash garlic powder (optional)
1½ tablespoons fresh dill, chopped,
   or 1 teaspoon dried dill
   weed

Wash finnan haddie and cut into sections. Place in large saucepan with 3 cups of cold water and boil for 10 minutes, or until fish flakes easily. Drain fish and reserve liquid. You will need 2 cups of fish stock, so if you have more, boil and reduce. When the fish is cooled, flake and return to the stock. Add diced carrot, celery and potato to fish and stock. Cover pan and simmer slowly for about 20 minutes, or until the vegetables are tender.

In a small skillet, heat oil and sauté onion until it turns golden brown. Add to soup mixture. Add the dash of garlic powder and white pepper. Pour skim milk, reserving ½ cup or so for the flour paste you will make with 1 tablespoon of flour. Add dill and simmer slowly for 10 minutes. Add smooth flour paste, taste for seasoning. Simmer, but do not boil, another 5 minutes. I have omitted any mention of salt, but if the finnan haddie was not too salty, and sometimes it isn't, you may want to add a scant teaspoon or so. Serve hot.

Serves 4 or 5

Quick Clam Chowder

1 10½-ounce can minced clams,
   undrained
1 cup nonfat milk solids
2½ cups water
2 tablespoons oil
1½ teaspoons salt
freshly ground pepper

2 medium-sized potatoes
6 scallions, chopped
2 carrots, grated
1 tablespoon chopped fresh dill,
   or ¾ teaspoon dried dill
   weed
⅓ cup white wine

Pare potatoes, cut into eighths, and cook in very little boiling salted water in covered pot. When done, cut into ½-inch cubes and reserve liquid.

In a 2-quart saucepan, combine nonfat milk solids, 2½ cups water, and minced clams and juice. Add oil, salt, pepper and dill and heat over low flame for 10 minutes. Add potato cubes and water in which they were cooked, grated carrots and chopped scallions and simmer slowly 15 minutes longer. Add wine, heat through and serve.

Serves 4

Borscht (Beet Soup)

In addition to the fact that this Russian beet soup is equally delicious served hot or cold, strained or thick with the vegetables in it, it boasts the distinction of being one of the few pronounceable words around that contains five consonants in consecutive order, beginning with its third letter.

There are as many variations of borscht as Russian folk costumes, but the traditional soup always had cabbage in it.

2 onions, chopped
2 tablespoons oil
6 beets, grated, or 1 1-pound
  can julienne beets, drained
1 cup beet juice
2 tablespoons tomato paste
2 cups cabbage, finely shredded
4 cups beef stock, or 3 10½-
  ounce cans consommé

1 No. 1 can tomatoes
clove of garlic, minced
2 teaspoons lemon juice
1 teaspoon vinegar
1 teaspoon sugar (or more)
2 teaspoons salt

If you are using fresh beets, cook the grated beets in 2 cups of water and reserve the liquid. You will need 1 cup.

In a large soup kettle, heat oil and add chopped onions. Sauté over low flame until limp and golden—about 10 minutes. Add finely shredded cabbage, drained beets and beef stock or consommé. Boil slowly for 15 minutes.

Add tomato paste, tomatoes and minced garlic and cook slowly for 25 minutes. Add beet juice, lemon juice, vinegar and sugar. Simmer for 5 minutes. Add salt and taste to correct seasoning.

Serves 5

Cold Quick Borscht

1 quart prepared beet soup
2 heaping tablespoons cottage cheese
2 teaspoons lemon juice

A blender will make short shrift of this in exactly 2 minutes. If you don't have a blender, beat the cottage cheese with a rotary beater until it is smooth and fluffy. Add half the soup, strained of beets, and beat together until uniformly mixed. Combine with the rest of the soup and blend well. Add lemon juice. Serve chilled.

Serves 4 or 5

Gazpacho

A perfect hot-weather soup of Spanish origin. It is made of raw vegetables and requires no cooking. A blender simplifies the preparation and gives a better result, although it is not an absolute necessity. I venture to say that gazpacho was made in Spain long before Mr. Waring dreamed up his invention.

1 10½-ounce can chicken broth, skimmed of fat
2 small cloves of garlic, minced
2 tablespoons lemon juice
1 slice day-old white or dark bread, crumbled
1 tablespoon oil
1 teaspoon sugar
5 large ripe tomatoes

4 or 5 scallions
1 green pepper
1½ teaspoons salt
freshly ground pepper
1 medium cucumber
2 tablespoons snipped fresh dill, or 1 teaspoon dried dill weed

Blend together oil, lemon juice, minced garlic and dill. Add crumbled bread and beat until fluffy. Peel, seed and cut up tomatoes and green pepper. Cut up scallions and peeled cucumber. (Be cautious with the cucumber: too much can overpower the other flavors in the soup so don't splurge with a great big one.) Purée the vegetables and bread mixture through food mill or blender. Add salt, pepper, sugar, and chicken broth. Taste and correct seasoning. Blend well and chill 4 or 5 hours.

Reserve a tablespoon of the green pepper, scallions and cucumber. Chop them fine and sprinkle on each portion of soup.

Serves 6

Jellied Clam Soup

3 cups jellied madrilene
1½ cups clam juice
2 tablespoons lemon juice
1 tablespoon chopped fresh dill, or ½ teaspoon dried dill weed
1 tablespoon scallions, finely chopped
1 teaspoon grated lemon rind
⅛ teaspoon dried tarragon
½ cup skim milk yogurt
1 tablespoon chopped parsley

Combine jellied madrilene with clam juice, lemon juice, dill, scallions, lemon rind and tarragon. Refrigerate for a few hours, or until well chilled. Before serving, beat in the yogurt with a wire whisk until thoroughly blended. Sprinkle with parsley and serve cold.

Serves 4 to 6

Cream of Potato and Leek Soup

It's only my eternal striving for Truth that keeps me from classifying this as Vichyssoise. The absence of certain nameless ingredients (like a pint and a half of heavy cream) is what makes the difference —but you'll never miss it. This is equally good hot or cold.

4 leeks
1 medium onion, thinly sliced
3 tablespoons oil
3 medium potatoes, peeled and sliced
3 cups chicken broth
2 teaspoons salt
white pepper
2 tablespoons flour
1 quart skim milk
finely chopped chives

Trim off roots of leeks and cut off the top part, leaving about 2½ inches of the green part. Split them to about ⅛ inch from the root end so that you can wash thoroughly. Slice the white and green parts of the leek very finely. In a large heavy pot, heat oil and cook sliced leeks and onion until transparent and beginning to take on a golden color. Add potatoes, chicken broth, salt and pepper. Cover and cook slowly for 40 minutes.

Rub the mixture through a sieve or food mill. Return the puréed mixture to pot. Make a smooth paste with flour and ½ cup of the milk. Add flour mixture and the remainder of the milk to pot and cook for 5 minutes over low flame, stirring constantly. Taste and correct seasoning.

Once more, to be assured of a perfectly smooth, creamy soup, rub the entire mixture through a fine sieve. Keep hot over simmering water. Serve sprinkled with chopped chives.

Serves 6

Cream of Bean Soup

2 cups of navy beans
4 shallots or 2 small onions, chopped
1 teaspoon salt
¼ teaspoon marjoram
½ teaspoon curry powder
3 cups chicken stock (or dissolved broth powders)

2 tablespoons flour
3 tablespoons oil
3 cups water mixed with 1½ cups nonfat milk solids
freshly ground pepper
¼ teaspoon paprika
2 tablespoons chopped chives

Wash beans and soak overnight in cold water to cover. Drain. In a 3-quart kettle, heat chicken stock to the boiling point. Add the drained beans, onions or shallots, salt, curry powder, marjoram, and simmer slowly until the beans are mushy. Add more water if needed. When soft, force the bean mixture through sieve or blend in electric blender until smooth.

In the soup kettle, heat oil and blend in flour. Slowly stir in the 3 cups of skim milk and cook, stirring constantly, until smooth and thickened. Add the bean purée and heat through, but don't allow to boil. Add pepper and paprika and taste for seasoning. Serve hot, sprinkled with chopped chives.

Serves 6

Cream of Broccoli Soup

1 10-ounce package frozen
  broccoli
1 small onion, chopped
3 tablespoons oil
2 tablespoons flour
1 10-ounce can consommé

⅔ cup nonfat milk solids
1½ cups water
1 teaspoon salt
¼ teaspoon Lawry's seasoned salt
¼ teaspoon nutmeg

Steam broccoli until thawed and heated through, about 10 minutes. Cook chopped onion in 1 tablespoon oil until very well browned. Force broccoli and browned onion through food mill and set purée aside.

In a medium-sized saucepan, heat 2 tablespoons of oil. Blend in flour, salts and mix well. Slowly add consommé and stir constantly until thick and smooth. Add nonfat milk solids and water. Bring to a boil, reduce heat and simmer for 3 minutes. Remove from heat. Strain through wire strainer and return to saucepan. Add the broccoli purée to contents of saucepan. Add nutmeg. Taste and correct seasoning. Keep hot over low flame until serving time, but do not boil.

Serves 3

Cream of Carrot Soup

5 or 6 carrots, scraped and thinly
  sliced
4 tablespoons oil
1 teaspoon sugar (or a few drops
  sweetener)
1 teaspoon salt
¼ cup water

1 tablespoon fresh dill, chopped,
  or ½ teaspoon dried dill
  weed
2 tablespoons flour
freshly ground pepper
3½ cups skim milk

In a heavy saucepan, cook thinly sliced carrots with 2 tablespoons oil, dill, ½ teaspoon salt, 1 teaspoon sugar (or equivalent sweetener) and ¼ cup water. Cover pan and cook until the carrots are tender, about 20 minutes. Set aside a few of the carrot slices and dice them as a garnish for the soup.

Place top half of double boiler over direct heat and heat the remaining 2 tablespoons of oil. Blend in flour, stirring until smooth. Add the remaining ½ teaspoon of salt, pepper and slowly add milk, stirring constantly. When the mixture boils and thickens, cook and stir another minute. Place pot over simmering water on medium flame, add the carrots and cook for 45 minutes. Pass the mixture through sieve, food mill, or whir in electric blender. Add the diced carrots, heat, sprinkle with chopped parsley and serve.

Serves 4

Cream of Corn Soup

2 1-pound cans cream-style corn
¼ cup oil
1 medium onion, chopped
3 tablespoons flour
1 teaspoon salt
freshly ground pepper

1½ cups nonfat milk solids
3½ cups water
1 10½-ounce can consommé
dash nutmeg (optional)
3 tablespoons chopped parsley

Purée corn through food mill or buzz in blender.

Heat oil in a 2-quart saucepan, add chopped onion and cook slowly until transparent. Stir in flour, salt, pepper and nutmeg. Add corn and consommé, and mix well. Add water and nonfat milk solids and cook and stir until smooth and thickened. Serve hot, sprinkled with chopped parsley.

Corn Chowder: To convert this into a corn chowder, add 1 can of corn niblets to the completed soup.

Serves 6

Shrimp and Corn Chowder

While my fish dealer's comment that "canned shrimp were invented by people who hate shrimp" may be impelled by personal reasons (he doesn't sell any canned things), I am nevertheless obliged to agree with him. I've never been able to find a thing to do with canned shrimp—except for this agreeable chowder, which can be assembled in a minute and does nicely for a quick lunch or a meager dinner. You'll find that soaking the canned shrimp in ice water for an hour before using will improve the flavor.

1 1-pound can cream-style corn
2 cups chicken consommé
salt and pepper

1 4-ounce can shrimp
1 teaspoon snipped fresh dill
1 teaspoon parsley, chopped

Combine corn and chicken consommé in saucepan and simmer for 5 minutes. Taste for seasoning and add salt and pepper if needed. (This depends on the amount of seasoning in the chicken consommé.) Add deveined shrimp, dill, and parsley, and simmer, but do not boil, for 3 minutes longer. Serve hot.

Serves 4

Cream of Tomato Soup

It wasn't until we had cream of tomato soup made with fresh tomatoes that we really understood what tomato soup was all about. This is no reflection on the canned soups but—to quote the cigarette ad—"You can taste the difference." This may be made with canned tomatoes, but it won't be as good.

4 tablespoons oil	freshly ground pepper
2 onions, sliced	1 14-ounce can chicken broth
4 or 5 large tomatoes (or 2 cups drained canned)	2 tablespoons nonfat milk solids
	2 tablespoons flour
2 teaspoons sugar	6 tablespoons water
½ teaspoon salt	2 tablespoons chopped chives

Refrigerate chicken broth so that the blob of fat can be easily skimmed when you are ready to use it.

Heat 2 of the tablespoons of oil in a large saucepan. Add onions and cook until they are soft and slightly browned. Add cut-up tomatoes, sugar, salt and pepper. Cover and simmer over low flame for 20 minutes. When cool, purée through food mill and set purée aside.

In a small saucepan, heat the remaining 2 tablespoons oil. Blend flour thoroughly over small flame, and add skimmed chicken broth, stirring constantly until the mixture thickens and bubbles. Add nonfat milk solids and the water and cook 3 minutes longer.

Pour the chicken broth mixture through wire strainer and return to saucepan. Just before you're ready to serve, combine the tomato purée with the broth mixture and heat through. If you put them together too early, the soup may curdle. Taste and correct seasoning. Sprinkle with chopped chives.

Serves 4

Mushroom Bisque

½ ounce dried mushrooms,
   ground (equivalent of ½
   cup)
1 pound fresh mushrooms,
   ground
2 cups stock or consommé
1 large onion, ground
3 tablespoons oil
3 tablespoons flour
4 cups fortified skim milk
dash garlic powder (optional)
1 8-ounce can tomato sauce
1½ teaspoons salt
freshly ground pepper
1 tablespoon chopped fresh dill

Wash dried mushrooms well and soak for 1 hour or more. Drain, but reserve 2 tablespoons of the liquid. Put mushrooms and onions through food chopper. In a saucepan, combine chopped mushroom and onion mixture with the 2 cups of stock and the 2 tablespoons of mushroom liquid and simmer slowly for 30 minutes.

Heat the 3 tablespoons of oil in 3-quart kettle. Add fresh mushrooms which have been put through food grinder and cook for 15 minutes, or until brown. Blend in flour, mixing well. Add the 4 cups of milk and tomato sauce. Add the dried mushroom and stock mixture, garlic powder, salt, pepper and chopped dill. Taste and correct seasoning. Simmer slowly for 15 minutes. Serve hot.

Serves 6

9

Meats

MEAT poses one of the biggest problems for a low-fat diet because of the high proportion of saturated fat contained in most cuts. However, a combination of careful selection, proper preparation and SMALL PORTIONS can do much to overcome this.

It is difficult to be specific about the amount of saturated fats in different meats. This varies, depending on the ages of the animals and what they were fed in their barnyard or grazing stages. Since meats don't come equipped with this kind of case history, our safest procedure is to choose the leanest cuts possible, cut off all visible fat, and cook them long and slowly to give the remaining fat ample opportunity to drain off. In the eating, leave all visible fat on the plate where it is guaranteed not to affect our cholesterol level. But even all these precautions cannot eliminate the invisible fat contained within the fiber of the meat itself. It is this which limits the quantity we may safely eat.

Beef stands at the top of the list, not only in degree of popularity among the eating public, but also, unfortunately, in the amount of saturated fat it contains. The prized black Angus can indeed be the "bête noire" of our friendly fat program. Contrary to the usual rule about the best being none too good, less choice cuts from stock less pampered and well-nourished are apt to be better for our purposes. Not for the likes of us are the roast and steak "richly marbled with creamy fat" that food writers drool over, or the cooking method that keeps them in the oven just long enough to remove the chill and char the outside. This may sound like a dismal prospect for rare roast beef, and indeed it is. Since the long and slow cooking will make the roast beef end up like pot roast, you're better off with pot roast to begin with. It's cheaper. We save our roast beef eating for occasions when we're dining out and have no choice. And, just as if I hadn't said this before, we take small portions, no seconds, and leave the visible fat on our plates.

When buying your meats, select the leanest cuts you can find. Your butcher will get accustomed to you after a while and even become co-operative. Mine did. It took some doing but now he knows exactly what I mean by "lean." Don't be afraid that these meats will be dry and stringy when cooked. We'll make them succulent and satisfying with gravies made with a friendly fat base, implemented with wine, herbs, mushrooms, tomatoes and other kitchen magic that won't out-rage your arteries.

For hamburger and meat loaf, choose the leanest round steak your butcher has, and watch him while he trims it—and I mean TRIM—before grinding. This procedure takes hamburger out of the class of budget spreaders, but it also takes it out of the sixty to seventy-five per cent saturated fat items.

Try to make it a rule to prepare pot roasts and stews the day before you use them. By refrigerating them overnight, you can do a really complete job of removing the crusted fat, far better than swooshing any amount of paper towels, lettuce leaves, or egg shells in your bub-bling cauldron. There is an additional advantage, also, in carving roasts when cold. You can cut paper-thin slices which are more eye-filling, and consequently, more satisfying, than a single thickish one. To keep our meat portions within the prescribed four- to six-ounce limit, never hesitate to resort to harmless stratagems which help make a little look like a lot. Stews and ragouts, in which you can stretch limited portions of meat with large portions of vegetables and pastas, are a great help in this direction.

Liver has much to offer nutritionally, but its high cholesterol con-tent restricts its use to once every three weeks. Heart and kidneys are very low in fat but high in cholesterol and should be, also, a once-in-a-while thing. Other animal organs should be avoided.

This is to serve notice that in this book sausages, frankfurters, salami, delicatessen meats and the like will be conspicuous by their absence. It's quite possible that your serum cholesterol level won't go

shooting up like Vesuvius erupting if you succumb to their blandish-
ments once in a while, but on the other hand, with all the wonderful things in the world to eat, why waste time with the less-than-good-
for-you ones? It seems to me that the salamis in delicatessen store
windows glare back at me with the same scorn I feel when I look at
them and their pasty gray fat globules. It's a personal vendetta, and
you might do well to cultivate your own with the whole sausage
family.

You may notice a discrepancy between the four- to six-ounce portions of meat recommended for the prudent dieter, and the amounts
suggested in the recipes. I have taken into account general family
needs—picture serving a male teen-ager four ounces of meat! Consequently, the amounts in relation to the number of portions do not
reflect ideal quantities for adults. Let your good judgment and your
better self be your guide.

Dr. and Mrs. Ancel Keys, in their excellent book *Eat Well and
Keep Well*, make a suggestion which I have found most helpful in
limiting meat portions. They recommend a filling first course such as
a hearty soup, or in the Italian style, some pasta, which will fill up
the diner so that he will be content with only a small amount of meat
in the course that follows. "Make the accompanying items of food as
tasty as possible, offer them in generous amount," they tell us, "and
the meat consumption will decrease."

BEEF

Sweet and Sour Pot Roast

The combination of maple syrup and vinegar may sound weird, but
they blend together beautifully and give the meat a delicate and distinctive flavor. Dumplings are a fine accompaniment for this.

4 to 5 pounds lean pot roast (eye round, top or bottom round)	20 peppercorns
1 teaspoon salt	2 large onions, chopped
1 teaspoon Lawry's seasoned salt	3 tablespoons real maple syrup
½ teaspoon ground allspice	3 tablespoons cider vinegar
1 bay leaf	2 cups consommé
	2 tablespoons flour

88   · LIVE HIGH ON LOW FAT ·

Use your fine artist's eye to remove every bit of fat your butcher missed when he trimmed the roast. Heat heavy stewing kettle or large Dutch oven on top of stove and sear meat on all sides, turning frequently to ensure even browning. When thoroughly seared, remove meat from pot and wipe pot clean of fat with paper towel. Replace meat, add salts, allspice, bay leaf, peppercorns, chopped onions, maple syrup and vinegar, cover pot and simmer slowly for 30 minutes.

Heat 2 cups of consommé or beef stock to the boiling point and add to meat. Cover pot and cook slowly for 3 to 3½ hours or until meat is tender. Refrigerate overnight.

When ready to serve, carve cold meat in thin slices. Skim fat from gravy and place skimmed gravy in large skillet over low flame. Make a paste of 2 tablespoons of flour mixed with ¼ cup of gravy. Add slowly to gravy in skillet, stirring constantly until it thickens and bubbles. Cook a minute longer. Taste and correct seasoning. Place the sliced meat in the hot gravy and heat thoroughly. Remove to warmed platter. Pour a little of the hot gravy over the meat and serve the extra gravy in a sauce boat.

Serves 8

Plain Pot Roast

This plain pot roast is as basic in the annals of good eating as simple addition in the field of mathematics.

4- to 5-pound boneless pot roast of beef (top, bottom or eye round)	freshly ground pepper
	2 carrots, grated
	2 stalks celery, grated
2 cups stock or consommé	4 onions, cut fine
1 clove garlic, minced	8 whole carrots, peeled
1 teaspoon salt	12 small white onions, peeled
1 teaspoon Lawry's seasoned salt	6 medium-sized potatoes, peeled

After you've chosen the leanest pot roast your butcher has to offer, ask him to omit the usual strip of suet. This will break his heart, but be firm. Trim it again when you get home. Butchers always miss a snippet of fat here and there. Heat heavy stewing kettle or large Dutch oven on top of stove and sear meat on all sides, turning frequently to ensure even browning.

Remove meat from kettle, pour off any fat that has collected and wipe it dry with paper towel. Place rack on bottom of kettle and replace meat. Add liquid, seasonings, grated carrot and celery, cut-up onions and garlic. Cover pot and simmer slowly for three hours. You will find that the grated vegetables will make a lovely rich gravy that requires no thickening.

Add whole onions, carrots, potatoes and taste for seasonings. (Try a teaspoon of sugar at this point—we think it's good.) You may want to add some additional garlic powder also. Continue simmering for another hour, when it should be fork-tender.

Refrigerate overnight, with the gravy in a separate container. When ready to serve, skim fat from gravy and return it to kettle. Slice meat thin and place in kettle with vegetables. Heat through, and transfer to warm platter. Cover meat and vegetables with some of the gravy and serve the rest in a gravy boat.

Serves 8 generously

Baked Steak

Another party favorite that requires no last-minute attention at mealtime.

3½- to 4-inch sirloin steak (7 to 8 pounds)
1 teaspoon salt
freshly ground pepper
3 teaspoons dry mustard
paprika
1½ tablespoons Worcestershire sauce
1 12-ounce bottle chili sauce
1 large onion, sliced paper thin
1 lemon, thinly sliced

Have your butcher cut steak from top section of sirloin. He will trim it, of course, butcher-fashion, but that will be merely a prelude to what you will cut off in your own kitchen. Salt and pepper both sides of steak. Make a paste of the dry mustard and Worcestershire sauce and spread half on each side of the steak. Place steak in large roasting pan, cover with chili sauce, and slices of onion and lemon. Dust surface lightly with paprika. Marinate in refrigerator for at least three hours. Bake uncovered in 375-degree oven for two hours. This will yield outside slices medium to well done, with the inside rare. To serve, slice with the grain of the meat into ¼-inch slices.

Serves 10 to 12

Boeuf Bourguignon

The literal translation of this would be Beef in Burgundy, I suppose, or Beef Stew in Wine—which wouldn't begin to do justice to the fabulous fragrance it emits while cooking. It has always seemed to me that the French perfume manufacturers missed the boat when they didn't bottle this—it might catch more husbands for willing ladies than "Joy."

2½ pounds lean, trimmed beef, cut in 1½-inch cubes
6 tablespoons oil
2 tablespoons flour
1½ cups dry red wine
1 teaspoon salt
freshly ground pepper
½ teaspoon sugar
3 medium-sized onions

1 carrot, chopped
1 clove garlic, minced
4 or 5 shallots, sliced
½ teaspoon thyme
1 cup (or more) water or consommé (part of this may be Madeira wine)
1½ ounces brandy
1 bay leaf

For garnish:

½ pound mushrooms, sliced
2 tablespoons oil
1 tablespoon lemon juice
2 tablespoons chopped parsley

Cut meat into 1½-inch cubes, trimming every bit of fat away. Heat 4 tablespoons of oil in a heavy stewing kettle, like a Dutch oven. Add beef and brown thoroughly, turning a number of times. Remove meat with slotted spoon and set aside.

Add flour to pot and brown it over high heat, stirring to keep it smooth. Reduce heat and slowly add 1½ cups dry red wine, stirring all the while to make a well-blended sauce. Add salt, pepper and sugar.

In small skillet, cook chopped onions in 2 tablespoons of oil until transparent. Add chopped carrot, minced garlic, and sliced shallots and cook 3 to 5 minutes longer, stirring constantly, until all the vegetables are slightly brown. Add browned vegetables to the large kettle and replace meat cubes. Add thyme and bay leaf. Add water or consommé (with wine, if you have it) to barely cover the meat.

Cover pot and simmer slowly for three to four hours until the meat is deliciously tender. Half an hour before serving, add brandy to the meat.

Just before serving, heat 2 tablespoons of oil in small skillet, add sliced mushrooms and cook for 5 minutes, or until brown. Turn them a few times. Sprinkle with lemon juice and heat through.

To serve, turn meat and sauce into heated bowl. Garnish with chopped parsley and a border of the sautéed mushrooms.

Or serve in a casserole—an earthenware one, if you have it (just to make it look as authentic as it tastes).

Serve with tiny new potatoes or broad noodles.

Serves 6

Beef with Olives in Casserole

This may be made well in advance—even the day before—which makes it a favorite Sunday night supper choice.

¼ cup oil	1 clove garlic, crushed
3 pounds lean top sirloin or round steak, 1½ inch thick	½ teaspoon thyme
⅓ cup flour	1½ cups consommé (or
1 teaspoon salt	¾ cup consommé and
freshly ground pepper	¾ cup dry red wine)
12 small white onions	½ cup pitted black olives
	¼ cup chopped parsley

Select leanest slices of round steak or top sirloin and cut into 1½-inch cubes yourself. That way, you'll catch every bit of fat which might have escaped your butcher. Trim ruthlessly every vestige of the unfriendly white stuff you see.

Preheat oven to 300 degrees. Mix flour, salt and pepper in paper bag and toss beef cubes in it—not too many at a time—so that each piece will be well coated. Heat oil in large heavy skillet and brown meat quickly. Transfer meat to casserole and add onions and garlic to skillet. Brown them lightly—five minutes will take care of this operation. Add onions and garlic to casserole, sprinkle with thyme and add consommé and wine.

Cover the casserole tightly and bake in a 300-degree oven for 1½ hours. Remove cover and add olives and parsley to meat. Cover and continue baking for another 40 to 50 minutes, or until meat is tender. Taste and correct seasoning. If the sauce seems thin, make a paste of a a little flour, some of the meat gravy and a splash of oil and add it slowly to the simmering sauce in the casserole.

Serves 8

Chinese Beef and Vegetables

Most Chinese dishes, in bits and pieces as they are, and thus not requiring a knife, make excellent buffet fare. This is no exception.

It's a twenty-minute dish from start to end, if you have the meat and vegetables cut and ready. It should be served immediately so that the vegetables, in true Oriental style, will be crisp. DON'T OVER-COOK—follow the directions exactly.

2 pounds lean, boneless sirloin or round steak, ¾ inch thick
2 tablespoons cornstarch
¼ cup cold water
3 cloves garlic, crushed
1 teaspoon powdered ginger
⅔ cup oil
2 medium tomatoes, cut in eighths

2 green peppers, cut into very thin strips
2 medium onions, chopped
1 cup chicken consommé (or broth powder dissolved in boiling water)
1½ teaspoons sugar
1 teaspoon salt
freshly ground pepper
4 tablespoons sherry

Unless you're sure the meat is tender, you might treat it with one of the tenderizing agents, used according to directions. Trim every bit of fat from meat and cut into thin strips, about ¼ inch wide, and 3 inches long. Heat oil in heavy skillet. Make a paste of water and cornstarch, and combine in bowl with meat, garlic and ginger, coating the meat thoroughly. Cook for ten minutes over medium heat, stirring all the while. Remove meat from pan with slotted spoon and set aside. Leave the remainder of oil in skillet.

Add tomatoes, green peppers and onions to skillet and cook for 2 minutes, stirring a few times. Add consommé, sugar, salt, pepper, sherry, stirring constantly, and cook an additional 3 minutes. Add meat and cook another 2 minutes. Serve at once with fluffy rice.

Serves 6

Sweet and Sour Stuffed Cabbage

Recipes for stuffed cabbage are as numerous as jelly beans at Easter time. Women vie with each other like mad in their claims for the excellence of their particular formulas. So please understand that it is with becoming modesty that I concede that this is positively the best. It was my mother's and I have yet to meet up with one I liked better. If you have the time, I suggest that you double the recipe and freeze the other half.

1 pound lean round steak, ground
1 pound chopped lean veal
1 onion, grated
¾ cup bread crumbs
¾ cup cold water
1 No. 2 can apricot halves
1 10½-ounce can consommé
10 prunes
 2 tablespoons cooked rice
 2 cups tomato sauce

freshly ground pepper
1 teaspoon salt
1 large head cabbage
½ cup orange juice
juice of ½ lemon (or more)
2 tablespoons brown sugar
¼ cup raisins
1 small onion, cut up
salt, pepper, paprika
ginger snaps (optional)

Cut out core of cabbage, pour boiling water over it, cover, and let cook gently for about 5 minutes, or until leaves are flexible enough to handle. You may want to keep the water simmering in the pot, since, sometimes, if the cabbage is tough, the inner leaves, when you get to them, need an additional few minutes of immersion.

While the cabbage is being softened, combine meat, cooked rice, grated onion, bread crumbs, water, salt and pepper and beat well, until spongy and light.

Cut out veins in center of cabbage leaves and fill leaves with mounds of the meat mixture, about the size of a large egg. Roll and fasten with toothpicks. Place in large covered kettle with cut-up onion. Add juice from apricots, orange juice, and consommé. Add prunes, apricot halves and raisins. Season with salt, pepper and paprika. Let come to a boil. Then add just enough water to barely come within an inch of the top of the cabbage rolls. Cook slowly, uncovered, for an hour. Add tomato sauce, lemon juice and brown sugar.

Taste and add more of whatever you think it needs. Let simmer slowly for two hours, covered.

Remove cabbage rolls from kettle and place in roaster, cover with some of the sauce, tuck fruits among them and bake in 300-degree oven for about 50 minutes until glazed and golden brown.

If the remainder of the sauce seems thin, thicken with crumbled-up ginger snaps. When ready to serve, remove cabbage rolls to large heated platter, cover with sauce. Serve extra sauce in gravy boat.

Serves 8 generously

Meat Loaf Supreme with Mushroom Sauce

As a change from the conventional meat loaf shape, you might bake this in a ring mold, and fill the center with peas and mushrooms, Brussels sprouts or string beans.

1 pound lean round steak, ground	1 large onion, grated
1 pound lean veal, ground	2 tablespoons Worcestershire
1 teaspoon salt	sauce
½ teaspoon Lawry's seasoned salt	3 tablespoons chili sauce
freshly ground pepper	1 clove garlic, minced
3 slices white bread, soaked in	1 teaspoon dry mustard
½ cup skim milk	

Combine meats, salts, pepper, soaked bread, grated onion, Worcestershire sauce, chili sauce, garlic and mustard. Mix well and beat until you're tired, but don't get tired until the meat mixture is light and spongy. Oil flat baking dish and pat meat into loaf shape. Bake for 50 minutes to an hour in 375-degree oven. Transfer to serving platter and cover with mushroom sauce.

For the ring form, oil 6-cup ring mold generously. Fill it with the meat mixture, loosely packed. Place mold in a pan of hot water and bake in 375-degree oven for 1¼ hours. To unmold, loosen meat loaf from the sides of the form with spatula and invert the form on a round platter. The meat loaf should slide out easily. Fill the center with a vegetable of choice and cover meat loaf with the mushroom sauce.

Serves 6 to 8

Mushroom Sauce

7 tablespoons oil
4 tablespoons flour
2 cups skim milk
1 teaspoon salt
1 teaspoon paprika

1 small clove garlic, minced
1 beef broth powder, dissolved
   in ½ cup hot water
½ pound mushrooms

Heat 4 tablespoons of the oil in small saucepan and blend with flour over low flame, but don't let it brown. Add salt, paprika and minced garlic. Add skim milk, stirring constantly until the mixture thickens and bubbles. Reduce heat and cook a minute longer. Add dissolved broth powder, mix well and remove from heat.

Wipe mushrooms with damp cloth. Chop stems and slice caps thinly. Sauté caps and stems with remaining 3 tablespoons oil about 4 to 5 minutes. Add to sauce and mix well. Keep sauce hot over just-simmering water. If it gets too thick, thin out with a little water or consommé.

Makes 2½ cups sauce

Swedish Meat Balls

In the one-inch size, these make a splendid chafing dish hors d'oeuvre. For a main dinner course, make them a bit larger.

1 pound lean veal, ground
½ pound lean round steak, ground
3 slices white bread
½ cup skim milk
1 teaspoon salt
1 clove garlic, minced

1 small onion, grated
freshly ground pepper
¼ teaspoon nutmeg
1 carrot, finely grated
4 tablespoons oil

Sauce

2 tablespoons flour
¾ teaspoon salt
freshly ground pepper

2 cups skim milk
1 teaspoon Kitchen Bouquet

Remove crusts from bread and soak bread in skim milk. In a large bowl, mix together chopped veal and chopped beef. Add grated onion, garlic, salt, pepper, nutmeg and grated carrot. Beat bread and milk together until fluffy and add to meat mixture. Beat well and work with your hands until it is smooth and light. Form into small balls, dipping your hands into cold water to avoid sticking, as you form the balls between your palms. Chill in refrigerator for an hour or so before cooking.

Heat oil in large heavy skillet and cook the meat balls until golden brown. Remove them with slotted spoon and set aside.

Use the oil remaining in the skillet for the sauce. You need about 2 tablespoons, so add a little if there doesn't seem to be enough. Scrape up whatever little crusts there are on the bottom of the pan— they'll do the sauce nothing but good. Blend in flour, salt and pepper, stir well, and add milk slowly, stirring constantly, until the mixture thickens and bubbles. Add Kitchen Bouquet and cook over low flame a minute longer. Place meat balls back into the sauce and simmer, covered, over low flame 20 to 25 minutes longer. Taste and correct seasoning.

Serves 10 to 12 as an hors d'oeuvre;
5 to 8 as a main course

Pilaf with Chopped Beef

This is an excellent meat stretcher that compensates with good flavor for a small portion.

1 pound lean round steak, ground
2 tablespoons oil
½ cup chopped black olives
⅓ cup green pepper, finely chopped
⅓ cup onion, finely chopped
1 clove garlic, minced
2 cups consommé

½ cup uncooked rice
1 6-ounce can tomato paste (Italian style)
1½ teaspoons salt
½ teaspoon sugar
freshly ground pepper
2 tablespoons chopped parsley

In large heavy skillet with cover, heat oil and brown meat, mixing well to keep it separated and crumbly. Add remaining ingredients, mix well, and cover tightly. Cook over low flame, stirring a few times, until the rice is tender. Remove to warm serving bowl, sprinkle with parsley and serve hot.

Serves 4

Canadian Bacon in Wine Sauce

1 pound Canadian bacon, sliced

Sauce

1½ tablespoons oil	pinch dried thyme
1½ tablespoons flour	pinch dried sweet basil
1 10½-ounce can consommé	2 tablespoons sherry

Heat heavy skillet and cook slices of Canadian bacon for about 5 minutes, turning them often. You will find that the fat, when done, is a light golden brown and different in color from the lean meat which is a reddish brown. Remove the offending portion and discard.

For the sauce, heat oil in small saucepan. Blend in flour and brown slowly. Add consommé, stirring slowly and constantly to keep the sauce smooth. Add thyme and basil and simmer for 15 minutes over low flame. Strain through wire strainer and add sherry. Pour over bacon slices.

Serves 3

Chicken Livers with Mushrooms

4 tablespoons oil	1 cup chicken broth
1 pound chicken livers	⅓ cup sherry
1 small onion, chopped	salt and freshly ground pepper
1 pound mushrooms, sliced	1 tablespoon lemon juice
3 tablespoons flour	

Wash, trim and drain livers well on absorbent paper. Heat oil in heavy skillet. Dredge the livers lightly in flour and cook them over a brisk flame until well browned and crisp all around. Remove with slotted spoon and set aside. Add chopped onion, cook for 2 or 3 minutes, until it begins to turn golden, and add sliced mushrooms. Cook until the mushrooms brown a bit. Add chicken broth slowly, stirring all the while and gathering up all the little crispy things on the bottom of the pan. Add sherry. Taste to see if you need any salt and pepper—a well-seasoned chicken stock may make additional seasonings unnecessary. Add lemon juice. Return chicken livers to the pan and cook over low heat another 5 minutes, covered. If the sauce is too thin, uncover pan and let it cook down. Serve hot on fluffy rice.

Serves 4

Chicken Livers Ah Linn

1 pound chicken livers
3 tablespoons soy sauce
4 tablespoons oil
1 cup pineapple tidbits, drained
½ cup blanched almonds
1¼ cups pineapple juice

2 tablespoons cornstarch
¼ cup sugar
¼ cup vinegar
¼ teaspoon salt
1 10-ounce package frozen tiny green peas

Trim livers, cutting away all traces of fat. Cut in half. Marinate the halves in soy sauce for a few minutes, mixing well, so that all the livers are seasoned with the sauce.

Heat oil in large heavy skillet and add livers. Cook for 10 minutes, or until no blood runs out when pricked. Turn them frequently to brown evenly. Add pineapple tidbits and blanched almonds, and simmer over low heat while you prepare the sauce.

Place frozen green peas in ½ cup boiling salted water and cook only until thawed—no longer. They should be crisply undercooked. Drain and set aside.

Make a paste of cornstarch with a few tablespoons of the pineapple juice. Place the remainder of the pineapple juice in small saucepan. Add sugar, vinegar, salt and cornstarch paste and cook over low flame, stirring constantly, until sauce thickens and becomes transparent. Add this sauce to chicken livers. Add green peas. Mix well and cook together 3 minutes longer. Serve at once with fluffy boiled rice.

Serves 3 to 4

Calves' Liver Sauté

1 pound calves' liver, thinly sliced
¼ cup flour
½ teaspoon salt
freshly ground pepper
3 tablespoons oil

½ cup chicken stock
2 tablespoons tomato purée
½ teaspoon sugar
1 tablespoon chopped parsley

Heat oil in heavy skillet. Remove outer skin from liver slices, sprinkle them with salt and pepper and lightly dredge with flour. Add liver to the hot oil and fry 4 minutes on each side. Remove liver from pan, add chicken stock, tomato purée and sugar. Mix well and scrape bottom of pan to blend the particles clinging to it. Cook 1 minute. Return liver to pan and cook 2 or 3 minutes longer. Sprinkle with chopped parsley.

Serves 4

Leg of Lamb with Apricots

small leg of spring lamb (6 to 7 pounds)
1 medium onion, thinly sliced
2 cloves garlic, cut into thin slivers
1 teaspoon salt
freshly ground pepper
2 tablespoons oil
1 cup water
½ pound dried apricots

Trim leg of lamb mercilessly, cutting off all fat and every bit of the parchment-like skin which envelopes it. Make a few gashes in the leg of lamb and insert a sliver of garlic into each. Place lamb on rack in shallow baking pan. Sprinkle with salt and pepper, dribble oil over lamb, and add water and sliced onion. Bake uncovered in 275-degree oven for 2 hours, adding water if pan gets too dry.

Meanwhile, steam apricots in just enough water to cover, for about 25 minutes until soft. Purée them through food mill.

After lamb has cooked for 2 hours, pour off gravy and allow to cool. Skim fat. Add apricot purée to gravy, return lamb to oven and cook another hour, basting frequently so that lamb is glazed and golden brown. Slice thin, place on warmed platter and cover with gravy. Serve additional gravy in gravy boat.

Serves 8

Sirloin of Pork Filets in Mushroom Sauce

3 pounds sirloin of pork, lean
¼ teaspoon dried rosemary
¼ cup flour
1 teaspoon salt
freshly ground pepper
3 tablespoons oil
1 onion, sliced
1 clove garlic, minced
½ cup nonfat milk solids, dissolved in ¾ cup water
½ pound sliced mushrooms
2 tablespoons lemon juice
2 tablespoons chopped parsley

Have your butcher remove bones from loin of pork. This will leave you a long strip of meat, from which either you or he (preferably, both) will trim the fat bordering it. Cut the strip crosswise into slices 1 inch thick.

Place slices in large heavy skillet and heat slowly 5 minutes on each side. Remove meat from pan and set aside. Drain skillet of grease and wipe dry. Heat oil in skillet and sauté sliced onion and minced garlic for 3 or 4 minutes until the onion is limp.

Combine flour with salt, pepper and dried rosemary. Lightly sprinkle both sides of meat slices with seasoned flour and return them to skillet. Brown in the hot oil.

In a small saucepan, combine nonfat milk solids with water and heat until it reaches the boiling point. Pour this over meat slices. Add sliced mushrooms, cover skillet and cook for 50 minutes. Add lemon juice to the pan gravy. Taste and correct seasoning. Garnish with chopped parsley.

Serves 4 to 5

Ham Slice with Pineapple

center slice of lean, smoked ham, ½ inch thick (about 1 pound)
2 slices drained canned pineapple
2 teaspoons brown sugar
¼ teaspoon cinnamon
oil
⅓ cup pineapple juice

Lightly oil bottom of heavy skillet which has a cover. Heat over low flame. Trim ham slice, increase heat under pan, and sear meat on both sides. Remove ham and wipe pan with paper towel. Replace in pan, adding just enough oil to keep it from sticking. Cover with sliced pineapple, sprinkle with brown sugar and cinnamon, and add the pineapple juice. Cover pan and simmer for 10 minutes. It should be nearly done in this time—but different varieties of ham require different cooking times, so you'll have to be the judge. For the last 3 or 4 minutes of cooking, uncover and baste with the juice a few times.

Serves 2 or 3

Kidney Stew

2 medium-sized beef kidneys
1 tablespoon vinegar
¼ cup flour
2 tablespoons oil
½ cup chopped onions
½ cup coarsely chopped celery

1 can tomatoes (2½ cups)
1 green pepper, cut in julienne
   strips
1 teaspoon salt
⅛ teaspoon red pepper

Remove fat from kidneys. Split lengthwise and cut out the white center and tubes. Curved scissors do this job easily. Cut kidneys in ½-inch slices and sprinkle with vinegar and flour.

Heat oil in heavy skillet. Add onions and celery and cook for 3 minutes. Add kidney slices and brown them with the onions and celery. When brown, cover skillet and simmer over low flame for 10 minutes.

In a saucepan, heat tomatoes with green pepper. Add salt and red pepper. When heated through, add tomato mixture to kidneys, cover pan and simmer for 15 minutes. Stir often.

Serves 4

Potted Calves' Hearts

Veal hearts may also be used. They require half the cooking time.

2 calves' hearts
2 tablespoons oil
1 large onion, sliced
2 carrots, sliced
½ cup chopped celery
1 tablespoon chopped parsley

½ bay leaf, crumbled
6 peppercorns
½ teaspoon salt
1 cup chicken stock or
   consommé
1 tablespoon flour

Remove fat from hearts and cut away veins and arteries and wash well. Cut into ½-inch cubes or thin slices. Heat oil in heavy skillet and brown hearts in it, turning frequently to ensure even browning. Sprinkle with flour and let flour brown a little. Transfer to ovenproof baking dish. Add onion, carrot, celery, parsley, bay leaf, peppercorns, salt and stock. Cover casserole and bake in 325-degree oven for 2 hours. Serve with fluffy rice or noodles.

Serves 4

Baked Rabbit

Hunting wild rabbit is apparently a popular sport in these United States. A recent statistic indicated that over forty million cottontails were bagged in one year, and, I assume, eaten. They are highly unsaturated, as is most wild game, so this is all to the good.

An English friend sent me the following description of one of her favorite dishes which she calls "jugged hare": "The jugged hare is marinated first in white wine, a little brandy, bay leaves, thyme, cloves, onion and garlic, then cut in pieces which are fried brown, afterward cooked in a casserole with a little port added at the last, and served with forcemeat balls and red currant jelly." In view of the spirituous ingredients involved in this, don't you think it would be more accurate to call this hare "potted"?

1 rabbit, cleaned and dressed	1 teaspoon salt
2 slices onion	1 tablespoon Worcestershire
1 bay leaf	sauce
1 stalk celery, finely minced	1 tablespoon capers
¼ cup oil	6 pitted black olives
2 tablespoons flour	2 tablespoons chopped parsley
2 cups chicken stock	

Place rabbit in baking pan. Brush with some of the oil and add slices of onion, minced celery and bay leaf. Bake for 30 minutes in 450-degree oven. Remove rabbit from pan and set aside for a moment while you prepare the sauce.

With the pan over a low flame on top of the stove, add flour and the rest of the oil. Stir and cook until it becomes brown. Add chicken stock and stir well until smooth. Add salt, Worcestershire sauce, drained capers and olives. Return meat to pan, cover tightly, and reduce heat in oven to 350 degrees. Cook for 30 minutes, or until tender. To serve, remove rabbit to warmed serving platter. Strain sauce and pour over it. Sprinkle with chopped parsley and garnish with olives.

Serves 4 to 6

VEAL

Since animals, like humans, tend to grow fatter as they grow older, it is easy to see why the meat from an immature animal like the calf is well suited to a low-fat dietary.

Like chicken, veal lends itself to such a variety of methods of preparation and can be used in conjunction with so many different herbs, wines, seasonings, vegetables and fruits that its frequent use need never become monotonous. Whether it comes to your table as a tender scaloppine, bathed in a wine sauce and embellished with mushrooms and fresh tomatoes, or a hearty stew, a succulent roast, or perhaps a savory curry, it can satisfy a jaded appetite and please a demanding palate.

The milky-white, most desirable-looking veal is to be found, naturally, in the choice and prime grades, carried generally by butchers who specialize in prime meats. Prime cuts, like the rib eye and boneless loin are—naturally—expensive and small comfort for housewives who budget. And how few of us don't! I realize it isn't very chic to talk about how much things cost, but it's hard to be chic in the face of food prices. On the other hand, the good and standard grades of veal which you are more likely to find at the neighborhood butcher or supermarket chains can be perfectly satisfactory.

The shoulder, rump and leg, well trimmed and, if you wish, the bone removed, make fine roasts, more desirable than the breast, which is pretty well larded and not too easily trimmed. For stews, I generally buy a rump or shoulder and cut it up myself. That way, I'm sure it will be manicured to a fare-thee-well. Unless you trust your butcher as you do your own father, use great caution when purchasing chopped veal. If you have any doubt in your mind, it might be safer to buy a rump, shoulder, or some other lean cut, trim it yourself, and put it through your own food grinder. Then you can be sure there won't be any fat or trimmings in your chopped meat.

One of the best cuts of meat obtainable for the low-fat dieter is the veal scallop, or scaloppine as its Italian originators call it. Born out of the stringencies of the limited meat supply in Italy, these tender little slices are a shining example of a necessity being turned into a virtue. The scaloppine are generally cut from the leg, trimmed of all fat, and pounded thin. One pound will serve three or four adults most adequately. Further proof of how our debt to the Italians extends beyond our gratitude to them for sharing with us Michelangelo, Leonardo, pasta, and double knits.

If your own butcher isn't able to supply you with good scaloppine, shop around a bit until you find who can. I did—and found Walter.

This might be the moment for a disparaging comment on the prepackaged breaded veal patties one finds in frozen food departments. In addition to their questionable content, their flavor is unlikely to swell the ranks of veal lovers, a cult which would do well to increase in number.

Scaloppine in Wine

Ten minutes of preparation is all that is needed for this noteworthy main course.

1 pound veal scaloppine (Italian style, pounded thin)	3 tablespoons oil
	½ bay leaf, crumbled
¼ cup flour	pinch dried sage
1 teaspoon salt	½ cup dry white wine or Marsala
freshly ground pepper	1 tablespoon chopped parsley

Combine flour, salt and pepper. Lightly dust meat slices with the seasoned flour. Heat oil in heavy skillet, add meat slices and brown. If they are thin enough, they will need only 2 or 3 minutes on each side. Transfer them to ovenproof dish and keep warm in a slow oven while you prepare the sauce.

To the fat remaining in the skillet, add the half bay leaf, crumbled, sage, and wine. Swish this around in the skillet, gathering up the brown particles on the bottom of the pan. Simmer for just a minute, and pour sauce over meat slices. Sprinkle with chopped parsley.

Serves 3 or 4

Roast of Veal

The rump, shoulder, eye of the rib, boneless loin or a portion of the leg are all suitable for roasting. The rump or shoulder with the bone removed are generally easily available cuts. (Make sure you collect the bone from the butcher—it makes wonderful minestrone soup.) Since there may be a good deal of waste on a veal roast, get a large one. By the time the bone is removed and the fat trimmed, it won't be *that* big.

4- to 5-pound rump or shoulder of veal, bone removed
1 onion, chopped
1 carrot, grated
1 stalk celery, grated
1 teaspoon Lawry's seasoned salt
3 tablespoons oil

For sauce:
½ cup dry white wine
½ teaspoon salt
freshly ground pepper
¼ teaspoon garlic powder
½ teaspoon dried sweet basil
½ teaspoon sugar

Trim every vestige of fat and sinew from veal roast. Sprinkle with Lawry's seasoned salt. Preheat oven to 450 degrees. Pour oil in roasting pan with cover and place meat in it. Sear meat, uncovered, in oven for 20 minutes, turning frequently to brown all over. Spread chopped onion, grated carrot and celery over top of meat, cover, and reduce heat to 300 degrees. Cook for 2 hours, or until meat is tender. Remove meat from roasting pan and set aside to cool. Place gravy in bowl and refrigerate as soon as it is cool.

Half an hour before you are ready to serve, skim whatever fat there is (there won't be much) from the gravy. Rub gravy and vegetables through strainer or whir in blender. Place gravy in large, heavy skillet. Add wine, garlic powder, basil, salt, pepper and sugar. Mix well, taste and correct seasoning. If the gravy is too thick, thin it with water or consommé. Keep warm over low flame. Slice veal in thin slices and place in hot gravy. Warm through and serve.

Serves 6 to 8

Breaded Veal Cutlets with
Artichoke Hearts and Tomatoes

1½ pounds scaloppine
½ cup flour
1 teaspoon salt
freshly ground pepper
½ cup skim milk fortified with additional dry skim milk powder

½ cup fine bread crumbs
3 tablespoons oil
1 10-ounce package frozen artichoke hearts
2 fresh tomatoes

Have scaloppine cut in large portion-sized pieces and pounded very thin. Combine flour, salt and pepper. Dip slices lightly in the seasoned flour, milk and bread crumbs and refrigerate for 1 hour to give the coating time to adhere well.

Cook artichoke hearts according to directions on package. Drain and set aside. Peel tomatoes and cut into eighths.

Heat oil in large heavy skillet. Sauté the breaded scaloppine until golden—about 5 minutes on each side. When done, transfer to shallow ovenproof baking dish.

In the same skillet, add cooked artichoke hearts and tomato wedges and cook until heated through—about 5 minutes. Keep tossing them so they do not scorch. Add more oil if needed and a couple of tablespoons of water or consommé to dissolve the crusty brown particles clinging to the bottom of the pan. Pour pan gravy, artichoke hearts and tomatoes over scaloppine, cover the baking dish with aluminum foil and place in 350-degree oven for 20 minutes.

Serves 4

Broiled Veal Chops

Start with the leanest chops you can get (naturally), at least 1½ inches thick. Trim them well, season with salt, pepper, paprika and perhaps a pinch of either basil, thyme or rosemary. Place in a shallow pan with a couple tablespoons of water. Brush well with oil a few times during the broiling process. Place broiling pan 3 inches below flame and broil for 35 to 40 minutes, or until tender, turning once. Sprinkle with chopped parsley.

Braised Veal Chops

4 large lean veal chops
½ cup oil
½ cup flour
1 teaspoon salt
freshly ground pepper
1 onion, finely chopped
½ cup chicken consommé
¼ cup sherry

½ pound mushrooms, sliced and
    sautéed in oil
2 tablespoons lemon juice
2 cups tiny potatoes or potato
    balls (canned, if desired)
paprika
½ teaspoon dried tarragon
2 tablespoons chopped parsley

Trim chops of all fat, season with salt and pepper and dip in flour.
In a skillet, heat 3 tablespoons of oil and sauté chops for 10 minutes
on each side until well browned. Remove to oiled, flat baking dish
and place in 350-degree oven for 45 minutes.

To pan in which chops were cooked, add 1 tablespoon oil, chopped
onion, and cook until the onion is limp. Add consommé and sherry
and stir well. Pour this sauce over chops in oven.

Using the same skillet and additional oil, brown the potato balls
and sprinkle with paprika.

For the last ten minutes of cooking, cover chops with a layer of
sautéed mushrooms which have been lightly sprinkled with lemon
juice. Surround chops with border of the browned potatoes. Sprinkle
with chopped parsley and tarragon over top.

Serves 4

Vealburgers

These meat patties have superseded hamburgers for us.

1 pound lean ground veal
½ teaspoon salt
½ teaspoon Lawry's seasoned salt
¼ teaspoon thyme
1 egg white
freshly ground pepper
2 slices bread, crusts removed
½ cup skim milk

2 tablespoons finely chopped
    green pepper
1 tablespoon pimento, finely
    chopped
1 tablespoon oil
corn flake crumbs
oil for frying

Place veal in bowl and add salts, pepper and thyme. Heat the tablespoon of oil in small skillet and cook pimento and green pepper for 5 minutes, stirring it from time to time. Add to meat. Soak bread in milk and beat it to make it fluffy and absorb the liquid. Add bread and egg white to the meat mixture and beat it until it is light and spongy. Form into 4 patties. Dip patties in corn flake crumbs. I prefer these to bread crumbs, particularly because veal is a little on the pale side and corn flake crumbs have a nice healthy glow. In large, heavy skillet, heat enough oil to cover bottom, and fry vealburgers until they are nicely brown on each side (about 5 minutes). Place in 350-degree oven 15 minutes longer.

Serves 3 or 4

Chafing Dish Veal Sauté

A festive but simple version of veal scaloppine that can be prepared in a chafing dish in full view of guests or family. A noodle or barley casserole warming in the oven and a mixed salad chilling in the refrigerator will round out the dinner nicely, with your guests busying themselves with some nibbles and aperitifs while the meat is cooking.

2 pounds veal, cut thin in Italian style	1 cup dry white wine
4 tablespoons oil	4 small onions, peeled and chopped
1 teaspoon salt	3 tablespoons chopped parsley
freshly ground pepper	1 cup sliced fresh mushrooms
2 tablespoons flour	

Have the scaloppine cut in pieces about 6 inches square, and thoroughly trimmed of all fat and gristle. Chop onions and parsley. Wash and peel mushrooms and slice them. Flanked by salt, pepper mill, flour, oil, wine, mushrooms, and chopped onions and parsley, you are ready to begin.

Remove hot water pan from chafing dish—this should cook over direct heat. Pour oil into chafing dish and heat for 3 minutes. Add veal pieces and brown well on both sides. Sprinkle salt, pepper and flour over the meat, shaking pan to distribute the seasonings. Pour wine over meat, a little at a time. Add onions and parsley and cover.

Allow this to simmer for 15 minutes. Add mushrooms and cook, covered, 15 minutes longer. Serve at once.

Serves 6

Veal Annie

Annie is our daughter. Like most young people who combine home-making with a full-time job, she has no time to indulge in wasted motions and elaborate preparations. She calls this dish "Veal Mish-mash," but I prefer to call it Veal Annie.

1½ pounds veal cutlets, cut thin in Italian style (scaloppine)
2 cups peeled Italian tomatoes, canned
1 large green pepper, cut in 1-inch strips
1 large onion, sliced thin

½ pound mushrooms, sliced
2 tablespoons oil
1 teaspoon salt
freshly ground pepper
pinch each oregano, basil
1½ tablespoons flour

Have your butcher pound cutlets very thin, with every smidgin of fat removed. Cut veal into pieces about 6 inches square. Heat oil in skillet and when hot, add veal and brown thoroughly on both sides. When well browned, add tomatoes and onion, mushrooms and green pepper. Add salt, pepper, oregano and basil. Sprinkle flour over all. Cook uncovered for 20 minutes, stirring frequently.

Serves 4

Veal Rolls, Marsala

2 pounds veal cutlets, cut thin (Italian style) into 12 pieces
¼ pound chicken livers
4 tablespoons oil
1 tablespoon chopped parsley
1 tablespoon flour

1 teaspoon salt
freshly ground pepper
4 tablespoons Marsala wine (or sherry)
12 slices French bread, toasted
¾ cup consommé

Sauté chicken livers in 2 tablespoons oil until well cooked—about 10 minutes. Chop fine and combine with parsley. Add salt and pepper. Spread the liver mixture on each slice of veal, roll and fasten with toothpicks. Heat remaining 2 tablespoons oil in large skillet. When hot, put in veal rolls and cook until well browned. Sprinkle flour over rolls, add 2 tablespoons wine and cook until wine is nearly evaporated. Toast French bread and place on a serving platter. Place a veal roll on each slice of toast.

Add consommé to gravy in pan. Add remaining 2 tablespoons of wine—more if you wish—and blend well. Pour this sauce over veal rolls and serve hot.

Serves 6 to 8

Hawaiian Veal Scallops

One more variation of this gentle meat which has an affinity for ever so many fruits, vegetables, wines, herbs—whatever your mood. This treatment could serve as a tribute to the fiftieth state of our nation. You can prepare this in the morning and refrigerate it in the baking dish, ready to be popped into the oven for the last forty minutes of baking.

2 pounds veal cutlet ¼ inch thick
2 tablespoons oil
2 tablespoons chopped onion
½ pound mushrooms, sliced
1 teaspoon salt
freshly ground pepper
½ teaspoon powdered ginger

¼ teaspoon paprika
1 tablespoon lemon juice
2 tablespoons flour
¾ cup chicken broth
1 cup pineapple chunks, drained
½ cup sherry

Trim veal carefully and cut into 3-inch pieces. Heat oil in large skillet. Add meat and onions and cook over moderate heat until well browned. Add more oil if pan gets too dry. Remove to shallow baking dish.

Sauté mushrooms in same pan until golden. Add salt, pepper, ginger, paprika and lemon juice. Sprinkle with flour and mix well over low heat.

Add broth slowly, stirring constantly, being sure to pick up all the little crusty things in the pan. Pour over veal. Add pineapple chunks and sherry, mixing lightly. Cover baking dish and bake at 375 degrees about 40 minutes.

Serves 6

Curried Veal

3 pounds lean veal (from rump or shoulder)
½ cup flour
1 teaspoon salt
white pepper
5 tablespoons oil
4 large onions, chopped
2 cloves garlic, minced
2 tablespoons curry powder (or to taste)
1 10½-ounce can consommé
⅓ cup nonfat milk solids
1 tablespoon brown sugar
1 teaspoon white sugar
1 lemon, thinly sliced and seeded
4 pieces of ginger root, thinly sliced, or ½ teaspoon powdered ginger
¼ cup seedless raisins
3 large apples, pared and coarsely chopped

Cut veal into 1½-inch cubes, trimming away sinew and fat. Coat meat by shaking it in paper bag with flour, salt and pepper.

In large heavy kettle, like a Dutch oven, heat 2 tablespoons of oil and cook chopped onion and garlic about 10 minutes, or until the onions are limp but not brown. Remove onions from pan with slotted spoon and set aside. Add 3 tablespoons of oil and sear meat well over medium-high flame. Turn meat frequently so that each piece will have its turn at the bottom of the pan. Sprinkle curry powder over meat and mix thoroughly. These powders vary in intensity, so I hope you know your own strength. Add the consommé and the nonfat milk solids and stir until evenly blended. Return onions and garlic to kettle. Add sugars and sliced lemon with the skin left on, raisins and ginger. Cover and cook over low heat until meat is tender, or about 45 to 50 minutes. About halfway through this cooking process, add chopped apples. If the sauce seems too thick, you can add another ½ cup or so of water. Taste and correct seasoning. Serve in ring of boiled rice on hot platter or in chafing dish.

If you plan this for a buffet dinner, surround your chafing dish with small bowls, like individual salad bowls, for instance, with as many of the following condiments as you can manage: chutney (a must), chopped hard-cooked egg white, slivered toasted almonds, chopped cucumber, chopped sweet white onion, radishes, black or white raisins, kumquats, chopped sweet pickles, tomato chunks, and sliced green pepper.   Serves 6 or 8

Sweet and Pungent Veal

1 slice of veal cutlet, 1 inch thick (about 1½ pounds)
2 cups chicken stock (or dissolved chicken broth powder)
4 tablespoons soy sauce
1 clove garlic, minced
⅓ cup sugar
4 tablespoons cornstarch
4 tablespoons cider vinegar
⅓ cup pineapple juice
⅔ cup pineapple chunks
3 tablespoons sherry

Trim meat thoroughly and cut into 1-inch cubes. In skillet with cover, place veal, chicken stock, soy sauce and garlic and simmer gently for 40 minutes, or until tender. Drain off liquid and reserve.

In a large saucepan, blend sugar, cornstarch, vinegar and pineapple juice until smooth. Gradually stir in liquid from meat and cook until sauce is smooth and transparent. Taste to see if you need additional salt. This depends on the degree of seasoning in the chicken stock. Add cooked veal, pineapple chunks and sherry. Heat thoroughly. Serve on fluffy rice.

Serves 4

Veal with Ripe Olives

2 pounds lean, trimmed veal
4 tablespoons oil
1 clove garlic, minced
1 small onion, sliced
⅔ teaspoon dried rosemary
½ cup dry white wine
1 tablespoon tomato paste
1 cup chicken stock
12 pitted black olives, sliced
½ cup flour
1 teaspoon salt
freshly ground pepper
chopped parsley

Cut veal into 1½-inch cubes, trimming away all fat. Combine flour, salt and pepper in a paper bag and shake the veal in it until thoroughly coated.

Pour oil in heavy skillet, heat and brown meat in it, turning frequently until all sides have been in contact with bottom of pan. Add garlic and onion and cook 3 minutes longer. Transfer meat to baking dish, add rosemary, wine, tomato paste and enough stock to cover meat. Cover casserole securely and bake in 300-degree oven for 1 hour. Add olives and cook 30 minutes more. Sprinkle with parsley.

Serves 4 to 6

Veal and Peppers

5 tablespoons oil
2½ to 3 pounds lean, trimmed
   veal
2 tablespoons flour
1 teaspoon salt
freshly ground pepper
2 cups canned tomatoes

4 large peppers (green and red,
   if you can get them)
1 large onion
⅓ cup oil
⅔ cup chicken consommé (⅓
   cup of this may be Marsala
   wine)

Trim meat carefully, remove all fat, and cut into 1½-inch cubes.
Heat the 5 tablespoons of oil in heavy kettle or Dutch oven. Add
veal and cook over moderate heat for 10 minutes, turning frequently
until well browned. Sprinkle salt, pepper and flour over meat and mix
well. Add tomatoes and bring to a boil. Reduce heat, cover pot and
simmer slowly for 30 minutes.

While this is cooking, wash, core and seed peppers. Cut them into
julienne strips ¼ inch wide and 1 inch long. Peel onion and slice
very thin. Heat the ⅓ cup of oil in medium-sized skillet. Add cut-up
peppers and onion and cook over low heat for 15 minutes, or until
peppers are tender. You'll have to watch this carefully and stir often
so that the vegetables won't scorch.

Add cooked vegetables to the veal. Add broth (with wine, if desired). Taste to correct seasoning. Cover and simmer gently for another 15 minutes. Serve with noodles or rice.

Serves 6

Braised Veal and Mushrooms in Caper Sauce

2 tablespoons oil
2 pounds boneless veal, cut into
   1½-inch cubes
½ pound sliced mushrooms
2 tablespoons flour
1 cup chicken stock
3 tablespoons skim milk

½ teaspoon salt
freshly ground pepper
⅓ cup white wine
2½ tablespoons capers, chopped
   fine
2 tablespoons parsley, chopped

Heat oil in heavy skillet with cover. Add cubed veal, thoroughly
trimmed of all fat and gristle, and mushrooms. Cook over medium

heat until veal is well seared, stirring constantly. Sprinkle flour over meat and mushrooms, and blend. Add stock and milk, salt and pepper, and mix well. Cover pan and turn heat low. Simmer until meat is tender—about 40 minutes. Add wine and capers and cook 5 minutes longer. Taste and correct seasonings. Sprinkle with chopped parsley. Serve with rice or cooked noodles.

Serves 4 to 5

Veal Stew with Lima Beans

A tossed green salad and a simple fruit dessert turn this hearty meal-in-one-dish into a satisfying family dinner.

½ cup flour
1 teaspoon salt
freshly ground pepper
1 to 1½ pounds veal, trimmed and cut in 1-inch cubes
2 tablespoons oil
1 cup hot water
1 cup Burgundy wine

1 cup large dry lima beans
1 bay leaf
½ cup diced carrot
½ cup chopped celery
1 teaspoon Worcestershire sauce
1 teaspoon salt
1 8-ounce can tomato sauce

Combine flour, salt and pepper in paper bag and shake veal, a few cubes at a time, to coat thoroughly. Heat oil in large, heavy skillet that has a tightly fitting cover, and brown veal. Add water, wine, lima beans and bay leaf, cover skillet and cook slowly for 1½ hours. Add carrots, celery, seasonings and tomato sauce, and cook for ½ hour longer, or until beans and veal are tender. Taste for seasoning and correct.

Serves 4

Veal Stew with Dumplings

2 pounds lean, trimmed veal, cut in 1-inch cubes
½ cup flour
3 tablespoons oil
4 cups hot water
2 chicken broth powders
2 10-ounce packages frozen peas and carrots
½ cup chopped celery

½ cup chopped onion
1 bay leaf
1 teaspoon Worcestershire sauce
1 teaspoon salt
½ teaspoon sugar
freshly ground pepper
2 8-ounce cans tomato sauce
1 tablespoon chopped parsley
¼ teaspoon thyme

After meat cubes have been completely denuded of every vestige of fat, shake in bag with flour. Heat oil in large kettle or Dutch oven and sear meat pieces, turning until all sides are browned. Dissolve broth powders in hot water and add to the meat. Cover pot and cook slowly for 1 hour. You may prepare this in the morning and refrigerate until time for dinner. It will need only 45 minutes longer.

Add celery, onion, peas and carrots, bay leaf, thyme, Worcestershire sauce, salt, pepper and sugar and continue cooking uncovered for exactly 30 minutes longer over low flame. Do not overcook. Add tomato sauce and bring to boil. Drop dumplings from spoon into sauce. Cover pot tightly and continue cooking for 15 minutes, undisturbed and without removing cover. To serve, place stew in large bowl or deep serving platter, sprinkle parsley over top and surround with dumplings.

Serves 6

DUMPLINGS

1 cup sifted all-purpose flour
½ teaspoon salt
1½ teaspoons baking powder

½ cup water
2 tablespoons oil

Mix all ingredients together to make a soft dough. Drop by small tablespoonfuls into boiling stew and proceed as described above.

10

Poultry

"CHICKEN EVERY SUNDAY" may certainly be expanded to include a few more appearances during the week with profit for seekers after a low-fat diet. Happily, young chickens are plentiful and inexpensive, lending themselves to guises for our table more numerous than Bluebeard's wives, and just as friendly.

Let us concentrate our use on the broilers and fryers in preference to fat hens or capons, for obvious reasons. Even these young things harbor strips of fat under the skin at the neck and cavity openings, so be profligate and reckless about lopping off the loose tabs of skin and searching out the bits of yellow stuff lurking underneath.

Since the white meat of poultry is more unsaturated than the dark, chicken breasts are ideally suited for our purposes. They are generally easily available in shops which sell poultry parts. I like to keep a supply of them on hand in my freezer as insurance against hurricanes, blizzards and unexpected company. Trim them carefully and prepare them with or without the skins; I prefer the latter for most dishes.

Young turkeys may be served frequently, with the white meat earmarked for the prudent dieter. Let the children have the legs and second joints. Their arteries can take it better than ours. Duck is acceptable when it is cooked long and slowly to give the fat plenty of time to drain off. (See recipe on page 128) Leave the skin, however.

Most wild game—pheasant, quail, rabbit and venison, among others—is extremely low in saturated fat. This is due to the diet of plants and berries instead of the artificially processed grains on which domestic stock is nourished. This happy state of unsaturation may give hunters further reason to pursue their sport.

Serve young poultry and serve it often. The recipes on the pages which follow will act as a guide for all the lovely gastronomic languages it speaks in addition to our own—Continental, Oriental and Latin American.

Oven-Fried Chicken

Nothing could be simpler than the preparation for this crisp golden chicken. And if you do what I do, and bake the chicken pieces on a cookie tin covered by a sheet of aluminum foil, you won't even have a pot to wash!

2 1½-pound broilers, cut in quarters, or 2 whole chicken breasts, cut in halves
½ cup oil
1 teaspoon Lawry's seasoned salt
freshly ground pepper
1 clove garlic, minced (optional)
½ teaspoon paprika
1 cup corn flake crumbs

I generally use boned, skinned chicken breasts for this dish, but it does very well also for carefully trimmed, quartered broilers, with the skin left on, if you wish.

Season oil with Lawry's salt, pepper, paprika and garlic. Using pastry brush, apply the seasoned oil to chicken pieces and roll them in the corn flake crumbs. Place the chicken pieces in shallow pan and bake in 350-degree oven for 1¼ hours.

Serves 4

Barbecued Chicken

2½-pound broiler, cut into quarters

Sauce

1 teaspoon salt
freshly ground pepper
1 tablespoon sugar
1 tablespoon paprika
1 tablespoon flour
1 medium onion, chopped fine
½ cup ketchup
½ cup chili sauce
½ teaspoon prepared mustard
⅓ cup oil
½ cup hot water
⅓ cup lemon juice
1 tablespoon Worcestershire sauce

Preheat oven to 350 degrees.

To make the barbecue sauce, combine salt, flour, pepper, paprika and sugar in medium-sized saucepan. Add onion, ketchup, mustard, chili sauce, oil and water. Heat to boiling point, stirring constantly. Remove from heat and mix in lemon juice and Worcestershire sauce.

Trim all traces of fat from chicken and arrange quarters in oiled baking pan. Brush with sauce, cover pan tightly with sheet of aluminum foil, and bake for 40 minutes. Remove foil and pour remainder of sauce over chicken. Continue baking for about 45 to 50 minutes longer, basting with barbecue sauce every 10 minutes or so. Don't let the barbecue sauce cook down—if it appears to be on the wane, add water. To give the chicken the charred barbecued look, run it under the broiler for the last five minutes of cooking.

Serves 3 or 4

Buttermilk Fried Chicken

The flour-buttermilk coating makes a tender, crisp crust and gravy.

2 1½- to 2-pound broilers, quartered
1½ cups skim milk buttermilk
½ cup flour
1½ teaspoons salt
freshly ground pepper
½ teaspoon dried rosemary, crumbled
⅓ cup oil

Trim chicken of all fat and loose tabs of skin. Combine flour, salt, pepper, and dried rosemary. Dip chicken into buttermilk and roll in flour mixture. Refrigerate for 1 hour.

Heat oil in heavy skillet and brown chicken until crisp and golden. Pour remainder of buttermilk into shallow baking dish, add browned chicken and bake uncovered in 300-degree oven until tender, about 1½ hours.

Serves 4 to 5

Glazed Chicken

3 whole chicken breasts, split and skinned
½ teaspoon salt
freshly ground pepper
2 tablespoons oil
1 10-ounce glass currant jelly
6 ounces water
1 teaspoon ground allspice
1 tablespoon Worcestershire sauce
2 tablespoons lemon juice
1 tablespoon cornstarch

Brush chicken breasts lightly with oil and sprinkle with salt and pepper. Arrange them in oiled baking dish.

To make the sauce, combine jelly, allspice, water, Worcestershire sauce and lemon juice in small saucepan over low flame, until jelly is melted and heated through. Make a paste of cornstarch and a tablespoon of cold water and add to jelly mixture. Cook slowly, stirring constantly, until it thickens and boils.

Heat oven to 450 degrees. Pour sauce over chicken breasts and bake for fifteen minutes in oven. Reduce heat to 350 degrees and continue baking for another fifty to sixty minutes, or until chicken is tender. Baste frequently with sauce. If the sauce cooks down and gets too thick, thin it out with a little water or consommé.

Serves 6

Chicken Cacciatore

2 1½-pound broilers, split
½ teaspoon Lawry's seasoned salt
2 small onions, chopped
2 cloves garlic, minced
½ cup oil
½ cup flour
1 teaspoon salt
freshly ground pepper

1 pound mushrooms, sliced
2 tablespoons parsley, chopped
½ teaspoon basil
1 No. 3 can Italian tomatoes (4 cups)
⅔ cup white wine, or ½ cup Marsala

Trim broilers carefully of all fat. Sprinkle with Lawry's seasoned salt and dredge with flour. Heat oil in large skillet, add broilers, and cook until golden brown. Remove to ovenproof casserole.

In the same skillet, sauté onions, garlic and mushrooms until the onions are limp and golden. Add basil and parsley. Strain tomatoes, adding only the pulp to the onion mixture. Cook five minutes, or until the tomatoes are liquefied. Add salt and freshly ground pepper and bring to a boil. Add wine and heat through. Pour this sauce over chicken and bake, covered, in 350-degree oven for 45 to 50 minutes, or until the chicken is completely tender.

Serves 4

Chicken Divan

This all-in-one-dish meal can be prepared in advance and refrigerated.

4 whole chicken breasts, cut in half and skinned
cold water
1 small onion, cut into quarters
1 teaspoon salt
freshly ground pepper
1 bunch broccoli (or 2 packages frozen broccoli spears)
5 tablespoons oil
5 tablespoons flour
3 cups chicken stock
½ cup nonfat milk solids
salt and pepper
¼ cup sherry
2 tablespoons grated sapsago or Parmesan cheese
2 tablespoons chopped parsley

Wash, skin and trim chicken breasts, leaving the meat on the bone. Place in large saucepan and just barely cover with water. Add salt, pepper and cut-up onion. Cover pot and simmer slowly for 30 minutes, or until chicken is tender. Remove chicken and when cool enough to handle, strip breastbones away, leaving chicken in one piece. Discard onion and reserve broth. When cool, chill and skim off any surface fat. Strain broth.

If you are using fresh broccoli, divide it into thin stubby stalks. Cook or steam with half a teaspoon of salt, making sure not to overcook. It is better to err on the underdone side than to risk a tired, faded-looking vegetable. The frozen variety must be watched with the same end in view. Drain broccoli well and set aside.

You will need 3 cups of chicken broth for the sauce. Measure the broth you just made, add the required amount of water and fortify it with a chicken bouillon cube or chicken broth powder.

Using the same saucepan in which you cooked the chicken, heat oil, add flour and stir until it bubbles. Add broth, stirring constantly, over low heat. Add the nonfat milk solids and cook and stir until it thickens. Season to taste with salt and pepper and add sherry.

Oil large, shallow, ovenproof serving dish. I use a 9½ x 14" oval porcelain-on-metal one for dishes of this kind, and I hope you have one too. They look lovely when brought to the table and don't mind oven heat one bit. Place broccoli in ring around the dish and cover with half the sauce. Place chicken on top of broccoli. Half an hour before you are ready to serve, add grated cheese to remaining sauce and pour over chicken breasts. Cover dish tightly with aluminum foil and heat in 350-degree oven about 30 minutes until heated through.

Dust lightly with paprika and sprinkle chopped parsley over all. Fill center of dish with Confetti Rice (see page 167)—or Mushrooms Trifolati (see page 183).

Serves 6 to 8

Chicken à la King

Ladies' luncheons may have turned this into a cliché but it's good anyway.

2 cups cooked chicken, cut in bite-size cubes
½ pound mushrooms, sliced
¼ cup pimento, chopped
3 cups skimmed chicken stock
4 tablespoons flour

3 tablespoons oil
1 teaspoon salt
freshly ground pepper
⅓ cup nonfat milk solids
4 tablespoons sherry (optional)
1 tablespoon parsley, chopped

In a medium-sized saucepan, heat 3 tablespoons of oil. Blend in flour over small flame, but don't let it brown. Add salt, pepper, and slowly add chicken stock, stirring constantly. Increase heat to medium flame and keep stirring until the mixture thickens and bubbles. Add nonfat milk solids and cook a minute longer. Sauté sliced mushrooms in a little oil for five minutes. Add to the cream sauce, along with chicken and pimento. Cook over low flame until heated through. Add sherry and taste to correct seasoning. Serve on toast triangles. Garnish with chopped parsley.

Serves 4 to 6

Chicken with Almonds

3 whole breasts of chicken, halved, skinned and boned
4 tablespoons oil
2 tablespoons brandy
1 tablespoon minced scallions
1 teaspoon tomato paste

1 cup almonds, blanched
1½ tablespoons flour
1½ cups chicken stock
1½ cups dry white wine
salt and pepper to taste
½ teaspoon dried tarragon

In a skillet, brown halved, boned and skinned chicken breasts in 3 tablespoons of oil and sprinkle with brandy. (For directions on boning, see Chicken Kiev on page 126.) Put chicken aside. Add remaining oil to skillet, cook scallions for just half a minute, and add half the almonds. When almonds begin to brown, slowly stir in tomato paste and flour. Gradually add chicken stock and wine, stirring constantly. Sprinkle with salt and pepper and continue stirring until mixture boils.

Return chicken to skillet and add tarragon. Cook, covered, for 40 minutes over low flame.

Serve breasts on a bed of fluffy rice, pour sauce over all and sprinkle with remaining almonds which have been slivered and browned in oil.

Serves 6

Chicken Marsala

2 1½-pound broilers, quartered and trimmed
½ teaspoon salt
freshly ground pepper
¾ cup flour

1 cup or more Marsala wine
1 sweet onion
1 4-ounce can sliced mushrooms, drained
3 tablespoons oil

Heat oil in heavy skillet which has a cover. Toss chicken pieces in a paper bag with flour seasoned with salt and pepper. Place chicken pieces in skillet and cook over medium flame until nicely browned. Add wine, cover, and cook for thirty minutes. If the liquid in the pan seems to be running low, add more wine. Pour drained sliced mushrooms over chicken and add sweet onion, cut into thin slices. Cook another twenty or twenty-five minutes, or until chicken is tender. Remove to warm platter and pour sauce over chicken.

Serves 4

Chicken in Orange Sauce

1 2½-pound broiler, cut in serving pieces
1 teaspoon salt
4 tablespoons oil
2 tablespoons flour
¼ teaspoon cinnamon
¼ teaspoon salt

dash of ground cloves
1½ cups orange juice
¼ teaspoon Tabasco sauce
½ cup chopped almonds
½ cup raisins
1 orange, sectioned, or 1 can mandarin orange slices

Trim all traces of fat from chicken and sprinkle lightly with 1 teaspoon salt.

In large, heavy skillet with cover, heat oil and brown chicken pieces well. Remove from pan and set aside. To the drippings in the pan, add flour, salt, cinnamon and cloves. Stir to a smooth paste over low flame. Add orange juice and Tabasco sauce and cook, stirring constantly until the mixture thickens and comes to a boil.

Replace chicken in skillet together with raisins and almonds, cover pan, and simmer over low heat until chicken is tender—about fifty minutes. Add orange sections for the last five minutes of cooking.

To serve, place chicken on warmed platter and spoon some of the sauce and all of the fruit over it. Serve the remaining sauce with fluffy hot rice.

Serves 2 or 3

Chicken with Bing Cherries

3 1½-pound broilers cut in halves	1 large onion, finely chopped
1 cup flour	1½ cups chicken stock
1 teaspoon salt	1 No. 2½ can black Bing cherries,
freshly ground pepper	pitted
½ teaspoon paprika	2 tablespoons cornstarch
¼ teaspoon ground ginger	½ cup sherry
½ cup oil	salt and pepper

Trim fat from broilers. Dredge them in flour which has been seasoned with salt, pepper, paprika and ginger. In heavy skillet, heat ¼ cup oil and brown chicken halves. Add more oil if needed. Place chicken in roasting pan with the other ¼ cup oil, ½ cup chicken stock and half the chopped onion. Cover pan and bake in 350-degree oven for 35 minutes, basting frequently. Remove cover and let the chicken brown again for half an hour.

While the chicken is minding its own business in the oven, you can prepare the sauce. For this, you will use the oil remaining in the pan in which you browned the chicken. Place remainder of chopped onion in pan, and brown. Blend 2 tablespoons of cornstarch with Bing cherry juice and the other cup of chicken stock. Add to browned onion and boil three minutes, stirring all the while. Your sauce will look more elegant if you put it through a wire strainer at this point,

to remove the residue of the onion. Add cherries, sherry, and taste
for seasoning. Pour part of the sauce over chicken on platter, and serve
the rest in a gravy boat.

Serves 6

Chicken Breasts in Wine and Tomato Sauce

3 whole chicken breasts
5 tablespoons oil
1 medium-sized onion, finely
  chopped
5 tablespoons flour
1 cup tomato juice
1 cup chicken stock

½ teaspoon salt
freshly ground pepper
1 4-ounce can sliced mushrooms
  (and liquid)
¼ cup sherry
2 tablespoons chopped parsley

Skin breasts, trimming off every bit of fat. Cut in half with poultry
shears. Combine salt, pepper and flour. Heat oil in heavy skillet with
tight lid and brown chicken breasts which have been dipped in the
seasoned flour. When golden brown, set them aside. Lightly brown
chopped onion in same pan. Add chicken, tomato juice, can of mushrooms and liquid, chicken stock, parsley and wine. Cover and simmer
over medium heat for about 50 minutes, or until the chicken is tender.

Serves 6

Chicken Orientale

This is a handsome addition to a party buffet table. You might also
consider it even without the provocation of a party or a buffet—just
some leftover chicken or a couple chicken breasts. It can be prepared
in the morning and heated at dinnertime.

2 cups cooked, diced chicken (or
  2 whole chicken breasts)
1 cup sliced celery
2½ cups chicken stock (canned
  or broth powder)
1 10-ounce package frozen green
  peas
½ pound mushrooms
¼ cup oil

6 tablespoons flour
salt (to taste)
freshly ground pepper
1 5-ounce can water chestnuts
1 5-ounce can bamboo shoots
  (optional)
1 tablespoon soy sauce
dash Tabasco sauce
1 cup Chinese noodles

If you are starting with uncooked chicken breasts, trim them of all fat. Place in 2-quart skillet, cover with cold water and add a tea-spoon of salt, pepper, and a small sliced onion. Simmer slowly until tender, about 30 minutes. Skim broth a few times. The last 10 min-utes, add a cup of celery cut into half-inch lengths. When done, re-move and reserve chicken breasts, celery and onion. If you have more than 2½ cups of broth, continue to simmer until reduced to the re-quired amount. Strain and cool. Skim congealed fat from broth when cooled. If stock seems weak, add a chicken broth powder—or even 2. When chicken breasts have cooled, cut in bite-sized pieces or largish flat slices—I prefer the latter.

Now for the Chicken Orientale. Prepare the vegetables first. Cook the green peas only until they are beautifully green—2 or 3 minutes after they come to a boil. The celery too should be crisp and under-done—10 minutes are all it needs. Wash and dry mushrooms, trim away a slice from the stem end and slice stems and caps. Sauté sliced mushrooms in 1½ tablespoons of oil for 6 minutes, covered, stirring them a few times so they'll cook evenly. Drain water chestnuts and slice. Drain bamboo shoots.

In a large skillet, heat ¼ cup of oil and blend in flour, stirring until smooth. Add the chicken stock slowly, stirring constantly until the sauce thickens and bubbles. Add soy sauce, Tabasco, and pepper. Add the chicken, peas, celery, mushrooms, water chestnuts, bamboo shoots and mix through. Taste to see if you need more salt. Transfer to oiled 2-quart casserole, cover with a layer of Chinese noodles and bake in 350-degree oven for 20 minutes, or until hot and bubbly. Serve with hot, fluffy rice.

Serves 6

Chicken Paprika

2 2½-pound broilers, cut into serving pieces
2 large onions, chopped
4 tablespoons oil
2 tablespoons mild paprika
½ teaspoon salt
½ teaspoon Lawry's seasoned salt
freshly ground pepper

1 10-ounce can chicken consommé, skimmed
1 medium green pepper, cut into strips ¼ inch wide and 1 inch long
1 large tomato, peeled and cut into small wedges
2 teaspoons tomato paste
⅓ cup nonfat milk solids

Trim chicken carefully, cutting away all fat. In large kettle or Dutch oven, heat oil and sauté onions until golden brown. Add chicken pieces and sear lightly for 5 minutes. Add paprika and seasonings, cover kettle and simmer for 10 minutes.

Add skimmed chicken consommé, green pepper strips, tomato wedges, tomato paste and milk solids. Cover kettle and cook over low heat for 1 hour, or until chicken is tender. Stir occasionally. Taste and correct seasoning. Serve with cooked broad noodles.

Serves 4 to 6

Chicken Kiev

This has the added virtue of being able to be prepared the day before you use it, a great time saver the day of the party.

3 whole chicken breasts
¼ cup flour
2 egg whites, lightly beaten
1 cup bread crumbs
oil for frying
salt and pepper

Liver and Mushroom Stuffing
1 small onion, finely chopped
2 tablespoons oil
½ pound chicken livers
8 large mushrooms
salt and pepper
1 tablespoon parsley, finely chopped

Split chicken breasts in half. If your butcher is uncooperative about boning breasts, it is of no consequence—you can do it yourself. Your fingers and a small paring knife are all you need. With chicken breasts on a flat surface, pull off skin. Make a small incision between meat and breastbone at one of the outside surfaces, and using fingers and knife, carefully pull, scrape and coax away meat from bones, taking care not to tear the meat. You can use bones for stock for a gravy if you want one, although this recipe does very well without it.

Place each breast between two sheets of waxed paper and pound thin with wooden mallet. Do not split flesh. Remove paper.

For the liver and mushroom stuffing, cook onion in oil until transparent. Add chicken livers and cook ten minutes. Remove livers. Add mushrooms to pan and brown lightly. Put onions, livers and mushrooms through your food grinder, using medium knife. Season with salt and pepper, and add parsley. Shape into six finger-shaped pieces about 1½ inches long.

Place a finger of the stuffing in the middle of each chicken breast, sprinkle with salt and pepper, and roll up envelope fashion, making the sides overlap. Fasten with a toothpick.

Dust each roll lightly with flour, brush with beaten egg whites and roll in bread crumbs. Refrigerate for an hour or more so that the crumbs will stick. If you are planning to cook them the following day, cover them with aluminum foil and store in refrigerator.

To cook: pour an inch of oil into frying pan. When hot but not smoking (360 degrees) fry 5 minutes or until golden brown all around. Remove, drain on brown paper. Put in shallow pan and cover with aluminum foil. Bake in 325-degree oven for 45 minutes.

Serves 6

Cornish Hens with Wild Rice Stuffing

Buy the little ones that weigh a pound. Larger than that is too big for a single portion, and splitting them robs them of some of their style (half of it, anyway).

4 1-pound Cornish hens	*Wild Rice Stuffing*
1 6-ounce can frozen orange juice	½ cup wild rice
½ cup sherry	½ teaspoon salt
1 teaspoon salt	2 cups cold water
freshly ground pepper	2 onions, chopped
½ teaspoon garlic powder	½ pound mushrooms, sliced
(optional)	1 teaspoon salt
3 tablespoons oil	4 tablespoons oil
	2 tablespoons chopped fresh dill, or 1 teaspoon dried dill weed
	¼ teaspoon thyme
	freshly ground pepper
	1 slice bread, crusts removed, finely shredded

Wash rice thoroughly in three or four waters, until no foreign particles appear and the water is clear. Drain rice and place in covered kettle with 2 cups of cold water and ½ teaspoon salt. Bring to a boil slowly. When boiling, remove cover and cook briskly over medium-high flame, without stirring, for 40 minutes, or until soft. The water should be all absorbed.

Heat oil in heavy skillet and add chopped onions. Cook for 5 minutes and add sliced mushrooms. Continue cooking until onions are golden brown. Add salt, pepper, dill, thyme, and combine with wild rice and shredded bread. Mix thoroughly and taste for seasoning.

Clean hens and trim away the little tabs of fat at necks and ends of breasts. Rub cavities with salt and sprinkle a little garlic powder if desired. Stuff hens with wild rice stuffing and skewer closed. Tie wings to body with string, and tie feet together. Brush hens with oil and sprinkle lightly with salt and pepper.

Place hens breast side up in covered roasting pan, or baking pan covered with aluminum foil. Roast in 325-degree oven for 50 minutes. Uncover pan and add concentrated orange juice to the gravy. Add more water if you think there isn't enough gravy, but chances are you won't need it. Continue baking, uncovered, for another 45 minutes. Turn hens once to give the underside time to brown. Baste often. The last 15 minutes, add sherry to pan gravy and continue to baste. The hens should be brown, glazed, and very tender. Transfer to warmed platter, pour the gravy over them, and sprinkle with a little chopped parsley.

Serves 4

Glazed Duck with Bing Cherry Sauce

By steaming the bird first, a kind of Turkish bath reducing treatment, we eliminate much of the fat that ordinarily distinguishes it. The slow roasting process will make an assault on what remains—but even so, let the prudent dieter in the household leave the skin on his plate. The delicious fruit sauce will compensate for any dryness.

5- to 6-pound duckling	2 stalks celery
1 teaspoon salt	1 cup or more water
freshly ground pepper	1 cup orange juice
1 large onion	

Salt and pepper duckling thoroughly, inside and out. Place on rack in large soup kettle with cover. Add water to pot to the depth of 2 inches. Add cut-up onion and celery cut into 2-inch lengths. Cover tightly, bring to boil and reduce heat. Cook slowly for 1½ hours.

Preheat oven to 325 degrees. After duck is steamed, remove from soup pot and drain thoroughly. Cut duck into quarters with poultry shears. Place pieces on rack in baking pan and roast uncovered for 1½ hours or until skin is crisp and brown. Pour off fat two or three times while it is cooking. The last 20 minutes, add orange juice and baste a few times.

Remove duck to warmed serving platter and cover with sauce and cherries. Serve extra sauce in gravy boat.

Serves 4

Bing Cherry Sauce

¾ cup brown sugar
1 6-ounce can frozen orange juice
6 ounces cherry juice from 1 No. 2 can pitted Bing cherries
1 teaspoon prepared mustard
1 tablespoon cornstarch
¼ cup cold water
¾ cup sherry

Combine brown sugar, undiluted frozen orange juice and cherry juice in saucepan. Bring to a boil and let simmer for a minute. Add cherries and prepared mustard. Thicken with cornstarch dissolved in ¼ cup cold water and simmer together for 5 minutes. Just before serving, add sherry.

11

Fish and Sea Food

THIS might very well turn out to be a panegyric about all the things that live in the sea, since even the fattest fish contain less fat than the leanest meats, and abound in unsaturated fatty acids besides. In addition, fish contain only half the amount of calories lurking in an equal weight of beef or pork, their protein content is highly concentrated, and they offer tantalizing flavors for the gourmet and opportunities for culinary virtuosity to the cook.

In our household, we have made lunch synonymous with fish. This makes meal planning as simple as a breeze, eliminating as it does the need for a major decision. For this generally light noontime meal, your grocer can be as helpful as your fish market, and is probably more accessible. The tins of sardines, tuna fish, salmon, herring and sardines in tomato sauce, and the like which line his shelves are just a can opener away from your table where they await your pleasure with all their friendly fat advantages. The shellfish—shrimp, crab meat and lobster—may be used occasionally.

There is scarcely a luncheon or dinner course, with the possible exception of dessert, for which sea food or fish cannot provide a solution. Starting with kippers for breakfast and continuing through luncheon, tea or cocktail time and dinner, you can find in the endless variety of sea food and fish, either frozen, dried, smoked, pickled, canned, salted or fresh, the basic material for some memorable snacks and meals.

I believe that many households which are "fish resistant," for want of a better way to describe this sad state, suffer only from underexposure to interesting fish cookery. Their reluctance or lack of interest often develops as a result of uninspired and pedestrian treatment. It is a myth that only experts can prepare fish properly, since almost anyone with a willingness to make an effort and the ability to tell time can become an expert.

The last is important because fish, unlike many meat and poultry dishes, does not improve with a long wait between preparation and serving. If you think your dinner might have to be delayed, time your preparations accordingly. Your family will hold up better after a ten- or fifteen-minute delay than the fish will. One of the secrets of the excellence of the sea food specialty restaurants is their practice of cooking-to-order.

If you should happen to live on the banks of a well-stocked trout stream, ignore the recipes. All you need is a frying pan, some polyunsaturated oil and salt and pepper. The rest of us will do well to experiment with all forms and shapes of crustaceans and the finny things.

Since it would be exceedingly difficult, if not impossible, to plan a dietary rich in protein and low in saturated fat without the frequent appearance of the fish and sea food family, please forgive me my poor joke about our need for a fish-ician in the successful management of our friendly fat regime.

Busy Day Fish Bake

Takes just a few minutes for preparation and not too much more for cooking.

2 pounds fish filets, fresh or frozen; sole, haddock or perch
½ teaspoon salt
freshly ground pepper
½ cup oil
1 cup corn flake crumbs

Salt and pepper fish filets. Dip in oil and coat with corn flake crumbs. Arrange filets in a single layer in lightly oiled shallow baking dish. Bake in 350-degree oven for 30 minutes or more, until fish flakes easily. Serve with tartare sauce and lemon wedges.

Serves 4

Baked Stuffed Fish
(Bass or Red Snapper)

3 pound bass or red snapper
½ teaspoon salt
freshly ground pepper
½ pound fresh shrimp, cooked and coarsely chopped
1 4-ounce can mushrooms, coarsely chopped

½ cup bread crumbs
sprinkle of dried dill
½ cup white wine
¼ cup water in which shrimp was cooked
¼ teaspoon Lawry's seasoned salt

Have fish scaled, cleaned and boned. Preheat oven to 450 degrees. Rinse and drain fish well. Salt and pepper inside and out.

Combine shrimp, mushrooms, sprinkling of dill, bread crumbs, ¼ cup white wine, and Lawry's seasoned salt. Mix well. Stuff into body cavity of fish. Sew opening with needle and thread or close with skewers.

Cut three diagonal gashes in the skin. This will keep the fish in shape during cooking. Place on rack in large, flat baking pan, basting every 15 minutes with remaining wine and water. After the first 15 minutes, reduce heat to 350 degrees. Bake until fish is flaky, which should take 40 to 50 minutes.

Serves 4

Baked Fish, Spanish Style

Any thick, white fish will do for this, but I particularly like halibut or a substantial haddock filet.

2 pounds halibut or filet of haddock, 1½ inches thick
1 teaspoon salt
freshly ground pepper
¼ teaspoon red pepper, or ½ teaspoon Tabasco sauce
6 tablespoons oil
2 large onions, thinly sliced
2 tablespoons pimento, diced

4 thick slices tomato
3 tablespoons chopped chives or scallions
½ pound mushrooms, thinly sliced
⅓ cup dry white wine
¾ cup bread crumbs
1 teaspoon Worcestershire sauce

Preheat oven to 350 degrees.

To cook fish, use large, shallow ovenproof baking dish that can be brought to the table. Spread 2 tablespoons of the oil over the bottom of dish, cover with layer of thinly sliced onions and pimento.

Wash fish and wipe dry. If you are using Tabasco sauce, sprinkle both sides of the fish with it, and rub it evenly over the whole surface. The red pepper should be mixed with the salt and pepper and the surfaces sprinkled with it. Cut fish into 4 portions and arrange seasoned slices on top of onion. Cover each piece of fish with a tomato slice and sprinkle with chopped chives or scallions. Scatter mushrooms over all. Add wine.

Heat remaining 4 tablespoons oil in small skillet, add Worcestershire sauce and brown the bread crumbs. Sprinkle over top of fish. Bake uncovered in 350-degree oven for 35 to 40 minutes, or until fish flakes easily with fork. Serve at once.

Serves 4

Baked Halibut with Clam Sauce

2 pounds halibut steak	½ teaspoon dry mustard
3 tablespoons flour	2 teaspoons Worcestershire sauce
3 tablespoons oil	1 10½-ounce can minced clams
2 cups skim milk	(save liquid)
1 teaspoon salt	2 tablespoons chopped parsley
freshly ground pepper	

Lightly oil large shallow baking dish that can be brought to the table. Salt fish lightly, sprinkle with paprika and dribble a little oil over it. Bake in 350-degree oven for 35 to 40 minutes, or until fish flakes easily.

For the clam sauce, heat the 3 tablespoons of oil in a small saucepan and blend in flour. Add salt, pepper, mustard, Worcestershire sauce and blend well. Add skim milk and liquid which has been drained from the clams, stirring constantly until the sauce thickens and bubbles. Add minced clams and chopped parsley. Taste to correct seasoning.

Cover fish with clam sauce for the last 15 minutes of baking in oven.

Serves 4

Baked Stuffed Mackerel

1 2½-pound mackerel, cleaned
    and split
1 teaspoon salt
1 large onion, finely chopped
2 cups packed soft bread crumbs

½ teaspoon thyme
3 tablespoons oil
freshly ground pepper
2 tablespoons minced parsley

Preheat oven to 400 degrees. Rub cavity of fish with salt. Mix onion, bread crumbs, oil, thyme, the 1 teaspoon salt, pepper and parsley together. Stuff fish with the mixture and close the opening with skewers or tie with string. Cut 3 diagonal gashes in the skin to keep fish flat during cooking.

Take a piece of aluminum foil large enough to hold the fish. Place stuffed fish in the center, sprinkle with a little freshly ground pepper and dribble oil over top. Bring foil up over fish, overlap it and close. Make the package secure so that the juices will remain inside. Place fish package on baking sheet and bake for 30 minutes. Open foil and fold back top. Continue baking for another 10 or 15 minutes, or until fish flakes easily when tested with fork. Baste with juices in foil package.

Transfer to hot serving platter in its foil wrapping. Garnish with lemon wedges and parsley. Serve with tartare sauce.

Serves 3

Codfish Portuguese

This is a famous Portuguese dish. Its official name is Bacalhau a Gomes de Sá—but we just call it Bacalhau—which, by a curious coincidence, means "codfish" in, as you might guess, Portuguese.

1 pound dried codfish
3 unpeeled potatoes
⅔ cup oil
1 clove garlic, crushed
2 large onions, sliced

¼ cup black olives, chopped
⅓ cup dry white wine
freshly ground pepper
½ teaspoon dill seed
chopped parsley for garnish

Soak codfish in cold water overnight. If you can get around to it conveniently, you can change the water a couple of times—the fish is salty. After soaking, discard water, drain fish, and place in medium-sized saucepan. Put in enough cold water to cover and boil for 20 minutes, or until fish flakes easily with fork. Reserve liquid and boil potatoes in it until tender. Flake fish, removing skin and bones, if there are any. When potatoes are done and cool enough to handle, peel and slice.

In a large skillet, heat oil and cook garlic and onions in it for about 8 minutes, until limp but not brown. Add olives, flaked fish and sliced potatoes. Add dill seed, wine, and season with pepper. Cook for about 5 minutes, stirring the whole time. Put mixture into well-oiled casserole and bake in 400-degree oven for 15 minutes. Garnish with parsley. Serve hot.

Serves 4

Filet of Sole, Amandine

2 pounds filet of sole or flounder
2 tablespoons flour
1 teaspoon salt
freshly ground pepper
½ cup oil
⅓ cup blanched slivered almonds
½ teaspoon Lawry's seasoned salt
3 tablespoons lemon juice
1 tablespoon chopped parsley
lemon wedges

Wash and dry fish filets. Sprinkle with flour seasoned with salt and pepper. Heat oil in large skillet. Add fish and fry over medium heat until golden on both sides. Remove fish to platter and keep warm in oven while you lightly brown almonds in the same pan. Sprinkle with Lawry's seasoned salt and lemon juice, heat through and pour over fish. Garnish with wedges of lemon and parsley. Serve at once.

Serves 4 or 5

Filet of Sole, Anchovy

Anchovies add a pleasant piquancy to many dishes. This can be made with any thin fish filet.

2 pounds fish filets
1 1-ounce can anchovy filets
1 tablespoon chopped parsley
5 tablespoons oil
lemon wedges

Wash fish filets and wipe dry with paper towel. Mash anchovies into a paste and mix with oil and parsley. Heat this mixture in large skillet for 5 minutes over very low flame. Add filets and cook over medium heat until golden brown on both sides. The time will vary with the thickness of the fish, but it should cook in 15 to 20 minutes. Remove fish to warm platter and pour sauce over it.

Garnish with lemon wedges lightly dusted with paprika.

Serves 4

Filet of Sole Shelly

For additional elegance try this with the shrimp sauce on page 208 or the lobster sauce on page 209.

6 filets of sole (about 2½ pounds)
2 stalks celery
1 medium-sized onion
1 clove garlic, crushed
5 tablespoons oil
½ cup blanched almonds, finely chopped
½ cup chicken stock

2 slices white bread, crumbed
pinch of nutmeg
pinch of mace
1 teaspoon salt
freshly ground pepper
juice of ½ lemon
½ cup dry white wine

For the stuffing, chop celery and onion very fine. Add garlic and almonds. Sauté this for 5 minutes in medium-sized skillet in 2 tablespoons of the oil, or until nuts are light brown. Add to the mixture chicken stock and crumbs made from bread. Season with mace, nutmeg and 1 teaspoon salt.

Place the 6 filets on flat surface and sprinkle lightly with salt and pepper. Divide dressing into 6 equal portions and spread on each of the filets. Roll up and secure with toothpick. Pour remaining 3 tablespoons oil in flat baking dish and arrange stuffed filets in it. Sprinkle with lemon juice and wine. Bake in 425-degree oven for 5 minutes, turn filets, dust lightly with paprika, and bake an additional 15 minutes, until fish is cooked through, and browned on top.

Serves 6

Fish Filets in Mustard Sauce

2 pounds fish filets
3 tablespoons oil
1½ cups tomato juice
1 clove garlic, crushed
2 tablespoons finely chopped
    onion
1 tablespoon finely chopped
    parsley

2 tablespoons prepared mustard
½ teaspoon salt
freshly ground pepper
2 tablespoons cornstarch
2 tablespoons water
¼ cup bread crumbs browned
    in 2 tablespoons oil

Combine the 3 tablespoons oil with tomato juice, crushed garlic, chopped onion, parsley, mustard, salt and pepper in saucepan and heat to boiling point. In a cup, stir together cornstarch and water. Add a bit of the hot sauce to cornstarch mixture and return the combination to saucepan, stirring constantly, until it thickens. Lightly oil shallow baking dish and arrange fish filets in it in a single layer. Spoon sauce over fish. Brown bread crumbs in 2 tablespoons of oil and scatter over the sauce. Bake in 350-degree oven for 30 minutes or more, until fish flakes easily and crumbs are brown.

Serves 4

Poached Fish Filets in Wine Sauce

1 pound fish filets
1½ tablespoons flour
1½ tablespoons oil
⅓ cup dry white wine

⅓ cup water
dash salt and pepper
pinch thyme, marjoram, dried
    parsley, savory

In a skillet with a tightly fitting cover, heat oil, add flour and blend. Add water, wine, salt and pepper and stir until perfectly smooth. Add herb seasonings, stir, and place fish in skillet. Cover and allow to simmer gently until done. This should take about 7 minutes. When fish flakes at the touch of a fork, it is ready for the heated serving platter. Pour sauce from pan over it.

Serves 2

Baked or Broiled Fish, Chinois
(Halibut, Salmon, Haddock, Cod)

2 pounds fish steaks
3 tablespoons soy sauce
½ cup sherry
2 tablespoons lemon juice

1 clove garlic, crushed
1 tablespoon oil
2 tablespoons fine bread crumbs

Mix soy sauce, sherry, lemon juice, garlic and oil together in flat baking dish. Wash fish steaks and pat dry. Place in sauce and marinate in refrigerator for an hour or longer. Sprinkle bread crumbs over top. Bake or broil in the usual way at moderate temperature. Baste with sauce a few times. Cook until fish flakes easily with fork. The time will vary, depending on the thickness of the fish. Transfer to warmed platter and serve at once.

Serves 4

Baked Fish Filets with Mushrooms and Noodles

An all-in-one dish that everyone likes.

8 ounces medium noodles
2 pounds fish filets (flounder or sole)
4 tablespoons oil
2 tablespoons flour
1¾ cup skim milk
1 teaspoon salt

freshly ground pepper
1 cup mushrooms, sliced
½ to ¾ cup sherry
3 tablespoons corn flake crumbs
½ teaspoon Lawry's seasoned salt
parsley for garnish

Cook ½ pound of medium noodles for 8 minutes, according to directions on package. Rinse and drain well. Lightly oil large shallow baking dish and spread cooked noodles evenly on the bottom.

In medium-sized saucepan, heat 2 tablespoons of the oil, blend in the flour, add salt and pepper. Add skim milk, stirring constantly until the mixture thickens and bubbles. Reduce heat and cook a minute longer. In small skillet, sauté sliced mushrooms in remaining 2 tablespoons oil for 3 minutes, add to sauce and mix well. Pour sauce on noodles.

Heat sherry in large skillet. While simmering, add fish filets. Poach over medium heat until they lose their raw look. With a slotted spoon, carefully remove them and arrange on the noodles. Pour the wine left in the pan on fish. Sprinkle with Lawry's seasoned salt, corn flake crumbs and chopped parsley. Bake in 350-degree oven for 10 minutes.

Serves 4 to 6

Poached Finnan Haddie

If you are not yet familiar with this fish, do make its acquaintance. Its origin is haddock which has been smoked, and in the tradition of its source, contains no fat of any kind. It has a salty tang which serves it well in its role either as an appetizer, or with a delicate white sauce sparked with sherry as a main dish.

The filets I buy from my fish store—and I assume this is standard—weigh between ¾ and 1 pound each. They serve 4 adequately as a first course, 2 portions as a main course.

To Poach: put some skim milk to the depth of 1 inch into a shallow skillet with tight-fitting lid. When warm, add fish which has been cut into serving-size pieces. Simmer slowly, covered, for about 20 minutes, when it should flake easily. If not, 5 minutes more should do the trick. Serve warm.

Creamed Finnan Haddie

1 pound finnan haddie filet
1 tablespoon oil
1 tablespoon flour
freshly ground pepper

1 cup skim milk (using what was left from poaching)
1 tablespoon, or more, sherry
chopped parsley

Poach finnan haddie according to directions in preceding recipe. Remove poached fish to platter and keep warm in oven. In small saucepan, heat oil, add flour and blend well. Add milk, and stir constantly until the mixture thickens and bubbles. Add dash of pepper, chopped parsley and sherry to taste. Pour over fish and serve hot.

Fish Florentine

This is an excellent guise for either whiting, halibut or any filets, such as cod, haddock, sole or flounder.

2 pounds fish
1 cup water
¼ cup white wine
¼ cup lemon juice
3 tablespoons oil
3 tablespoons flour
1 cup skim milk
1 tablespoon Worcestershire
    sauce

1 package frozen chopped spinach
    (or 1½ cups, cooked and
    drained)
4 scallions, finely chopped
½ teaspoon salt
freshly ground pepper
bread crumbs

Place fish in shallow casserole or baking dish. Add water, wine, and lemon juice. Cover and boil for 5 minutes. Drain broth from fish into saucepan and boil, uncovered, until it is reduced to two-thirds. Set this stock aside and place 2 tablespoons of the oil and flour in the same pan. Stir over medium heat and add skim milk, stirring constantly until it becomes thickened. Add salt, pepper, fish stock, Worcestershire sauce, spinach and chopped scallions. Taste to correct seasoning and bring to boil. Remove from heat.

Sprinkle fish lightly with salt and pepper. If you have used the whiting, remove bones carefully, leaving fish in quite large pieces. Cover fish with the spinach sauce, and sprinkle with bread crumbs. Dribble a tablespoon of oil over all. Bake in 400-degree oven for 8 to 10 minutes, or until top is golden brown. Serve immediately.

Serves 4

Broiled Salmon

3 pounds salmon steak, ¾ inch
    thick
3 tablespoons oil
juice of a lemon

½ teaspoon salt
freshly ground pepper
rosemary or dill
lemon wedges

Dribble lemon juice on both sides of salmon steak, rub a soupçon of rosemary or dill, whichever you prefer, on fish and brush with oil.

Place in preheated, oiled flat baking dish. Place under broiler flame about 2 inches from heat unit. Broil for about 8 minutes, basting with oil in pan. Turn and broil for 8 minutes more, or until fish flakes easily. Season with salt and pepper, and place on heated serving dish. Serve with lemon wedges, dusted with paprika.

Serves 6

Salmon Mousse with Cucumber Sauce

I hope you have a fish mold—or know where you can borrow one when you make this mousse. With a slice of stuffed olive for an eye, and its delicate pink body curved around a bowl of green cucumber sauce, this bigger-than-life fish will look as flavorful as it tastes. It is equally effective as an appetizer course for dinner guests or a main course for a party luncheon.

2 pounds cooked salmon	1 teaspoon grated onion
1 stalk celery	1 egg, separated
1 onion	1½ tablespoons oil
1 teaspoon salt	1 cup skim milk
1½ tablespoons sugar	¼ cup cider vinegar
1 tablespoon flour	1½ tablespoons gelatine soaked in
½ teaspoon dry mustard	3 tablespoons cold water
2 teaspoons Worcestershire sauce	

Boil salmon in salted water to which you have added onion and the stalk of celery. When it flakes easily—this will take about 20 minutes—remove from pot and cool. Flake, making sure you get at all the bones. Salmon bones are tricky things, as you know.

In top of double boiler, mix salt, sugar, flour, dry mustard, Worcestershire sauce, grated onion, egg yolk, oil, milk and vinegar. Cook over boiling water, stirring constantly, until the mixture thickens. Add soaked gelatine and stir until dissolved. Add entire mixture to flaked salmon. Beat egg white until stiff and fold into the mixture. Taste for seasoning. Rub mold lightly with oil and pack with mixture. Chill for 5 hours. Unmold on round platter garnished with watercress. Serve cucumber sauce separately.

Serves 6 to 8 as appetizer
4 to 6 as main course

Cucumber Sauce

1 large cucumber, peeled and grated
1 cup mayonnaise
½ teaspoon prepared mustard
1 tablespoon lemon juice
1 tablespoon minced chives
few drops of green vegetable coloring

Blend ingredients together and chill.

Smelts Sauté

If you wish, you may cook these with the heads and tails left on.

1½ pounds smelts
¼ cup nonfat milk solids
¼ cup water
1 cup flour
1 teaspoon salt
freshly ground pepper
3 tablespoons lemon juice
4 anchovy filets, cut up and mashed
1 tablespoon corn flake crumbs
1 tablespoon chopped parsley
4 or 5 tablespoons oil

Wash smelts, and do whatever you want to about the heads and tails. Just be sure to clip off the little fins. Season fish with salt, pepper and 2 tablespoons of the lemon juice. Let them marinate for 10 or 15 minutes. Reserve this liquid which is left for the sauce. Combine nonfat milk solids with water and 1 tablespoon of the oil, and stir well. Dip fish in this mixture and roll in flour. Heat 3 tablespoons of oil in a large skillet. Fry smelts until they are brown and crisp—about 5 minutes on each side—adding extra oil if needed. Place on absorbent paper to drain and keep warm in oven while you prepare the sauce.

Add to the same skillet the reserved liquid, another tablespoon of oil if the oil has been all used up, 1 tablespoon lemon juice, mashed anchovy filets, corn flake crumbs and chopped parsley. Cook over low heat for 2 minutes, stirring constantly. Taste to correct seasoning—you may want to add a drop or two of sweetening. Remove fish to warmed serving platter and pour sauce over fish.

Serves 4

Sweet and Pungent Fish

1 pike, 2 to 2½ pounds, boned
2 slices canned pineapple
1 large green pepper
⅓ cup sugar
⅓ cup cider vinegar
1 teaspoon salt
1 teaspoon Chinese brown gravy
    sauce (bead molasses type)

For Fish Stock
bones, head and skin of fish
cold water to cover
¼ teaspoon salt
3 whole peppercorns
1 rib celery, cut into 2-inch
    lengths
1 small onion, quartered

¼ cup flour
¼ cup fish stock
2 rounded teaspoons cornstarch
oil for frying

Have your fish man filet pike and give you bones, head and skin. Place these in medium-sized saucepan, cover with cold water, add salt, peppercorns, celery and onion. Cover and simmer for 30 minutes. Strain. If you have more than ½ cup, cook down until liquid is reduced to that amount. Set stock aside.

Core and trim green pepper and cut into 8 strips. Cut each pineapple slice into 8 pieces.

Wash fish filets and dry. Cut into 1-inch squares and dip in flour. In your deep-fat fryer, heat 3 inches of oil to 380 degrees, or until a 1-inch piece of bread browns in 30 seconds. Fry until brown, a few pieces at a time, so as not to cool the oil suddenly. Each piece of fish takes approximately 8 to 10 minutes. Remove pieces with a slotted spoon as they are done and drain on absorbent paper.

While fish is cooking—and if you are near enough to watch it—you can prepare the sauce. In a medium-sized saucepan, combine vinegar and stock and bring to a boil. Add sugar and salt and stir. Add pineapple and green pepper and bring to a boil again. Mix cornstarch with a teaspoon or so of cold water to make a smooth paste and add to sauce with the brown sauce, stirring until smooth and thickened. Add fried fish and cook 2 minutes more.

Remove to warm serving bowl and serve with hot fluffy rice.

Serves 4

Broiled Swordfish Steak

2 pounds swordfish steaks
⅓ cup oil
3 tablespoons chopped scallions
3 tablespoons chopped parsley
¼ teaspoon paprika
1 tablespoon soy sauce

¼ teaspoon tarragon
¼ teaspoon sweet basil
juice and rind of 1 lemon
½ teaspoon salt
freshly ground pepper

Wash and dry swordfish steaks and place in shallow baking dish. In small skillet, heat oil, and add chopped scallions and parsley. Cook until scallions turn deep gold color. Add paprika, soy sauce, tarragon, basil, salt, pepper and lemon juice and rind. Simmer 2 minutes longer until thoroughly blended. Spread this sauce over fish and refrigerate for at least an hour. Heat broiler and broil fish steaks 4 inches below flame for 10 to 15 minutes on each side, depending on the thickness of the fish. Serve with lemon wedges lightly dusted with paprika.

Serves 4

Swordfish Steaks in Tomato Sauce

2 slices swordfish, each 1½
    inches thick (about 3 pounds)
3 tablespoons finely chopped
    parsley
½ cup oil

2 cloves garlic, crushed
¼ cup lemon juice
2 8-ounce cans tomato sauce
1 teaspoon salt
freshly ground pepper

Preheat oven to 425 degrees.

Oil large flat baking dish and place swordfish steaks in it. In a saucepan, simmer parsley, oil and garlic for 10 minutes. Stir occasionally. Add tomato sauce and lemon juice and heat through thoroughly. Add salt and pepper, and taste for seasoning. Pour sauce over fish and bake 25 minutes, or until fish flakes easily when tested with fork.

Serves 6

Crab Meat Casserole

1 pound fresh lump crab meat	½ teaspoon salt
1½ tablespoons flour	freshly ground pepper
1½ tablespoons oil	1 tablespoon horse-radish
1¼ cups skim milk	2 tablespoons chopped parsley
1 tablespoon lemon juice	½ cup bread crumbs, browned in
1 tablespoon Worcestershire sauce	2 tablespoons oil
2 tablespoons ketchup	

You can make this with canned crab meat, but it won't taste as good as it does with the fresh. Pick over crab meat, removing all shells.

In medium-sized saucepan, heat oil, blend with flour thoroughly over small flame, but don't let it brown. Add milk, stirring constantly, and cook until mixture thickens and bubbles. Add lemon juice, Worcestershire sauce, ketchup, salt, pepper, horse-radish and chopped parsley and mix well. Add sauce to crab meat and blend well. Place in lightly oiled 1½-quart casserole, cover with browned bread crumbs and bake in 350-degree oven for 20 minutes.

Serves 4

Note: Do not freeze leftover crab dishes. Cooked crab meat, unlike shrimp, lobster or scallops, does not take kindly to freezing. Its quality may be unimpaired, but it turns unappetizingly dark.

Southern Crab Cakes with Mustard Sauce

Made small, a lovely appetizer course—and equally satisfying in heartier portions as a main course.

1 pound fresh lump crab meat	1 tablespoon lemon juice
2 egg whites	1 slice white bread
½ cup mayonnaise	1 egg white, whipped to a froth
¼ cup minced scallions	½ cup flour
2 tablespoons finely minced celery	½ cup bread crumbs
1 teaspoon Worcestershire sauce	½ cup oil

Pick over crab meat to remove shells. Beat egg whites lightly and combine with crab meat, adding mayonnaise, scallions, celery, Worcestershire sauce and lemon juice. Remove crust from bread, crumble finely and add to crab meat mixture, mixing well. Form into round balls, the size of a walnut for the appetizer course, larger if they are to serve as the main course.

Beat egg white to a froth with 2 tablespoons of water. Dip crab cakes into flour, egg white and bread crumbs. Cover and refrigerate until ready to cook.

To cook crab cakes, heat oil in heavy skillet and brown on all sides. Add more oil if needed. Serve with mustard sauce.

Serves 4 to 6
(8 as appetizer)

Mustard Sauce

2 tablespoons flour
2 tablespoons oil
1 cup skim milk
½ cup consommé or dissolved
    broth powder

2 tablespoons prepared mustard
1½ tablespoons Worcestershire
    sauce
½ teaspoon instant onion
freshly ground pepper

In a small saucepan, heat oil. Blend flour and, stirring constantly, add skim milk. Allow to come to boil, reduce heat, and stir in ½ cup consommé. Add mustard, Worcestershire sauce, instant onion and pepper. Cook for 3 minutes over low flame, stirring constantly, until sauce is thick and smooth. Taste for seasoning—you may want a bit more mustard or Worcestershire sauce if you like it a bit spicier. Keep sauce warm until ready to serve, but do not let it boil. If it gets too thick, thin it out with a few additional tablespoons of consommé. Sauces should never be too thick and floury—the consistency of heavy rich cream is about right.

Yields 1½ cups sauce

Cold Lobster Mayonnaise

The social status of the lobster has come a long way since the early 1800's when prosperous New Englanders regarded it patronizingly as a staple to be eaten only by the poor people who couldn't help themselves. I suspect, though, that even the aristocracy of New Bedford would have relished this refreshing dish on a hot day.

2 fresh 1½-pound lobsters
boiling salted water
⅓ cup mayonnaise
½ teaspoon chopped chives
1 teaspoon lemon juice

freshly ground pepper
1 teaspoon chopped parsley
4 anchovy filets
strips of pimento

Plunge lobsters into kettle of boiling salted water and cook, tightly covered, for 7 minutes after the water has reached a boil again. More cooking than that will make them tough. Two-pound lobsters will require an extra minute.

When lobsters are cool, place on backs and slit lengthwise down the middle. Remove intestinal vein but reserve tomalley (the greenish liver) and lobster coral (the roe), and place back in the lobster. Crack claws to make it easier to remove meat.

Combine mayonnaise with lemon juice, chopped chives, parsley and pepper. Spread over lobster, decorate with anchovy filets and pimento, and chill until ready to serve.

Serves 2

Lobster Tails Thermidor

For the occasions when you're looking for something a little different, give a thought to these. As a main course, a half-pound tail is a generous serving. The four-ounce size is adequate as an appetizer or a buffet dish when there are other foods.

4 8-ounce frozen lobster tails
4 tablespoons oil
4 tablespoons flour
1 teaspoon salt
½ teaspoon paprika
½ teaspoon dry mustard
¼ teaspoon nutmeg
2 cups skim milk

⅓ cup nonfat milk solids
1 4-ounce can sliced mushrooms
3 tablespoons sherry
¾ cup bread crumbs browned in
   2 tablespoons oil
lemon wedges
chopped parsley

Place lobster tails in kettle of boiling, salted water. When water reaches a boil again, lower heat and cook exactly 9 minutes if tails are thawed, 11 minutes if frozen. Time this carefully or the meat will not be at its best. Lobster reacts to overcooking by getting tough and rubbery. (The thawed 4-ounce size needs to cook for only 5 minutes.)

Drain hot water from kettle and refill with cold. When thoroughly drenched and cool, remove tails, drain well. Cut through the under-shell with kitchen shears. Remove meat by inserting your fingers between shell and meat and pulling it firmly. It should come out easily in one piece. Dice meat into small bite-sized pieces and set aside. Reserve shells.

Heat 4 tablespoons oil in medium-sized saucepan. Blend in flour. Add salt, paprika, mustard and nutmeg. Slowly stir in 2 cups of milk, mixing well to make a smooth sauce. Add nonfat milk solids and cook for a minute or two until sauce thickens and bubbles. Taste and correct seasoning. Add diced lobster, drained, sliced mushrooms, and sherry. Refill shells with lobster and sauce. Cover with bread crumbs which have been browned in oil. Place under broiler for 10 minutes. Sprinkle lightly with chopped parsley, remove to warmed serving platter and garnish with lemon wedges.

Serves 4

Lobster and Scallop Kabobs with Tangy Sauce

2 pounds rock lobster tails (4 or 5)	8 large mushroom caps
½ pound scallops	1 green pepper

Snip under-shell of the lobster tail with scissors. Work meat out of shell. Cut meat into pieces the same size as scallops.

Wash green pepper and cut into 1½-inch squares. Simmer in boiling, salted water just long enough to soften a bit—no more than 5 minutes. On skewers, alternate chunks of the lobster meat, mushroom caps, scallops and green pepper. Preheat broiler.

Brush skewered foods with tangy sauce and broil for 5 minutes. Turn skewers, brush the other side with sauce and continue cooking 3 to 5 minutes longer. Serve with fluffy boiled rice and extra sauce.

Serves 4

Tangy Sauce

1 onion, chopped
2 tablespoons oil
1 cup ketchup
⅓ cup water
5 tablespoons lemon juice

2 tablespoons brown sugar
3 tablespoons sherry
1 tablespoon prepared mustard
1 tablespoon Worcestershire sauce

Heat oil. Add chopped onion and cook until limp and transparent. Add lemon juice, ketchup, water, sugar, sherry, mustard and Worcestershire sauce and blend well. Cover pan and cook over low heat for 20 minutes. Serve hot.

Makes 1⅔ cups

Boiled Shrimp

Shrimp, like all their sea food cousins, must never be overcooked. They respond to this indelicate treatment by getting tough—a poor return for our pains. Cooking them as described below will keep them tender and juicy.

Hardware stores sell a sharp-pointed plastic gadget designed for shelling and deveining shrimp which we find useful.

1 pound unpeeled raw shrimp
1 cup water
1 teaspoon salt

2 stalks celery, leaves and all, cut into 3-inch pieces
3 peppercorns

Make a stock of water, salt, cut-up celery and peppercorns. Bring to boil in covered kettle and simmer for 5 minutes.

Add shrimp, cover, bring to boil, reduce heat, and simmer for 3 minutes. (The frozen ones will need a few additional minutes before they thaw out, but as soon as they're pink, they're done.) Uncover and remove pot from heat. As soon as shrimp are cool enough to handle, peel and clean.

Serves 2 to 3

Grilled Shrimp

2 pounds uncooked jumbo shrimp	½ teaspoon oregano
½ cup oil	½ teaspoon basil
½ teaspoon salt	juice of ½ lemon
freshly ground pepper	½ teaspoon Lawry's seasoned salt
1 clove garlic, minced	½ teaspoon paprika
3 tablespoons minced parsley	2 tablespoons bread crumbs

Shell and devein raw shrimp, leaving tails. Rinse well under cold water and dry between paper towels. In shallow baking dish, combine oil, salt, pepper, garlic, parsley, oregano, basil and lemon juice. Marinate shrimp in this mixture for at least 20 minutes.

Remove shrimp from marinade and place on broiler pan. (I always cover broiler pan with aluminum foil. It makes cleaning up easier and saves all the juices.) Dust shrimp with Lawry's seasoned salt and paprika and place broiling pan on the highest rack, not more than 2 inches away from the flame. Broil for 3 minutes on each side.

Return shrimp to baking dish, sprinkle with bread crumbs, and place in 450-degree oven for 20 minutes, turning them once during the baking. Serve hot in the baking dish.

Serves 4 to 6

Shrimp Marinara

3 pounds shrimp, boiled and cleaned	1 cup tomato juice
	1 teaspoon salt
2 onions, chopped fine	2 teaspoons oregano
6 tablespoons oil	½ teaspoon basil
1 No. 2½ can Italian peeled tomatoes	½ teaspoon basil
	freshly ground pepper

Boil shrimp as described on page 149. Remove shells and devein. Sauté finely chopped onions in oil in heavy kettle with cover. When they are transparent, add canned tomatoes and tomato juice. Season with salt, oregano, basil and pepper. Cover and simmer slowly for 20 minutes. Taste and adjust seasoning. Tomato juices vary in degree of sweetness or saltiness, so you'll have to express your own preference. If the sauce seems at all thin, let it boil down a bit. Add shrimp and let simmer another 7 or 8 minutes until thoroughly heated. Serve with fluffy rice.

Serves 6 to 8

French-fried Shrimp
(Shrimp Tempura)

People who can't abide anything batter-fried are mad for these. They're puffy, delicate and crisp.

24 raw jumbo shrimp
6 tablespoons flour
6 tablespoons lukewarm water
1 tablespoon oil
1 teaspoon salt
2 egg whites
oil for deep-fat frying

Shell and devein shrimp, leaving the tails intact. Rinse and pat dry. Slash through the vein side a bit and flatten them out.

In a medium-sized bowl, combine flour and water and beat well. Add salt and oil and mix well. Allow this to rest at least an hour.

When you are ready to fry the shrimp, beat egg whites until stiff, but not dry, and fold into batter.

Heat at least 3 inches oil in deep-fat fryer to 380 degrees (or until a cube of day-old bread browns in 30 seconds). Hold each shrimp by the tail, dip into batter. Fry in hot fat. Do only 1 or 2 at a time. Otherwise the oil will cool and the shrimp will be soggy instead of crisp and delicate. They cook quickly and puff up so brown and beautiful, you won't even mind the time it takes. Drain on absorbent paper and keep warm in oven until serving time. Serve with tartare sauce and lemon wedges, or the hot barbecue sauce on page 117.

Serves 3 or 4

In place of the other sauces, we sometimes serve one of these to accompany the fried shrimp:

Chinese Mustard

¼ cup boiling water
3 tablespoons dry English mustard
¼ teaspoon salt
2 tablespoons oil

½ teaspoon Worcestershire sauce
Stir boiling water into mustard. Add salt, oil and Worcestershire sauce, and mix well.

Red Sauce

½ cup ketchup
⅓ cup chili sauce
1 or 2 tablespoons horse-radish
1 tablespoon lemon juice
3 tablespoons mayonnaise

dash Tabasco

Combine all ingredients and blend well with a rotary beater. Chill in refrigerator until serving time.

Shrimp Michael

Michael didn't originate this—he happens to be our son and is especially fond of the crustaceans fixed this way:

24 jumbo-sized shrimp
⅔ cup oil
6 cloves of garlic, crushed

⅔ cup lemon juice
2 teaspoons chopped parsley

These shrimp will be cooked in the shells, so we remove only the black vein—a sharp paring knife will do the trick. Wash well and drain. Place shrimp in a marinade made of the oil, garlic, lemon juice and parsley. Store overnight in refrigerator. When you are ready to cook them, remove from marinade and broil about 5 minutes on each side, or until the shells are brown. The shells will present no problem to the diners—they lift off easily with knife and fork.

Serves 4

Shrimp in White Wine Sauce

3 pounds cleaned raw shrimp
1 small onion, sliced
1 cup dry white wine
1 teaspoon salt
1 cup chicken stock
    (bouillon or canned broth)

½ cup oil
5 tablespoons flour
2 tablespoons celery leaves, finely
    chopped
1 cup skim milk
chopped parsley

Shell and devein the raw shrimp and wash well. Combine onion, wine, stock and salt in saucepan. Bring to a boil. Reduce heat, add shrimp and simmer until they are pink—about 3 minutes. Remove shrimp from pan and reserve liquid.

Heat oil over direct heat in top of 3-quart double boiler. Blend in flour, stirring until smooth, and add the reserved liquid. Bring to a boil, stirring constantly.

Place pan over simmering water in double boiler and add celery leaves and milk. Add shrimp, discarding any pieces of onion that may be clinging to them. Taste for seasoning and correct. Leave the mixture for at least 20 minutes over the simmering water so that all the delicate flavors have a chance to blend together. Remove to casserole or chafing dish for serving and sprinkle chopped parsley over top.

Serves 6

Sweet and Pungent Shrimp

2 pounds raw shrimp
¼ cup dark brown sugar
2 tablespoons cornstarch
½ teaspoon salt
¼ cup cider vinegar
1 tablespoon soy sauce

¼ teaspoon ground ginger
1 1-pound 4-ounce can pineapple chunks
1 green pepper, cut into strips
2 small onions, cut in rings

Boil shrimp according to recipe on page 149. Shell and devein. Set aside. In a saucepan, mix sugar, cornstarch and salt. Add to this the juice drained from pineapple chunks, vinegar, soy sauce and ginger. Cook over medium heat, stirring constantly, until slightly thick. Add green pepper, onion and pineapple. As dictated by rules of Chinese cookery, which will not countenance overcooked or mushy vegetables, simmer for 3 minutes only. Add shrimp and bring to a boil, stirring constantly. Serve at once with hot rice.

Serves 4

Oriental Shrimp

2 pounds raw shrimp
2 tablespoons oil
1 small onion, chopped
¾ cup chicken broth
½ cup water chestnuts, thinly sliced
1 tablespoon cornstarch

1 package frozen peas
4 thin slices ginger root (or ½ teaspoon powdered ginger)
1 teaspoon salt
2 tablespoons soy sauce
¼ cup sherry

Shell and devein raw shrimp. In heavy skillet with tightly fitting lid, heat oil and add shrimp and onion. Stir constantly and cook until onion is tender and shrimp turn pink. This will take about 2 minutes.

Add broth, water chestnuts, peas, ginger and salt. Cover and cook over medium flame for 4 or 5 minutes, until peas and shrimp are tender. Remove cover and stir in soy sauce, sherry and cornstarch which has been dissolved in a tablespoon of water. Cook until sauce is clear and thickened. Serve at once with fluffy rice.

Serves 4

Curried Sea Food

This can be the answer to "What will we have for company?"

2 pounds large uncooked shrimp
1 pound fresh or frozen lobster
    meat
1 pound scallops
⅔ cup oil
2 cloves garlic, crushed
1 onion, finely chopped
3½ cups skim milk
7 tablespoons flour

2 teaspoons salt
freshly ground pepper
2 teaspoons prepared mustard
2 tablespoons Worcestershire
    sauce
1 tablespoon curry powder (or
    more)
½ pound sautéed mushrooms

Wash scallops and, if they are large, cut in two. Shell and devein raw shrimp, wash and drain well. Cut lobster meat into bite-sized chunks. Wash, peel and slice ½ pound mushrooms and sauté in 2 tablespoons oil.

In large skillet, sauté shrimp and scallops in 2 tablespoons of the oil for 5 minutes, or until shrimp are pink.

Heat remainder of oil in large kettle and add crushed garlic and onion. Cook onion until transparent and blend in flour, stirring constantly. Add milk slowly and bring to a boil, stirring constantly. Add salt and pepper, mustard, Worcestershire sauce and curry powder. The amount of curry powder depends on how strong your curry powder is—they vary—and how strong a curry you like. Be gentle, however—you don't want to blast your family's palate. Add shrimp, scallops, lobster and sautéed mushrooms. Taste for seasoning and correct. Keep warm but do not boil. Serve with rice. I always serve this in a chafing dish so that we can come back for a second helping (and we do). Don't neglect the chutney with this.

Serves 6 to 8

This curried sea food also makes a nice first course, served in individual shells. It will serve 12 adequately. Divide curry into shells, sprinkle with bread crumbs and a dribble of oil, and place shells on baking dish in 450-degree oven for about 10 minutes, or until piping hot.

The same curry sauce will serve you in good stead for leftover chicken, veal, beef or lamb. To determine the quantity of sauce you need, figure on a cup of sauce to 2 cups of whatever your main ingredient is.

Sea Food Newburg

A delicate Newburg like this one turns in a good performance either as a main dish, a late supper or an appetizer course. It can be made with boiled haddock, cod, halibut, etc.—or lobster, crab meat, shrimp and scallops, either alone or in combination. In determining the amount of sauce needed, figure a cup of sauce to a pound of fish or sea food.

If you are boiling the fish or sea food for this Newburg, you may use the stock in which it has cooked and omit the scallops.

1 pound cleaned and cooked shrimp or other sea food or fish	1 teaspoon salt
	white pepper
	½ pound scallops
1½ heaping tablespoons flour	1 stalk celery
3½ tablespoons oil	2 tablespoons chili sauce
1 cup skim milk	½ pound mushrooms, sliced
½ cup fish stock	4 tablespoons sherry

Wash scallops, place in small saucepan with ¾ cup cold water. Add a stalk of celery cut into 3-inch lengths, a pinch of salt and pepper. Bring to a slow boil and cover. Cook only until done—and that is when they've stopped looking raw. Overcooking makes them tough, just as it does crab meat or shrimp. Remove scallops from saucepan. Reduce stock to ½ cup by boiling over medium flame and reserve. Discard celery.

Wash and slice mushrooms. In small skillet, heat 2 tablespoons of the oil. Add mushrooms and cook for 5 minutes.

In large-sized skillet, heat remaining 1½ tablespoons oil. Add 1½ tablespoons flour and blend over small flame, but don't let it brown. Add salt and pepper, stir constantly and add milk. Add fish stock and continue to stir until it thickens and boils. Add chili sauce and sautéed mushrooms. Add shrimp, scallops and sherry and heat through. Taste and correct seasoning. Remove to warmed serving dish or, preferably, chafing dish. Serve with toast triangles.

Serves 3 or 4

Sea Food Milano

This is a good buffet dish for a largish gathering. The left-over freezes beautifully.

5 tablespoons oil
2 cups chopped onion
3 cloves garlic, crushed
½ teaspoon oregano
½ teaspoon basil
7½ cups tomato juice
½ cup ketchup
½ cup chopped parsley

3 squirts hot pepper sauce (or Tabasco)

1½ teaspoons salt
1½ pounds scallops
4 pounds shrimp
1 pound fresh or frozen lobster meat
6 cups small-sized shell macaroni
3 tablespoons cornstarch
½ cup cold water
chopped parsley for garnish

Boil shrimp according to directions on page 149. Clean and shell.

Heat oil in saucepan. Add chopped onion, garlic, oregano and basil and sauté 3 minutes, stirring often. Add 7½ cups tomato juice, ketchup, chopped parsley, 3 squirts of hot pepper sauce and salt. You may need more salt than this, depending on the tomato juice, but taste as you proceed. Add raw scallops, cut into bite-sized pieces, boil for 5 minutes and thicken with 3 tablespoons cornstarch mixed with ½ cup cold water.

Bring large kettle of salted water to a rolling boil, add 6 cups of the small-sized shell macaroni and cook about 10 minutes or until slightly tender. Rinse with hot water and drain thoroughly. Combine with sauce, lobster and shrimp. Add more seasoning if needed. It is now ready for reheating, which can be done in very slow oven or on top of stove on low flame. Stir as little as possible, but be careful it does not stick. When ready to serve, the consistency should be quite moist but not runny. Add water if needed. Serve in chafing dish or large casserole and sprinkle top with chopped parsley.

Serves 12

Broiled Scallops

This is particularly good when made with the bay scallops—which are the tiny ones, about the size of 11-millimeter pearls (but not as expensive). The scallops should marinate in the sauce for a few hours in the refrigerator. At dinnertime, you can preheat the broiler, but don't put the scallops under it until the family has washed their respective hands and powdered their respective noses—the scallops won't wait.

2 pounds scallops
½ cup oil
2 tablespoons scallions, finely chopped
2 tablespoons parsley, finely chopped
½ teaspoon sweet basil
½ teaspoon tarragon, finely crumbled
2 cloves garlic, minced
2 tablespoons corn flake crumbs
½ teaspoon salt
freshly ground pepper

Wash scallops and drain on absorbent paper. In small skillet, heat oil, add chopped scallions, basil, tarragon, garlic, parsley, salt and pepper and cook for 2 minutes. Add the crumbs and cook a minute longer. Arrange scallops in flat shallow baking dish and pour the mixture over them, mixing well so scallops will be thoroughly drenched. Place pan on broiling rack about 4 inches from heat. Cook under medium heat. Turn scallops over to brown both sides. The larger sea scallops will need 10 to 12 minutes—the bay scallops only about 8. If they are not brown enough, turn broiler flame up higher at the very end. Turn into warmed serving bowl or deep platter. Serve with lemon wedges.

Serves 4

Scalloped Scallops

2 pounds scallops
1 scant cup water
1 teaspoon salt
freshly ground pepper
2 tablespoons oil
2 tablespoons flour
1 small clove garlic, crushed

1 cup skim milk
¼ cup dry white wine
1 tablespoon chopped dill or
   ½ teaspoon dried dill weed
½ cup bread crumbs browned in
2 tablespoons oil

Wash scallops and place in saucepan with a scant cup of cold water. Bring them to a boil slowly, and cook only until the scallops have lost their raw look—2 or 3 minutes. Remove with slotted spoon and set aside. Boil the remaining liquid until it is reduced to ½ cup. Set aside.

Heat 2 tablespoons of oil in a saucepan with the crushed garlic and blend in flour. When smooth, add skim milk slowly, stirring constantly until thick and smooth. Add salt, pepper and liquid from the scallops. Add wine and dill. Add scallops and taste to correct seasoning.

Pour scallops and sauce into lightly oiled baking dish and sprinkle with bread crumbs which have been browned in oil. Bake in 350-degree oven for 25 to 30 minutes.

Serves 4

12

Potatoes and Other Starches

FEW FOODS are as maligned as the potato, which has been made the patsy for all the additional calories heaped on it in the form of butter, cream and cheese.

Actually, a medium-sized potato, about two and a half inches in diameter, contains approximately 100 calories, the same amount as an apple, an orange, half a large grapefruit, or one slice of buttered toast. The starch content is fairly high, ranging from twelve to twenty per cent, but on the other hand, it is chock full of essential nutrients and vitamins.

The number of calories with which the potato ends up depends not only on its embellishment, but also on how it is cooked. For instance, three ounces of French-fried potatoes contain about 345 calories; the same amount, raw and pan-fried has 240; the same amount plain boiled, 71 calories.

The smallest loss of vitamin C in potatoes occurs when they are cooked in their skins for as short a time and in as little water as possible, in a tightly lidded pot. They should not be soaked in water or allowed to stand in their own steam. So much for the tuber which has kept entire nations alive in times of disaster.

The use of dried beans and peas should not be overlooked in a dietary where meats are limited. They are an excellent source of protein, next best to that found in animal products. They lend themselves to a variety of delicious dishes which may serve as a main course.

The other starches—rice, wild rice, and noodles, barley and groats, imaginatively prepared, can bring a considerable amount of glamour along with substance, to any meal.

Baked Stuffed Potatoes

Nothing lost if these are prepared in the morning and refrigerated until time to pop them in the oven.

6 medium potatoes	¼ cup (or less) hot water
1 teaspoon salt	1 egg white, stiffly beaten
freshly ground pepper	1 tablespoon chopped chives
2 tablespoons oil	chopped parsley for garnish
4 tablespoons nonfat milk solids	paprika

Preheat oven to 400 degrees.

Scrub potatoes well, oil them, and prick with knife or skewer. Bake until soft, about an hour. When done, cut a large oval slice off the top. Scoop out the insides and mash. Add oil, salt, pepper, nonfat milk solids and enough hot water to make them light and fluffy. Mix well. Add chopped chives and fold in stiffly beaten egg white. Taste and correct seasonings.

Refill potato shells with this mixture. Dust tops lightly with paprika and sprinkle with parsley. Lower oven heat to 350 degrees, replace potatoes in oven and bake until the tops are browned, about 20 to 25 minutes.

Serves 6

Pan-Crisped Potatoes

These are crunchy and crusty outside and mealy inside, a perfect state for a potato.

4 to 6 medium potatoes	sprinkle of paprika
½ teaspoon salt	freshly ground pepper
½ teaspoon Lawry's seasoned salt	oil for frying

Scrub potatoes and place in saucepan with as little boiling, salted water as possible. Cover pan and boil until tender, between 25 and 40 minutes. When soft, drain and cool. Remove skins and slice lengthwise into eighths.

Cover bottom of large, heavy skillet with ⅛ inch of oil and heat. Add potato segments. Sprinkle with salts, pepper and paprika. Cook over medium heat for 15 to 20 minutes, shaking pan frequently and turning potatoes with spatula so they will get brown and crusty all around. Serve hot.

Serves 4 to 6

Escalloped Potatoes

6 medium-sized potatoes peeled and sliced thin	1 tablespoon snipped fresh dill (or 1 teaspoon dried dill)
2 large onions, grated	1½ cups skim milk
1 teaspoon salt	4 tablespoons oil
freshly ground pepper	bread crumbs
1 tablespoon chopped chives	paprika

In oiled 1½-quart casserole, place a layer of potatoes; cover with grated onion, sprinkle with salt and pepper, chives and dill, and repeat until all potatoes are used. There should be about 3 layers. Finish with a layer of potatoes.

In small saucepan which has been rinsed with cold water but not dried, heat skim milk and oil to the boiling point. Pour over potatoes so that it comes to the top layer but does not cover top. Sprinkle with bread crumbs and dust with paprika. Bake in 375-degree oven for 1¼ hours until potatoes are tender.

Serves 6

Parsleyed New Potatoes

The small new potatoes, like debutantes, are at their best when dressed simply.

2 pounds new potatoes	2 tablespoons chopped parsley
1 teaspoon salt	2 tablespoons oil
freshly ground pepper	

Wash potatoes well and boil, unpeeled, in as little salted water as possible in a covered pot. Depending on size, they may take anywhere from 15 to 35 minutes, but watch them carefully and don't overcook. When cool enough to handle, peel and transfer to heated skillet. Shake them until they are dry, and over low flame, add oil, parsley and seasonings. Continue to toss until they are coated with oil and parsley. Serve hot.

Serves 6

New Potatoes with Caraway Seeds

2 pounds new potatoes
2 tablespoons oil
1 tablespoon caraway seeds
2 tablespoons flour
1 cup beef stock (or broth powder, dissolved)

½ teaspoon salt
dash white pepper
3 tablespoons nonfat milk solids, dissolved in
¼ cup water
1 teaspoon chopped parsley

Wash potatoes well and boil, unpeeled, in as little salted water as possible in a covered pot. Cook from 15 to 35 minutes (depending on size) but watch them carefully and don't overcook. Peel when cool enough to handle, and keep warm.

In small skillet, heat oil and add caraway seeds. Heat through for a minute and blend in flour. Stir in beef stock slowly and stir constantly over low heat until thickened. Add salt, pepper, liquefied skim milk and parsley, blend well and cook an additional minute. Pour over potatoes.

Serves 6

Cottage Cheese Potato Casserole

6 medium potatoes
2 cups cottage cheese
2 tablespoons oil
2 tablespoons flour
2 teaspoons chopped parsley
1 teaspoon salt
1 tablespoon grated onion
freshly ground pepper

1 tablespoon chopped dill or 1 teaspoon dried dill
⅓ cup skim milk
½ cup fine bread crumbs browned in 2 tablespoons oil
2 tablespoons grated sapsago cheese

Scrub potatoes and place in as little boiling, salted water as possible. Cover pan and cook until soft, 25 to 40 minutes. Drain. When cool, peel and slice thinly.

Beat cottage cheese with a rotary beater until fluffy. Add oil and mix well.

Combine flour, parsley, salt, grated onion, pepper and dill. Oil 1½-quart casserole and arrange a layer of thinly sliced potatoes on the bottom. Cover with a layer of cottage cheese, sprinkle with seasoned flour and repeat until all are used, ending with a layer of potatoes. Pour warmed milk over all, and cover with a layer of the browned bread crumbs. Bake in 350-degree oven for 25 minutes. Remove from oven and sprinkle with grated sapsago cheese. Return to oven for 5 minutes until the cheese browns.

Serves 6

Potato Pudding

4 or 5 large potatoes, grated
1 cup boiling water
½ medium onion, grated
1 egg, lightly beaten
1½ tablespoons flour

2 tablespoons oil
1 teaspoon salt
½ teaspoon Lawry's seasoned salt
freshly ground pepper

Preheat oven to 400 degrees.

Grate potatoes into good-sized bowl. And you really will have to grate them—a blender doesn't do the same job. Add a cup of boiling water and mix well. Strain through a wire strainer, discarding the liquid which drains off. (If some of the vitamins drain off with it— that's the price you pay for potato pudding.)

Pour 1 tablespoon of the oil in 8 x 8" baking dish and place in hot oven.

Add remaining tablespoon oil to the grated, drained potato along with onion, flour, egg, salts and pepper and mix well. Pour into heated, oiled baking dish and bake for 1 to 1½ hours, or until the pudding is crisp and brown on top.

Serves 4 to 5

Glazed Sweet Potatoes

4 medium-sized sweet potatoes,
    cooked and peeled
2 tablespoons oil

2 tablespoons dark brown sugar
1 No. 1 can apricot halves
½ cup apricot syrup

Preheat oven to 400 degrees.

Cut potatoes in two, lengthwise, and place the halves, cut side up, in oiled baking dish. Dribble oil and sprinkle brown sugar over them. Distribute drained apricot halves among the sweet potatoes and pour apricot syrup over all. Bake for about 25 minutes, basting a few times with the syrup, until potatoes are glazed and brown.

Serves 4 to 6

Prune and Sweet Potato Casserole

4 medium-sized sweet potatoes
1½ cups cooked prunes, pitted (unsweetened)
½ cup brown sugar

1 teaspoon salt
½ cup prune juice
3 tablespoons lemon juice
3 tablespoons oil

Cook sweet potatoes in a small amount of boiling water until tender. This will probably take about 30 to 35 minutes. Peel and cut lengthwise in slices about ⅜ of an inch thick. Place alternate layers of sweet potatoes and pitted prunes in oiled 1½-quart casserole, sprinkling each layer with brown sugar and salt. Combine prune juice with lemon juice and add to casserole. Pour oil over all. Bake, uncovered, in 350-degree oven for 40 to 45 minutes. Baste a few times with the syrup in the dish.

Serves 4 to 6

Sweet Potato Soufflé

6 medium-sized sweet potatoes
½ pound mushrooms
4 tablespoons oil
1 teaspoon salt
freshly ground pepper

⅓ cup orange juice
2 teaspoons grated orange rind
2 egg whites, stiffly beaten
cinnamon

Scrub potatoes well and bake in 375-degree oven until soft—about 1 hour. Split and scoop out. Rice potatoes through food mill so they will be completely smooth.

Wipe mushrooms, slice off the stem ends and slice them thin. Heat oil in small skillet and sauté mushrooms until just soft—about 5 minutes. Add to riced potatoes. Add salt, pepper, orange juice and grated orange rind and mix well. Fold in stiffly beaten egg whites. Turn into oiled 2-quart casserole and sprinkle lightly with cinnamon. Bake in 350-degree oven for 30 minutes, or until top is browned.

Serves 6

Noodles and Cabbage

Decisions such as whether to pigeonhole this Hungarian dish (properly known as "Kraut Fleckerl") as a vegetable or a starch, try men's souls. Also women's.

1 small head cabbage, coarsely shredded	1 8-ounce package broad noodles
1 onion, chopped	1 teaspoon salt
4 tablespoons oil	freshly ground pepper
	2 tablespoons caraway seeds

Cook noodles according to directions on package. Rinse with hot water and drain well.

Shred cabbage. Heat oil in heavy skillet. Add cabbage and onion and brown well, turning often. When browned, cover skillet and cook 5 minutes longer. Add drained noodles, salt, pepper and caraway seeds and heat through, mixing well. Serve hot.

Serves 4

Poppy Seed Noodle Casserole

½ cup blanched almonds, slivered and toasted	1 pound fine noodles
2 10½-ounce cans beef consommé	3 tablespoons oil
2 cans water	2½ tablespoons poppy seeds

Place slivered, blanched almonds on flat pan. Dribble 1 tablespoon of the oil over them and bake in 325-degree oven for about ½ hour, or as long as it takes them to become nicely brown. Shake pan frequently. When done, drain on brown paper.

In a large saucepan, bring condensed beef consommé and an equal quantity of water to a boil; drop in fine noodles. Cover and simmer until consommé is absorbed, which should take about 12 minutes. When noodles are done, add remaining 2 tablespoons oil and 2½ tablespoons poppy seeds and toss well. Place in oiled 2-quart ovenproof casserole, sprinkle with toasted almonds and keep warm in oven until ready to serve.

Serves 10 to 12

Pineapple Cream Noodle Pudding

This goes well with a simple fish dinner. With the addition of a cup of raisins and half a cup of chopped nuts, it can double in brass as a dessert.

½ pound medium or broad
    noodles
2 cups cottage cheese
1 cup crushed pineapple (save
    juice)

½ cup light brown sugar
2 tablespoons oil
1 tablespoon lemon juice
½ cup corn flake crumbs

Cook noodles for 8 minutes according to directions on box. Drain and rinse with hot water. Beat 1 cup cottage cheese in your electric beater, or by hand with rotary beater, until creamy smooth. Add oil and enough drained pineapple juice—2 or more tablespoons—to make it the consistency of thick cream. Stir in lemon juice, crushed pineapple and brown sugar. Fold in the other cup of cottage cheese, lumps and all. Add this mixture to drained noodles and toss lightly to distribute evenly.

Lightly oil 9 x 13" baking dish. Spread noodle mixture in dish, sprinkle corn flake crumbs on top and bake in 350-degree oven for 1 hour, until top is nicely browned. Serve hot.

Serves 8

Variation: If you wish to use this for dessert, sprinkle it with topping of ½ cup corn flake crumbs combined with ¼ cup of brown sugar and ½ teaspoon cinnamon.

Baked Rice

This isn't much more complicated than boiling rice, and it provides a nice change.

3 tablespoons oil
1 small onion, chopped
1 4-ounce can mushrooms,
   chopped

1 cup uncooked rice
2½ cups chicken broth
salt and pepper

Over low flame, heat oil in 1½-quart ovenproof casserole that has a cover. Add chopped onion and cook just until limp. Add drained, chopped mushrooms and cook 3 minutes longer, or until mushrooms are brown. Add cup of rice and stir until rice is coated with oil. Add chicken broth and taste to see how much salt you need. Season with required salt and pepper. Cover casserole and place in 350-degree oven for 1 hour. The liquid should be all absorbed and the rice tender. If this is not the case, continue baking 10 or 15 minutes longer.

Serves 4 or 5

Confetti Rice

The red and green bits in this make it look gay as a New Year's Eve party.

1⅓ cups rice
2 tablespoons oil
½ green pepper, cut into ⅛-inch cubes
2 tablespoons pimento, cut into ⅛-inch cubes

½ teaspoon Lawry's seasoned salt
1 4-ounce can sliced mushrooms, drained
2 tablespoons finely minced onion

Cook rice according to directions. In small saucepan, heat oil. Add onion and green pepper and cook for 5 minutes. Add seasoned salt, pimento and drained mushrooms and cook another 2 minutes, or until heated through. Combine with cooked rice and toss together. Taste and correct seasonings.

Serves 6

Mushroom Rice de Luxe

2 cups Uncle Ben's rice
1 pound fresh mushrooms
1 green pepper
1 onion
2 stalks celery
3 tablespoons oil

1 teaspoon salt
freshly ground pepper
½ cup blanched almonds, halved and toasted
1 tablespoon chopped parsley

Cook 2 cups of rice according to directions on package.

Wash mushrooms and pat dry. Seed and core green pepper and cut into quarters. Peel onion. Grind mushrooms, green pepper, onion and celery stalks in food grinder, using medium blade. The resulting purée may not look very tempting, but don't let that discourage you. Heat 3 tablespoons oil in large skillet and sauté puréed vegetables for 30 minutes, stirring frequently. Add salt and pepper. Oil 2-quart ovenproof casserole.

Toss together mushrooms, purée, rice and almonds and pack into casserole. Sprinkle chopped parsley on top. Place casserole in pan of hot water and bake for 45 minutes at 350 degrees.

Serves 8 to 10

Fried Chinese Rice

Leftover chicken was never put to better use than in this dish. It makes a fine starch dish for a buffet, or for a family dinner that needs some bolstering. As an accompaniment for a chicken dinner—just omit the chicken, use *half* the amount of broth, and there you are.

3 tablespoons oil
2 stalks celery, finely diced
1 onion, chopped fine
½ pound mushrooms, sliced
2 cups cooked chicken, diced

1 tablespoon (or more) soy sauce, according to taste
1 teaspoon cornstarch
1 cup chicken broth
4 cups cold cooked rice
salt and pepper to taste

Heat oil in large heavy skillet and sauté onion, celery and mushrooms for 5 minutes. In a bowl, mix cornstarch with chicken broth until smooth and add soy sauce. Add diced chicken to vegetables in skillet and brown. Add broth mixture and cook for a few minutes to reduce the amount. Add cold rice (it *must* be cold) and stir constantly until all the rice has been in contact with the bottom of the pan. Reduce heat and let it steam through gently, but stay with it and turn it frequently. Taste for seasoning, correct and serve at once. Like most Chinese dishes, this does not take kindly to waiting. It is at its best immediately after completion.

Serves 6

Wild Rice and Almond Casserole

1 cup wild rice
4 tablespoons oil
1 tablespoon chopped onion
1 tablespoon chopped chives
2 tablespoons finely chopped
  green pepper

1 tablespoon chopped parsley
2 cups chicken consommé
salt
freshly ground pepper
½ cup almonds, blanched and
  shredded

Wash rice in two or three waters, until no foreign particles appear. Drain thoroughly. In a large, heavy skillet, heat oil, and add finely chopped onion and chives, green pepper, and parsley. Heat through for 3 minutes, and add drained rice. Cook over low heat, stirring constantly, until the rice becomes a gold color. In a small saucepan, bring the chicken consommé to the boiling point and pour over rice in skillet. The amount of salt you need depends on the amount of seasoning of the chicken broth, so taste and correct. Add pepper. Add shredded almonds and mix thoroughly. Turn into lightly oiled 2-quart casserole, cover tightly, and bake in 350-degree oven for 1¼ hours, or until rice is tender. If it seems to be drying out, add an additional ¼ cup of hot consommé.

Serves 4 or 5

Rice and Noodle Pilaf

The crisp brown noodles in this pilaf provide a pleasant contrast in texture to the fluffy rice.

3 tablespoons oil
3 ounces fine noodles, uncooked
1½ cups Uncle Ben's rice,
  uncooked

3 cups chicken consommé or
  broth
freshly ground pepper
salt

Heat oil in large skillet and add noodles, turning them frequently. When they are crisp and browned, add rice, pepper and 2 cups of the consommé. The amount of salt needed is variable, depending on the seasoning in the broth, so you will have to use your own judgment. Cover skillet and cook over low flame for 10 minutes. Add remaining cup of broth, taste and correct seasoning. Cook, covered, until all the liquid is absorbed and the rice soft and fluffy—about 25 minutes in all.

Serves 4 to 6

Baked Beans

Baked beans seem to be a universal favorite. Some cold sliced meat loaf, a pot of succulent beans and a green salad can hold their own in any kind of weather or situation.

1 quart (4 cups) navy beans (or pea beans)
1 tablespoon salt
½ tablespoon dry mustard
3 tablespoons molasses
3 tablespoons sugar
1 cup boiling water
½ cup ketchup

Wash beans, cover with cold water and soak overnight. In the morning, drain and cover with fresh water. Cook slowly, covered, for not more than ½ hour. To test for done-ness, take a few on the tip of a spoon and blow on them. If they are done, the skins will pop. If not, on with the cooking, but don't overcook. Mushy baked beans are a bore. Drain well when done and place in lightly oiled casserole or bean pot.

In a small bowl, mix mustard, salt, molasses, sugar and ketchup and pour over beans. Mix well. Add enough boiling water to cover. Cover pot and bake in 350-degree oven for 1 hour. Uncover pot and bake another hour until browned on top.

Serves 10 to 12

Barley Pilaf

Barley is an interesting grain which rates consideration other than as an addendum to soup.

3 tablespoons oil
1 cup pearl barley, uncooked
½ cup finely chopped onion
¼ pound mushrooms, sliced
½ teaspoon meat extract
2 cups chicken broth or dissolved broth powder
½ teaspoon Lawry's seasoned salt
freshly ground pepper

In a heavy skillet, heat oil. Add onions, mushrooms and barley.

Over medium heat, cook slowly and turn the mixture continually until the barley is golden brown.

While this is cooking, bring chicken broth to a boil slowly. Dissolve meat extract in broth and stir gradually into the barley mixture. Add salt and pepper and correct seasoning. Transfer to lightly oiled casserole, cover and bake for 1 hour in 350-degree oven. If the casserole seems to be drying out, add more boiling water or chicken stock.

Serves 4 or 5

Escalloped Pea Beans and Tomatoes

1½ cups pea beans
1 medium-sized onion, sliced
1½ teaspoons salt
freshly ground pepper
2 tablespoons oil
3 tablespoons flour

1¼ cups skim milk
1 cup canned tomatoes, drained
½ cup bread crumbs browned in
    2 tablespoons oil
1 tablespoon minced parsley

Soak pea beans in cold water for 3 or 4 hours. Place in saucepan with the same water. Add sliced onion, salt and pepper and cook slowly until tender, and there is about ¼ cup liquid left.

In another saucepan, heat oil and blend in flour. Add skim milk gradually, stirring constantly, until the mixture thickens and bubbles.

Combine cooked beans, ¼ cup liquid and strained tomato pulp. Add to the cream sauce. Taste and correct seasoning. Turn into oiled 1½-quart baking dish. Cover with the bread crumbs which have been browned in oil and sprinkle parsley over top. Bake in 375-degree oven for 30 minutes.

Serves 6

Kasha Varnishkas
(Groats and Noodle Bows)

5 tablespoons oil
1 cup kasha (buckwheat groats)
boiling water
1 teaspoon salt
6 ounces noodle bows (the small
    ones, preferably)

1 large onion, minced
½ pound small mushrooms cut
    in chunks
½ teaspoon Lawry's seasoned salt
freshly ground pepper
1 tablespoon Kitchen Bouquet

In large skillet with cover, heat 1 of the tablespoons of oil and add groats. Over low heat, stir until brown. Meanwhile, have your teakettle boiling. When all the groats have had their turn at the bottom of the pan, add salt and enough boiling water to cover 1 inch above the groats. Remove pan from heat, cover tightly and allow to stand for about 30 minutes, or until all the water has been absorbed. Stir after 15 minutes.

In a medium saucepan, cook noodle bows for 12 minutes, or until just done. Don't let them get mushy. Rinse well with boiling water and drain.

Preheat oven to 350 degrees. Heat the remaining 4 tablespoons of oil in medium-sized skillet. Add onion and cook until transparent. Add cut-up mushrooms, seasoned salt, pepper and Kitchen Bouquet and cook 5 minutes longer. Lightly oil 1½-quart casserole. Combine groats, bows and onion and mushroom mixture and toss together evenly. Taste to correct seasoning. Place in casserole, cover and bake 20 minutes. Serve hot.

Serves 6 to 8

13

Vegetables

THE HONORS for delicious vegetables must be divided equally between a crisp, fresh state to begin with, and the method of preparation. A tired, limp vegetable won't improve with cooking, no matter what you do with it. Always start with the best and freshest vegetables your market has to offer. The younger they are, the less time they require for cooking and the better the flavor. If you are fortunate enough to have access to farm-fresh produce, use the simplest cooking method and seasonings. The natural flavors and textures of the lovely fresh things require little enhancing, although even the frozen vegetables are of high quality these days and can be most satisfactory.

Be generous in serving leafy green and yellow vegetables, in addition to all the others. Nature has been thoughtful in providing us with a color index for our nutritional needs. By mixing a rich palette of colors and contrasts with the vegetables we serve—green, red, yellow, white, orange, etc., we not only provide visual pleasure at meals, but fulfill our mineral and vitamin requirements at the same time.

Since a good deal of the vitamin content of vegetables is water soluble, it follows that the shortest immersion in water will do the least damage. Vegetables should be placed in the least amount of boiling, salted water possible, cooked briefly, and served at once, slightly underdone in preference to being boiled to a soggy, flaccid pulp. Adding a broth powder to the water in which you cook your vegetables is a good idea for extra flavor, particularly where sauces and fats are restricted for a low-calorie diet.

One of my favorite bits of kitchen equipment is a steamer in which

I cook our vegetables. It is made by the Wear-Ever people and consists of a round pot with a shallow insert which has a few holes around the rim, and a very heavy lid. The water is placed in the lower half of the pot, and whatever is to be cooked in the shallow pan. It works on the same steam principle as a pressure cooker, but since I am a confirmed pot-peeker and lid-lifter, I like this better than the mechanical contraption. The steamer cooks vegetables or fruits or fish in half the time it takes to boil them, and they're always just right. As a matter of fact, the first thing I did after our daughter and her young man set their important June date was to make a trip to Macy's basement to buy a steamer for them. The monogrammed towels waited for the following week. First things first.

If you have been serving a limited vegetable repertoire, try some unfamiliar ones. Run the gamut of the wide variety your produce market has to offer and experiment with new and different methods of preparation. I always suspect that somewhere in the past of most people who shrug their shoulders at vegetables lies a mess of soggy green peas and some drowned string beans. Properly cooked and seasoned vegetables, imaginatively combined and served, can be as great a gastronomic joy as the most elegant pâté, and pay better dividends.

Vegetables Amandine

The "amandine"—or "almondine"—refers simply to the addition of slivered toasted blanched almonds to a vegetable, fish or meat dish. They add an interesting texture and flavor to what might otherwise be a workaday preparation.

For a vegetable or meat serving for 4, from ⅓ to ½ cup of almonds are enough. Blanch them by covering with boiling water for about 5 minutes, after which you should be able to slip off the skins with no difficulty. While still warm, sliver them by cutting them in two, lengthwise. Heat 2 tablespoons of oil in a skillet and cook the almonds in the hot oil for 2 minutes, turning them a few times, until they turn a deep golden color.

Cauliflowerets, broccoli, string beans or asparagus do nicely with the toasted almonds. Cook or steam the vegetables as usual, being careful (as usual) not to overcook, season them with salt and pepper, and scatter the toasted almonds over them.

Vegetables Polonaise

To prepare vegetables "Polonaise," brown about ½ cup of fine bread crumbs in 2 tablespoons of heated oil, add 1 teaspoon of chopped parsley and mix well. Sprinkle over cooked vegetable in the serving dish. This will serve 4.

Asparagus, cauliflower and broccoli are favorites for this garniture.

Butternut Squash

It seems to me there are ever so many people who are unfamiliar with this flavorful vegetable. If you are one, you have a fine treat in store. In taste it is a cross between Hubbard squash and sweet potato, combining the best virtues of each.

2 pounds butternut squash	½ teaspoon salt
2 tablespoons oil	pepper
	1 teaspoon sugar

You may peel the squash either before or after it is cooked. (I peel it after; my staunch kitchen assistant, Bea, peels it first.) Cut squash into large hunks and boil or steam in as little water as possible until tender—20 to 30 minutes. Mash with potato ricer—and it needn't be too smooth. Add oil, salt, pepper and sugar and mix well. Taste for seasoning. Serve hot.

Serves 4

Butternut Squash Fritters

We often fix extra butternut squash, so we can have a cupful left over for these fritters which will do for dessert if you're so minded. Pumpkin may also be used.

1 cup cooked butternut squash, finely mashed	½ teaspoon baking powder
	¼ teaspoon cinnamon
1 cup flour, sifted	oil for deep frying
¼ cup sugar	

Combine finely mashed squash with flour, sugar, baking powder and cinnamon. Beat well. Heat 3 inches of oil to 375 degrees, or until a 1-inch cube of bread browns in 40 seconds. Drop squash mixture by teaspoonfuls and fry until browned. Drain well on absorbent paper. Sprinkle with superfine granulated sugar.

Makes about 30 small fritters

Beets in Orange Sauce

Use either diced or julienne canned beets for this.

1 1-pound can beets
2 tablespoons oil
2 tablespoons light brown sugar
1½ tablespoons flour

1 cup orange juice (fresh or
  frozen)
sliced orange peel
½ teaspoon salt

Drain beets and discard juice. Set aside. Heat oil in medium-sized saucepan, add sugar mixed with flour and stir until smooth. Add orange juice and orange peel and cook, stirring all the while, until thick. Add salt and drained beets and heat through.

Serves 3 to 4

Broccoli Sauté

1 bunch broccoli (about
  1½ pounds)
4 tablespoons oil
1 clove garlic, minced

4 scallions, tops and all, chopped
½ teaspoon salt
freshly ground pepper

Wash and drain broccoli. Divide into small stubby sections, trimming stems. Steam, or place in saucepan with ½ inch of salted, boiling water. Boil for 5 minutes, uncovered. Cover and cook 15 minutes, or until just barely done. Drain.

In a heavy skillet, heat oil and sauté garlic and scallions. Add broccoli, sprinkle with salt and pepper, cover skillet and cook over low heat for 5 minutes. Remove cover and let cook over low heat for another 5 minutes, stirring often.

Serves 4 or 5

Brussels Sprouts with Chestnut Sauce

2 pounds Brussels sprouts (or 2
    10-ounce packages frozen)
1½ tablespoons oil
1 tablespoon flour
1 cup chicken consommé

¼ teaspoon salt
pinch white pepper
⅛ teaspoon basil
1 cup cooked chestnuts, peeled
    and sliced

Trim off outer leaves from Brussels sprouts and wash well. Cook in small amount of salted water (or steam) until just done—10 or 12 minutes. Don't overcook. The frozen ones should be cooked according to directions on package, but the same rule about not overcooking applies here also.

For the sauce, heat oil in heavy skillet over low heat. Add flour, stirring until smooth. Add consommé slowly, stirring constantly until it thickens. Add salt, pepper and basil. Taste and correct seasoning.

Add sliced chestnuts to the cream sauce. Place drained Brussels sprouts in warm serving bowl and pour chestnut sauce over them.

Serves 5 or 6

Cabbage with Caraway Seeds

1 medium-sized head of cabbage,
    shredded
1 onion, sliced
4 tablespoons oil

½ cup water (or white wine,
    optional)
1 teaspoon salt
freshly ground pepper
1 teaspoon sugar
2 tablespoons caraway seeds

Cut out core of cabbage and shred. Wash and drain.

In a large heavy saucepan with a cover, heat oil and cook onion until transparent. Add water (or wine), cabbage, salt, pepper and sugar. Cover and cook over low flame until cabbage is done, 20 to 30 minutes. If the cabbage seems in danger of burning, add a little water or wine. The liquid should be absorbed when the cabbage is done. Sprinkle with caraway seeds and mix through. Remove to warm bowl to serve.

Serves 4

Sweet and Sour Red Cabbage

A traditional and excellent vegetable with pot roast.

1 medium-sized red cabbage (about 4 cups shredded)
2 tablespoons oil
½ cup cider vinegar
2 tablespoons brown sugar

1 large tart apple, peeled, cored and cut into cubes
1 teaspoon salt
freshly ground pepper

Remove core from head of red cabbage and slice medium fine. Wash cabbage and lightly drain, leaving whatever liquid adheres to the cabbage. Place in large heavy saucepan with cover. Add vinegar, sugar, oil, salt and pepper, cover, and cook over low flame for 10 minutes. Add cubed apple, cover, and continue cooking another 20 minutes, or until cabbage is tender. Taste and correct seasoning—it may need more sugar or a squirt of lemon juice—or both.

Serves 4 to 6

Carrot Casserole

1½ pounds fresh carrots, sliced
1 No. 2 can tomatoes (2½ cups), drained
1 teaspoon salt
freshly ground pepper

1 teaspoon marjoram
1 teaspoon sugar
2 tablespoons chopped parsley
½ cup dry bread crumbs
2 tablespoons oil

Lightly oil 1-quart casserole. Combine sliced carrots, drained tomatoes, salt, pepper, sugar and marjoram. Add enough liquid from tomatoes to come about halfway up in the casserole. Bake for 45 minutes in 350-degree oven, or until carrots are tender.

Brown bread crumbs in 2 tablespoons heated oil and sprinkle on top. Garnish with the chopped parsley.

Serves 4

Carrots Virginie

4 cups carrots, cut in julienne strips (about 8 carrots)
3 tablespoons oil
3 tablespoons orange juice

1 tablespoon lemon juice
1½ teaspoons salt
¼ teaspoon powdered ginger
4 tablespoons honey

In heavy skillet with cover, combine oil, orange juice, lemon juice, salt, ginger and honey. Mix well. Add carrot strips and cook, covered, over low flame for 25 minutes, or until carrots are tender. Keep your eye on them while they're cooking and stir frequently so they won't scorch.

Serves 6

The tiny canned Belgian carrots may also be used. Prepare the sauce as directed above, add drained carrots and heat through thoroughly. A 1-pound can serves 4.

Glazed Carrots

6 long carrots
2 tablespoons oil
2 tablespoons light brown sugar
2 tablespoons lemon juice
1 tablespoon chopped parsley

Scrape carrots and slice crosswise, about the thickness of a nickel. Boil in salted water (or steam) until barely tender—don't let them get soft. Drain. In medium-sized skillet, heat oil, add sugar, lemon juice and parsley and cook over low flame until it bubbles. Add sliced carrots and cook until all the liquid is absorbed. Turn slices often, so they will be evenly glazed.

Serves 4

Cauliflower with Anchovy Sauce

The anchovy flavor lends this a delightful piquancy.

1 small head of cauliflower
1 cup water
½ teaspoon salt
1 large clove garlic
6 tablespoons oil
4 anchovy filets, chopped
2½ tablespoons bread crumbs
freshly ground pepper

Wash cauliflower and separate into small flowerets. Cook (or steam) in boiling, salted water over medium heat until tender. This generally takes about 10 to 15 minutes. Make sure you don't overcook.

In a small skillet, brown garlic in oil for 3 minutes until brown. Discard garlic. Add chopped anchovies to oil and stir until anchovies are reduced to a paste. Add fine bread crumbs and cook another 2 minutes.

Place cooked cauliflower in warmed serving dish, sprinkle with pepper and pour anchovy sauce over it. Toss lightly and serve hot.

Serves 4

Cauliflower Sauté

1 small head of cauliflower	2 scallions, tops and all, chopped
4 tablespoons oil	1 teaspoon salt
large lettuce leaves	freshly ground pepper
1 clove garlic, minced	

Wash cauliflower and separate into small flowerets. Heat 1 tablespoon of the oil in heavy saucepan. Add cauliflower plus a few of the tender green leaves. Spread several dripping-wet leaves of lettuce over all. Cover pan tightly and cook over low heat for about 10 minutes, or until cauliflower is just tender. Discard leaves.

In a large skillet, heat remaining 3 tablespoons oil and sauté minced garlic and chopped scallions for 5 minutes. Add cauliflower, sprinkle with salt and freshly ground pepper, cover skillet, and cook over low heat for 20 minutes. Turn flowerets a few times, so that all of them come in contact with bottom of pan. Remove cover and let cook over low heat for another 5 minutes. Serve immediately.

Serves 4 to 6

Corn Pudding

2 12-ounce cans corn niblets	freshly ground pepper
1 tablespoon flour	3 tablespoons oil
1 tablespoon sugar	1 cup skim milk
1 teaspoon salt	2 egg whites, stiffly beaten

Preheat oven to 350 degrees.

Drain corn and place in medium-sized bowl. Add flour, sugar, salt, pepper, oil and skim milk and mix well. Fold in stiffly beaten egg whites, blending thoroughly. Pour into oiled 2-quart casserole and bake for an hour, or until pudding is set and a little brown on top.

Serves 6

Chestnuts

Of all the nut family, chestnuts are at the bottom of the ladder in terms of fat of any kind. They are low in calories and completely unsaturated. One of the few remaining provincial delights in New York is the hot chestnut vendors who stand on street corners in the fall and winter, their carts emitting shrill whistles and the lovely warm smell of chestnuts roasting. To avoid the questionable taste of eating hot chestnuts in the street, you can roast them at home.

Cut 2½-inch gashes on the flat side of each chestnut in the shape of the letter X. Place on a baking sheet, dribble a tablespoon of oil over them and bake in a 350-degree oven for 45 to 50 minutes, or until the skins peel off easily and the chestnuts are cooked through.

To prepare chestnuts for use in cooking, cut the X-shaped gashes described above. Cover the chestnuts with boiling water and boil briskly in a covered saucepan for 25 to 30 minutes. Hold them under cold running water while you peel off the shells. If the shells do not come off easily, boil them a bit longer.

Fried Cucumbers

These are good with any fish dish.

3 large cucumbers	¼ teaspoon Lawry's seasoned salt
½ cup flour	1 egg white, slightly beaten
½ teaspoon salt	bread crumbs
dash freshly ground pepper	oil

Pare cucumbers and slice lengthwise in slices ⅜ inch thick. Each cucumber should yield 4 slices. Pour oil into heavy skillet to the depth of ¼ inch and heat. Dip cucumber slices into flour which has been seasoned with the salts and pepper, then into egg white and bread crumbs. Fry in the hot oil about 5 minutes on each side, turning once. The lemon wedges which accompany the fish will do nicely for these also.

Serves 3 or 4

Eggplant and Zucchini Casserole

A vegetable mélange which may be prepared in advance and baked at dinnertime.

1 medium-sized eggplant, peeled and cut into 1-inch slices
3 large onions, thinly sliced
3 zucchini (about 1 pound), washed and sliced in ¼-inch slices
2 cloves garlic, minced
4 tablespoons oil
½ pound sliced mushrooms
3 large tomatoes, peeled and coarsely chopped
1 green pepper, seeded and cut in strips ¼ inch wide
2 teaspoons salt
1 tablespoon sugar
freshly ground pepper
1 bay leaf
¼ teaspoon oregano
¼ teaspoon sweet basil
½ cup fine bread crumbs browned in oil

Cover eggplant with boiling water and simmer gently for 10 minutes. Drain thoroughly.

In a large skillet, cook onions and garlic in oil until transparent. Add zucchini and cook, covered, for 10 minutes. Add mushrooms and cook, stirring, uncovered, for 5 minutes. Add tomatoes, bay leaf, oregano, basil, green pepper and seasonings and simmer 10 minutes longer. Remove bay leaf. Taste for seasoning—you might want to add a dollop more of garlic powder, sugar, salt or whatever you think it needs.

Oil 2-quart casserole and place a layer of eggplant on the bottom. Pour part of tomato and zucchini mixture over it. Make alternate layers of eggplant and tomato mixture until all are used, ending with tomato mixture. Cover with browned crumbs. Bake in slow oven, 275 degrees, for 1½ hours.

Serves

MUSHROOMS

Broiled Mushrooms

12 large mushroom caps
3 tablespoons bread crumbs
1 tablespoon chopped parsley
½ teaspoon Lawry's seasoned salt
dash freshly ground pepper
3 tablespoons oil
1 clove garlic, minced

Add minced garlic to oil and mix well.

Wash mushroom caps and dry well. Never peel them unless absolutely necessary since much of their fine flavor is in the smooth skin.

Make a mixture of bread crumbs, salt, pepper and parsley. Brush mushroom caps with the garlic oil and roll in seasoned bread crumbs. Place about 2 inches from broiler flame and broil 5 minutes on each side. If they seem a little dry, dribble a little more oil on them when you turn them.

Serves 4

Mushrooms Trifolati

Our affable host on the occasion of our dining at the Palazzi Restaurant, outside of Rome, suggested that we order "Funghi Trifolati," since they are a popular Roman dish—like spoon bread in the South, perhaps. The maître d' was genial and frustratingly vague about the recipe, but our host, true to his word, and after consultations with cooks of his acquaintance, filled us in on the missing ingredients via transatlantic mail.

1 pound mushrooms	2 tablespoons minced parsley
3 tablespoons oil	2 tablespoons lemon juice
1 clove garlic	toast rounds
4 anchovy filets, crushed	garlic oil

Trim off ends of stems of mushrooms. Wash mushrooms and dry them well. Slice stems and caps thinly. Heat oil in heavy skillet with garlic. When garlic is browned, remove it and add mushrooms. Cook over high heat, stirring often. After about 5 minutes, there will be a good bit of mushroom liquid in the pan. Stir a few tablespoons of this into the crushed anchovies, making a thick paste. Add this paste to the mushrooms, mixing thoroughly. Cook another 5 minutes, or until the liquid is absorbed. Add lemon juice, minced parsley and toss lightly. Serve on toast rounds which have been fried in garlic oil. This also makes an excellent appetizer course.

Serves 4

Fried Mushrooms

Add to the recipe for Mushroom Trifolati 2 small tomatoes, peeled and cut into chunks, and ½ teaspoon of chopped mint leaves. Omit parsley. Serve on toast.

Mushrooms in Ramekins

1 pound mushrooms	½ cup consommé
4 tablespoons oil	½ teaspoon meat extract
1 tablespoon chopped parsley	2 tablespoons oil
1 tablespoon flour	2 tablespoons bread crumbs

Snip off ends of mushroom stems. Wash mushrooms, dry thoroughly and slice. Heat 4 tablespoons oil in heavy skillet, add mushrooms and cook over medium heat for 5 minutes. Add flour and mix well. Add meat extract and broth and simmer another 10 minutes. Add parsley, mix and remove from fire. Lightly oil 4 ramekins and fill with mixture. Sprinkle with bread crumbs, dribble a bit of oil over each, and bake in 350-degree oven for 10 minutes. Serve with toast triangles.

Serves 4

Stuffed Mushrooms

12 large mushrooms	½ cup stock or consommé
2 tablespoons oil	½ teaspoon freshly ground pepper
1 small onion, chopped	2 slices bread, soaked in water
1 clove garlic, crushed	1 teaspoon mayonnaise
4 anchovy filets, chopped	2 tablespoons oil
1 tablespoon chopped parsley	2 tablespoons corn flake crumbs

Preheat oven to 400 degrees.

Remove stems from mushrooms and trim off ends. Wash and dry both the caps and stems. Chop stems and in a small skillet, cook in 2 tablespoons oil with chopped onion and garlic for 5 minutes. Add anchovies, parsley and pepper and cook another 5 minutes over high flame. Place in bowl and add the 2 slices of bread which have been soaked in water and squeezed dry. Add mayonnaise and mix until smooth. Oil shallow baking dish and arrange mushrooms in it, stem side up. Fill each cap with stuffing, making it round on top. Sprinkle with crumbs and dribble oil over all. Pour consommé on bottom of pan. Bake for 20 minutes. Serve hot.

Serves 4

ABOUT ONIONS

The succulent, small white onions deserve more than the seasonal rush given them at Thanksgiving time, followed by oblivion for the rest of the year. They are truly a delicious vegetable and rate encores in our meal planning.

Creamed Onions

2 pounds small white onions	½ teaspoon salt
3 tablespoons oil	pinch cayenne pepper
2 tablespoons flour	½ teaspoon dried thyme
2 cups skim milk	¼ cup bread crumbs

Peel and trim onions. Cook in boiling, salted water (or steam) until just done, about 15 minutes.

In a heavy saucepan, heat 2 tablespoons of the oil. Blend flour thoroughly over small flame, but don't let it brown. Add seasonings, and while stirring constantly over medium heat, stir in milk. Keep stirring until the mixture thickens and bubbles. Reduce heat and cook 1 minute longer. Add thyme and cayenne pepper.

In a small skillet, brown bread crumbs in remaining tablespoon oil. Transfer the onions and sauce to oiled baking dish. Mix well. Sprinkle with browned bread crumbs. Heat in 350-degree oven for 20 minutes.

Serves 4

Spiced Onions

2 pounds small white onions	3 tablespoons oil
⅔ teaspoon meat extract	2 teaspoons sugar
⅓ cup boiling water	pinch powdered cloves
½ teaspoon salt	¼ teaspoon cinnamon

Peel and trim onions and boil in salted water (or steam) until just done—about 15 minutes.

Combine meat extract with ⅓ cup boiling water; add oil, sugar, cloves, cinnamon and salt and simmer together for 5 minutes. Pour sauce over cooked onions and allow to heat together for about 10 minutes before serving.

Serves 4

Glazed Parsnips

1 pound parsnips
½ teaspoon salt
5 tablespoons orange juice

3 tablespoons light brown sugar
1 tablespoon grated lemon rind
1 tablespoon oil

Cook parsnips in small amount of water until soft. Drain and peel when cool. Slice them lengthwise, making 3 or 4 slices of each, and place slices in lightly oiled, shallow baking dish. Sprinkle salt over slices. Mix together orange juice, sugar, oil and grated lemon rind and pour over parsnips. Bake in 350-degree oven for 25 minutes.

Serves 3 to 4

Peas, Country Kitchen

1 1-pound 1-ounce can tiny
  French peas
2 cups lettuce, coarsely shredded
1 3-ounce can water chestnuts,
  drained
1 tablespoon oil

1 tablespoon flour
⅓ cup liquid drained from peas
½ teaspoon salt
freshly ground pepper
¼ teaspoon thyme
1 tablespoon chopped parsley

Drain liquid from peas, reserving ⅓ cup. Drain and slice water chestnuts. Heat oil in medium-sized saucepan. Add flour, mix well, and stir in the liquid drained from peas, blending well to make the sauce smooth. Add shredded lettuce and cook for 2 minutes until it wilts. Add drained peas, sliced water chestnuts, salt, pepper and thyme and heat through, or about 5 minutes longer, covered. Remove to heated bowl and sprinkle parsley over top.

Serves 4

Peas and Onions in Mustard Sauce

2 pounds small white onions
1 10-ounce package frozen peas
4 tablespoons oil
4 tablespoons flour
1½ cups skim milk
½ teaspoon salt

⅛ teaspoon white pepper
1½ tablespoons white vinegar
1½ tablespoons lemon juice
¼ teaspoon dry mustard
pinch saffron

Peel and trim onions. Cook in boiling, salted water (or steam) until just done—about 15 minutes. Cook peas according to directions on package.

In medium-sized saucepan, heat oil. Blend with flour thoroughly over small flame, but don't let it brown. Add milk, and over medium heat, while stirring constantly, add salt, pepper and vinegar. Cook until mixture bubbles and thickens and reduce heat. In a small bowl mix lemon juice, mustard and saffron. Add to sauce. Heat together for 2 minutes. Drain peas and onions and place in warm serving dish. Pour sauce over vegetables and mix lightly.

Serves 6

Hot Sauerkraut

1½ pounds sauerkraut	½ cup tomato purée
veal marrow bone	freshly ground pepper
½ green pepper, diced	½ teaspoon salt
1 large onion, chopped	1 teaspoon sugar
2 tablespoons oil	2 teaspoons flour

Cook sauerkraut with marrow bone for 1½ hours over low flame in covered kettle. Brown diced pepper with chopped onion in oil in large skillet. Add flour and stir well. Transfer sauerkraut to skillet and mix thoroughly, absorbing all the oil and distributing green pepper and onion. Add tomato purée, salt, pepper and sugar. Taste and correct seasoning.

Serves 4 to 5

Creamed Spinach

2 10-ounce packages frozen, chopped spinach	1 tablespoon flour
	1 cup skim milk
1 tablespoon oil	1 teaspoon salt
2 tablespoons finely chopped onion	freshly ground pepper
	⅛ teaspoon nutmeg

Cook or steam spinach according to directions on package, being careful not to overcook. Drain and set aside.

Using the same pan, heat oil. Add chopped onion and cook until golden over low flame. Blend in flour, stirring constantly. Slowly add milk, stirring until it becomes thickened and bubbly. Add salt, pepper and nutmeg. Add cooked, drained spinach and simmer until it is warmed through—2 or 3 minutes.

Serves 6

Spinach and Mushrooms

2 pounds spinach
1 large onion, chopped
2 tablespoons oil
½ pound fresh mushrooms, sliced

1 tablespoon lemon juice
1 teaspoon salt
½ teaspoon sugar
freshly ground pepper
⅛ teaspoon nutmeg

Heat 1 tablespoon of oil in medium-sized skillet and add onion. Cook until golden. Wash spinach carefully, cutting off the coarse stems. Chop coarsely and add to onions. Cover and cook over medium flame for 10 minutes.

In a small skillet, heat the remaining tablespoon of oil with lemon juice. Cook sliced mushrooms in this for 5 minutes. Add to the spinach with the salt, pepper, sugar and nutmeg. Toss together lightly. Taste for seasoning. Serve hot.

Serves 4

String Beans and Mushrooms

1 pound string beans
1 teaspoon salt
freshly ground pepper
paprika

2 small onions, finely chopped
1 pound mushrooms
2 tablespoons oil

Wash and cut string beans in very thin slices, diagonally, French style. Wash mushrooms, slice stems and cut caps into quarters. Cook string beans (or steam) in very little boiling water until just done. (The cooking time for string beans varies with their quality and variety—it may be anywhere from 15 to 30 minutes. The beans should be crisp and just tender, so taste them from time to time as they cook and consider them done when they reach that state.) Drain beans and season with salt, pepper and paprika.

In medium-sized skillet, sauté minced onion in oil until transparent. Add cut-up mushrooms and cook over medium heat for 3 minutes. Cover skillet and allow to steam for 10 minutes longer. Add the mushroom and onion, along with whatever liquid has collected, to the string beans. Pour into oiled casserole and heat in 350-degree oven for 10 minutes.

Serves 4 or 5

String Beans, Roman Style

Excellent with a veal roast.

1 pound fresh string beans or 1 10-ounce package frozen, French style	1 small clove garlic, minced
	2/3 teaspoon oregano
	1 cup tomato sauce
2 tablespoons oil	

If you are using fresh string beans, wash and drain them and cut lengthwise, French style. Steam or boil in a little boiling, salted water until tender but a little crunchy—do not overcook. Cook frozen string beans according to directions on package until just done. Drain well.

In medium-sized skillet, heat oil and add minced garlic and oregano. Cook until garlic turns golden. Add tomato sauce and simmer for 5 minutes. Pour sauce over beans and mix well.

Serves 4

Baked Stuffed Tomatoes

These always do well with baked steak or veal roast or chops.

6 large firm tomatoes	1/2 teaspoon salt
1 12-ounce can corn niblets	freshly ground pepper
3 tablespoons oil	1/2 cup fresh bread crumbs
1/3 cup chopped green pepper	Lawry's seasoned salt
1/2 cup onion, finely chopped	chopped parsley

Slice tops off tomatoes and scoop out the pulp and reserve, leaving a good-sized cavity in the tomatoes. Turn them upside down so that the rest of the juice will drain out. Heat oil in medium-sized skillet. Add green pepper and onion and cook for 3 or 4 minutes, or until the onion becomes limp and golden. Add 1/2 cup of the tomato pulp, diced, soft bread crumbs, corn niblets, salt and pepper. Season tomatoes with a bit of Lawry's seasoned salt, fill them with the corn mixture and bake in 350-degree oven for 20 to 25 minutes, or until tomatoes are cooked through but not limp. Sprinkle tops with chopped parsley.

Serves 6

Fried Tomatoes

Either the green or red tomatoes will do for this—as long as they are very firm.

4 firm tomatoes	¼ teaspoon basil
¼ cup flour	¼ teaspoon oregano
1 tablespoon corn meal	½ cup oil
½ teaspoon salt	pinch sugar
freshly ground pepper	

Mix flour, corn meal, salt, pepper, basil and oregano. Cut tomatoes into thick slices and coat with flour mixture. Heat oil in heavy skillet and brown tomatoes. They should cook in 8 to 10 minutes. Sprinkle a little sugar over the tops when done.

Serves 4 to 5

Zucchini Sauté

I think zucchini is one of the outstanding members of the squash family—good tasting, easily prepared, low in calories, and adaptable for so many methods of preparation. The lovely things don't even require peeling!

This is a quickie, and one of our favorites:

4 medium-sized zucchini	½ teaspoon sweet basil
4 medium-sized onions	½ teaspoon oregano
2 tablespoons oil	dash garlic powder (optional)
1 teaspoon salt	1 tablespoon chopped parsley
freshly ground pepper	

Wash zucchini well. Cut off stem end and bottom slice, and slice crosswise into 1-inch pieces. In a large skillet, heat oil and add sliced onions. Cook until golden and limp, but not brown. Add zucchini and cook over high flame for 5 minutes. Add salt, pepper, basil, oregano, garlic powder and parsley. Lower heat, cover, and cook 15 minutes longer, or until tender—but not the least mushy. Add a little water if necessary.   Serves 4 to 5

Variations and additions: A green and a red pepper, cut in ½-inch strips, cooked along with the onion.

Two fresh tomatoes, peeled and cut in eighths, added to the zucchini mixture the last 15 minutes of cooking.

Cold Zucchini Piquante

My mother had a theory that no matter how hot the day, and how cool and refreshing the main course, something catastrophic would happen to one's insides without one steaming dish, which we were obliged to eat. After my personal physician came into my life and dispelled the myth, I determined never to inflict like hardships on our children.

Which brings us to Cold Zucchini Piquante. Serve instead of hot string beans with the chilled crab meat salad when the thermometer registers way up there.

6 large zucchini	2 tablespoons chopped parsley
oil to the depth of 1 inch in skillet	½ teaspoon salt
2 cloves garlic, minced	freshly ground pepper
2 teaspoons sweet basil	¾ cup wine vinegar

Fill skillet with oil to the depth of 1 inch. Over low flame, heat for 5 or 6 minutes, or until a cube of bread will turn golden in 30 seconds. Scrub zucchini thoroughly and discard end slices. Cut into 1-inch slices and fry quickly in hot oil until light brown. Remove with slotted spoon and drain on absorbent paper. In glass or earthenware bowl (not metal), place 1 layer of zucchini, sprinkle with minced garlic, basil, parsley, salt and pepper, and repeat until all the zucchini are used.

In a small saucepan, heat vinegar and boil for 5 minutes. Pour immediately over zucchini. Allow this to marinate overnight in refrigerator. Drain and serve, garnished with watercress. (The zucchini will keep in this marinade for 2 weeks.)   Serves 8

14

Salads, Dressings, Sauces and Molds

FEW THINGS can add as much interest to a meal at such small effort, while returning as much in important nutritional value, as a good salad. And "good" doesn't mean exotic. Just everyday salad greens which have been washed, dried, crisped, broken to size, and tossed with loving care in a tasteful dressing.

Salads are a particularly valuable ally in our friendly fat program. The very nature of their raw state means that no overzealous cook has had time to boil out any of the vitamins they contain and they offer bulk and variety for the calorie watchers.

Homemade salad dressings offer an excellent means of including additional quantities of polyunsaturated oils in our diets. The commercially prepared dressings are approved by the Anti-Coronary Club when dining out, but since some of the oils used commercially may be of the monounsaturated types, we can do our cause more good with the dressings we make ourselves.

A delicious mayonnaise, a tart French, or a creamy garlic dressing (see recipes) are easily prepared. Good Seasons make a variety of agreeable dry salad mixes to which you add the oil and vinegar. Their cheese dressings are, of course, out of bounds. Hellman's also features a French dressing made with corn oil, in case you're not in the mood to mix your own.

It's a good idea always to use leftover vegetables like peas, carrots, string beans, broccoli, etc., in a cold salad, since a second heating further destroys their vitamin content. Laced with a tangy dressing and a bit of chopped onion, they'll do fine, but please don't throw them into the bowl of mixed greens. They'll lose their identity in the hodge-podge and dilute the crispness of the other ingredients.

Let the mixed salad *really* be mixed. The popular iceberg, or Simpson, is as dependable as a pair of old shoes, but like old shoes, it can be improved upon. Vary it with romaine, chicory, escarole, Belgian endive, Boston, Bibb, and don't neglect some dark green, tender young spinach leaves and shredded raw red cabbage. Bibb lettuce is a delicious green, but expensive and not always available. Fresh Boston lettuce has much the same quality and is easier to come by.

Greens should be washed as soon as you get them home and thoroughly drained. A flexible wire basket is excellent for this. Drain the moisture out of the greens and store them in the refrigerator in plastic bags. You can prepare them an hour or two in advance of dinner and keep them chilled. I'm sure you know all about tearing them by hand and never defiling their surfaces with a knife. The dressing can wait until the last minute, or you run the risk of a soggy salad, perish forbid.

Whether the salad appears as an appetizer course, or as a refreshing fruit, chicken or sea food to perk up a wilted diner on a hot day, or in the form of tossed mixed greens to add zest and variety to a meal, give it the benefit of your best. This means the best in the quality and freshness of the ingredients you buy and the best of your talent in making it as attractive as you can.

Tossed Green Salad

This may also be made with a prepared French dressing.

1 small head Boston lettuce	½ cup oil
small bunch romaine	1 teaspoon salt
1 cup (about) Belgian endive	3 tablespoons wine vinegar
2 cups (about) fresh spinach	1 clove garlic, minced
2 cups (about) chicory or escarole	freshly ground pepper
8 small artichoke hearts (optional)	¼ teaspoon dry mustard
6 filets of anchovies, diced	2 tablespoons sesame seeds

Use a salad bowl big enough to allow plenty of room for the tossing—or it will cramp the style of the tosser. Make sure that the greens are all perfectly dry. Break them into generous bite-sized pieces. Toss with oil, adding it gradually, and stopping when all the leaves glisten. Add diced anchovies and artichoke hearts. In a separate bowl or cruet, combine vinegar with salt, garlic, pepper and mustard, add to salad and toss again. Sprinkle with 2 tablespoons of sesame seeds which have been browned in 1 teaspoon of hot oil.

Serves 8 to 10

Tossed Salad with Herbs

After mixing the crisp salad greens and before adding the oil and vinegar, add 1 teaspoon each: fresh snipped dill, basil, marjoram and chervil, or ¼ teaspoon each of the dried herbs and proceed as above.

Tossed Greens and Grapefruit Salad

1 bunch watercress	½ cup diced green peppers
2 cups curly endive	1 small sweet onion, cut into rings
2 clusters Belgian endive	1 teaspoon salt
1 cup fresh grapefruit sections	4 tablespoons oil
½ cup sliced cucumber	2 tablespoons lemon juice

Tear watercress into sprays, discarding ends of stems. Separate leaves of Belgian endive and break the curly endive into bite-size pieces. Combine them with grapefruit, cucumbers, peppers and onion rings. Toss with oil, lemon juice and salt. Taste for seasoning and correct.

Garnish salad bowl with additional grapefruit sections, cucumbers and watercress.

Serves 6

Cucumber Salad with Cottage Cheese Dressing

What the doctor often orders with a fish dinner.

2 cucumbers	8 radishes
2 cups crisp greens	½ cup watercress
1 small red onion, thinly sliced	

Cottage Cheese Dressing

8 ounces skim milk cottage
   cheese
5 tablespoons oil
1½ tablespoons cider vinegar or
   2 tablespoons lemon juice

1 to 2 tablespoons sugar
½ teaspoon salt
1 small clove garlic, minced
⅛ teaspoon dry mustard
freshly ground pepper

If the cucumbers are farm fresh, leave the skins on. The ones we buy in our urban markets are protected by a waxy finish which is better dispensed with. Wash peeled or unpeeled cucumbers well and score them lengthwise with sharp-pronged fork. Slice cucumbers, red onion and unpeeled radishes, very thin. These may be sliced in advance and kept in the refrigerator with a few ice cubes on them. Just before serving, tear lettuce into bite-sized pieces and add to salad bowl with chilled vegetables.

For the dressing, beat cottage cheese until creamy in electric beater or with rotary hand beater. Add oil, vinegar, garlic and seasonings. Taste and correct seasoning. Toss salad with creamy dressing, garnish bowl with a few sprigs of watercress and serve at once.

Serves 4

Fruit Salad and Cottage Cheese Plate

This is just one version of a fruit combination plate that we use frequently.

1 honeydew melon
1 cantaloupe
1 box strawberries or raspberries
1½ cups white seedless grapes
2 navel oranges, peeled and cut
   in sections
2 bananas, quartered

1 large red apple, unpeeled and
   cut in thin segments
lemon juice
small can of peaches or pear
   halves (reserve juice)
1½ cups skim milk cottage cheese
curly endive or chicory

Slice honeydew melon crosswise to make four rings. Peel and remove center seeds and place on bed of curly endive or chicory on your prettiest luncheon-size plates. Place a small scoop of cottage cheese in center of ring. Scoop tiny melon balls from the remaining honeydew and cantaloupe.

Sprinkle peeled, quartered bananas with lemon juice to keep from discoloring.

Surround the slice of honeydew with a clump of cantaloupe balls, a mound of strawberries or raspberries, grapes, orange sections, apple crescents, banana quarters, etc. A few fresh blueberries sprinkled over all will add a nice touch of color. Chill well and serve cold.

Serves 4

This may be served with the fruit salad dressing (page 204) or the following:

½ cup skim milk cottage cheese
¼ cup mayonnaise

½ cup juice from canned fruit
1 teaspoon lemon juice

Beat or blend cottage cheese until smooth and creamy. Add mayonnaise, fruit syrup and lemon juice, and mix until well blended.

Makes 1¼ cups dressing

Raw Mushroom Salad

1 pound fresh mushrooms
2 cups Pascal celery, cut into
⅜ inch cubes
2 hard-boiled egg whites, cut into
⅜ inch cubes
3 tablespoons scallions, finely
minced
4 tablespoons pimento, finely
minced

¼ teaspoon marjoram
½ teaspoon salt
freshly ground pepper
1 teaspoon celery seed
1 cup oil
4 tablespoons wine vinegar
¼ teaspoon sugar
1 clove garlic, minced
lettuce leaves (or romaine)

Try to get the large snowy mushrooms with stubby short stems. Wash mushrooms and pat dry. Snip off ends of stems. It is better not to peel mushrooms because so much of their flavor is in the velvety skin. Cut mushrooms in man-sized bites, right through the stems. Place in large bowl. Add cut-up celery and egg whites, minced scallions and pimento. In another bowl combine oil, wine vinegar, marjoram, salt, pepper, celery seed, minced garlic and sugar and mix well. Add gradually to mushroom mélange, tossing well between additions. Taste and correct seasoning. Marinate in refrigerator for at least an hour.

Serve in either a large bowl or individual lettuce-lined salad bowls. Transfer to serving bowls with a slotted spoon, to eliminate the excess dressing.

Serves 6

Chef's Salad

1 whole cooked chicken breast, cut into julienne strips
4 cups assorted salad greens, broken into bite-sized pieces
3 tomatoes, cut into wedges
1 green pepper, cut into rings
4 or 5 sliced radishes
2 carrots, coarsely grated
1 tablespoon onion, finely minced
freshly ground pepper
1 tablespoon fresh dill, snipped
½ cup (or more) French dressing
watercress for garnish

In a large bowl, combine salad greens, tomatoes, green pepper, radishes, carrots, minced onion, ground pepper and snipped dill. Toss with sufficient French dressing to coat greens thoroughly. Arrange chicken strips on top. Garnish with watercress. Serve chilled.

Serves 4

Tomato Salad

3 large firm tomatoes
1 medium onion, chopped
⅓ cup cider vinegar
4 tablespoons oil
½ teaspoon salt
freshly ground pepper
½ teaspoon basil

Slice tomatoes about ⅓ inch thick. In a medium-sized bowl, combine vinegar, oil, chopped onion, salt, pepper and basil. Add tomato slices and chill in refrigerator, covered, at least 2 hours. Garnish with watercress and a sprinkle of parsley.

Serves 3

Pickled Beets

6 or 8 fresh-cooked beets, or 1 pound can sliced beets
6 tablespoons vinegar
2 tablespoons water
⅓ cup sugar
2 tablespoons honey

If you are starting with fresh beets leave them whole with the root ends and about two inches of the tops attached. Cook in boiling water to cover until tender, 25 to 35 minutes.

Remove beets from water and slip off skins. Slice them ¼ inch thick and place in bowl.

Combine vinegar, water, sugar and honey in saucepan and bring to a boil. Simmer until the sugar is completely dissolved. Pour this hot mixture over the beets. When cool, cover bowl and refrigerate at least 24 hours before using.

Pickled Beet and Endive Salad

2 cups sliced pickled beets
¼ cup beet liquid
1 sweet onion, sliced into thin rings

2 clusters Belgian endive
¼ cup French dressing
1 tablespoon chopped parsley

Slice clusters of Belgian endive crosswise into rings ¼ inch thick. Combine with pickled beets, liquid and onion and refrigerate for an hour. To serve, arrange beets, onion and endive on individual salad plates. Add French dressing to beet liquid, mix well, and pour over ingredients. Sprinkle lightly with parsley.

Serves 4 to 6

Aunt Rosa's Potato Salad

This is a particularly wonderful salad for party days when the refrigerator is crammed full, because it does not need to be refrigerated. More than that, it mustn't be.

3 pounds small potatoes
½ cup oil (or more)
½ cup vinegar (or more)
1 onion, chopped fine

1 teaspoon salt
freshly ground pepper
¼ teaspoon paprika
¼ cup chopped parsley

The essential in this preparation is warm vinegar on warm potatoes. Having established this keynote to your satisfaction and mine, scrub the potatoes well, place in as little boiling salted water as possible, cover pot and cook until done. Drain at once. While still warm, peel and slice potatoes. Add enough oil, tossing lightly, to coat potatoes and make them shiny. Heat vinegar to the boiling point and add slowly, using as much as you need to moisten the mixture. Add chopped onion, salt, pepper, paprika and chopped parsley. Toss well and taste for seasoning. You may want a bit more salt or a pinch of sugar. Arrange in a mound on platter, garnish with sprigs of parsley or watercress, green pepper rings and some strips of pimento. Serve at room temperature.

Serves 8

Coleslaw

3 cups finely shredded cabbage	2 tablespoons sugar
3 tablespoons oil	½ teaspoon dry mustard
⅓ cup warm vinegar	1 tablespoon finely chopped onion
1 teaspoon salt	1 tablespoon chopped pimento
freshly ground pepper	1 teaspoon celery seeds

Place shredded cabbage in a large bowl. Toss with oil and warm (not hot) vinegar. Add salt, pepper, sugar, dry mustard, chopped onion, pimento and celery seeds, and mix well. Cover bowl and chill in refrigerator. Garnish with green pepper rings and tiny tomatoes.

Serves 4

Mixed Vegetable Salad

This is an excellent accompaniment for cold smoked fish, herring or sardines.

1 cup cooked potatoes, diced	1 teaspoon fresh dill, chopped;
1 cup cooked string beans, diced	or ¼ teaspoon dried dill
1 cup beets, diced	weed
¾ cup French dressing	5 tablespoons mayonnaise
½ teaspoon dry mustard	2 tablespoons chopped chives
1 tablespoon onion, finely chopped	

Cook or warm diced potatoes, string beans and beets separately. Mix mustard, onion and dill with French dressing. Place string beans, potatoes and beets in 3 bowls and, while still warm, marinate each in ¼ cup of the French dressing. Chill well. Just before serving, toss them together with mayonnaise and serve in lettuce-lined bowl. Sprinkle chopped chives over top.   Serves 4 or 5

Waldorf Salad

There was a hiatus of a couple of decades during which I completely forgot about this apple-nut salad. Maybe it was because it used to appear with wearisome regularity when I was a little girl. My mother was a firm subscriber to the theory about "an apple a day," etc. At any rate, the friendly advantage of both apples and nuts have recalled it to me so it is now back in good standing, if not with the same frequency it enjoyed long ago.

2 large or 3 medium apples,
    peeled, cored and diced
1 cup chopped celery
½ cup broken walnut meats

juice of ½ lemon
⅓ cup raisins
mayonnaise

Squeeze lemon juice over diced apples. Add celery, nuts, raisins and as much mayonnaise as you need to hold the ingredients together. Chill well in refrigerator. Serve on crisp greens, garnished with a few strips of pimento.

Serves 4

String Bean Salad

1 pound fresh string beans
⅓ cup oil
3 tablespoons wine vinegar
½ teaspoon salt

freshly ground pepper
3 tablespoons fresh dill, chopped,
    or 2 teaspoons dried dill
    weed

Slice string beans lengthwise, French style. Place in saucepan with small amount of boiling, salted water and cook until just done. Do not overcook. When done, drain and transfer to bowl. Immediately, while string beans are still warm, add enough oil to coat beans and make them shiny. Add vinegar, salt, pepper and dill, and toss lightly. Cover bowl and chill in refrigerator a few hours before serving.

Serves 4

Crab Meat Salad

1 pound fresh lump crab meat
¾ cup celery, chopped
3 tablespoons green pepper, chopped
2 tablespoons chives, chopped
4 tablespoons French dressing
½ cup mayonnaise
½ teaspoon curry powder (or more)
lettuce
tomato wedges
2 tablespoons capers
parsley sprigs

Pick over crab meat and remove shells. Combine crab meat, chopped celery, green pepper, chives and French dressing and chill in the refrigerator for 2 hours.

When ready to serve, mix curry powder with mayonnaise and blend into crab mixture.

Line serving platter with lettuce, arrange crab meat on it in a mound and garnish with tomato wedges and parsley. (Lobster or chicken may be substituted for the crab meat.) Sprinkle capers over salad. Serve chilled.

Serves 4

Halibut Salad

1½ pounds fresh halibut
2 cups cold water
1 teaspoon mixed whole spices
1 tablespoon salt
1 large onion, quartered
1 tablespoon vinegar
¼ teaspoon sugar
⅓ cup celery, finely chopped
¼ cup green pepper, finely chopped
¼ cup mayonnaise
pinch curry powder (optional)
1 tablespoon dill, chopped, or ¾ teaspoon dried dill weed

In a medium-sized skillet, combine cold water, spices, salt, onion, sugar and vinegar. Bring to a boil, add halibut and cook, covered, for 30 minutes, or until the fish flakes easily. Remove from fire and leave fish in the stock until it is completely cold. The spices in the stock give the fish a lovely flavor, so give them plenty of time to permeate. When we're planning this salad for dinner, I like to cook the fish in the morning and refrigerate it in the stock all day until time to assemble it.

When cold, flake the halibut. Add celery, green pepper, enough mayonnaise to moisten (either with or without the curry powder) and dill. Toss lightly and serve on bed of lettuce. Garnish with tomato wedges, green pepper rings and cucumber slices.

Serves 4

Lima Bean Salad

This and some cold asparagus provide a pleasant diversion for a hot-weather lunch.

2 cups fresh or frozen lima beans	½ teaspoon salt
2 tablespoons chopped parsley	freshly ground pepper
1 clove garlic, minced	4 tablespoons oil
1 large sweet onion	1 tablespoon cider vinegar

Cook lima beans in a small amount of boiling salted water until tender but not mushy. Rinse with cold water and drain well. Place in bowl with chopped parsley and minced garlic. Add ⅓ of the onion, finely chopped. (Slice the remainder of onion thinly and use as a garnish.) Toss lightly. Add oil slowly until beans are well coated. Add vinegar by half-teaspoonfuls, tossing lightly until well blended. Don't splash the vinegar in or you'll ruin your salad. Add salt and pepper and blend. Taste and correct seasoning. Chill in refrigerator at least 1 hour. Serve on bed of lettuce, garnish with onion rings, tiny tomatoes and a sprinkle of paprika.

Serves 3 to 4

Scallops in Green Sauce

For some reason, we are likely to overlook scallops when planning something in the cold sea food department.

1 pound sea scallops, cut in half	¼ cup finely chopped parsley
1 small onion, chopped fine	½ cup finely chopped raw spinach
½ cup dry vermouth	¼ cup chopped chives or
sprig of parsley	scallions
bay leaf	1 tablespoon fresh dill, or
salt and pepper	½ teaspoon dill weed
1 cup mayonnaise	

In a saucepan, combine onion, vermouth, parsley, bay leaf, salt and pepper. Add washed scallops, cover pan, and simmer gently for 7 minutes. DON'T let the mixture boil, or you'll have nothing but a scorched pan and some tough scallops. When scallops are tender, drain and cool.

While scallops are cooking, combine mayonnaise with chopped parsley, spinach, chives and dill.

Line small salad bowl with lettuce leaves and place cooled scallops in it. Cover with the green sauce and top with a sprinkling of finely chopped parsley. Chill.

Serves 2 or 3

Salad Niçoise

We serve this either as an appetizer for dinner or a main luncheon course. Unexpected brunch callers on Sunday also get it—the fixings are usually in the house and it takes only a minute to assemble.

1 medium-sized head lettuce, or combination of romaine, chicory, escarole, etc. (about 3 cups)

2 7-ounce cans white meat tuna fish

2 tomatoes, cut into eighths, or ¼ cup coarsely chopped pimento

½ cup pitted black olives, cut in quarters

2 tablespoons capers, drained

4 artichoke hearts, cut in half (optional)

1 small cucumber, peeled and thinly sliced

1 1-ounce can anchovy filets, drained and cut in half

1 green pepper, trimmed and seeded, cut into ¼-inch strips

1 small sweet onion, thinly sliced

sufficient French dressing to moisten and coat greens

In a good-sized salad bowl, break crisp salad greens into bite-sized pieces. Add tuna fish, in good-sized chunks so it won't get lost. Add the rest of the ingredients. If there is going to be any delay in serving this, cover the bowl with waxed paper and refrigerate it without the French dressing. Nothing will happen to it if it chills a half hour or so, except that it will be nice and cold. Just before serving, toss lightly with the dressing so that all the greens are coated and ingredients well distributed.

Serves 6 as an appetizer—4 as a main course

Shrimp Salad, Indienne

This conventional shrimp salad is unconventionally spiced with an aromatic curry dressing. The dressing also does very well with chicken, lobster, crab meat or veal.

1½ pounds shrimp, cooked,
　　cleaned and deveined
3 stalks celery, finely diced
1 small onion, finely chopped
1 teaspoon capers

1 cup mayonnaise
1 tablespoon curry powder (or
　　more, according to taste)
juice of ½ lemon

Combine curry powder, mayonnaise and lemon juice. Mix thoroughly and add to shrimp, celery, onion and capers. Toss well. Chill and serve on bed of crisp greens, garnished with tomato wedges, cucumber slices and parsley.

Serves 2 to 4

Basic French Dressing

1 cup oil
¼ cup cider or wine vinegar
　　(or 2 tablespoons lemon
　　juice)
1 to 3 teaspoons sugar
freshly ground pepper

1 teaspoon salt
⅛ teaspoon paprika
½ teaspoon dry mustard
½ teaspoon Worcestershire
　　sauce (optional)
1 clove garlic (optional)

Measure all ingredients into a jar. Cover tightly and shake well. Chill for a few hours. Remove the garlic. Shake well before serving.

Yield: 1⅓ cups

Fruit Salad Dressing

⅓ cup undiluted frozen
　　lemonade concentrate,
　　thawed

2 tablespoons honey
⅓ cup oil
½ teaspoon celery seeds

Combine all ingredients in a small bowl and blend thoroughly until smooth.

Yield: ¾ cup

Betty's Garlic Cream Dressing

If you don't like garlic, I can't promise that this will reform your taste. However, if you feel about garlic as we do, you'll never be without a jar of this in your refrigerator. It's wonderful on any kind of salad, from mixed greens through cabbage, chicken, sea food, on tomato aspics—or as a dip for vegetables or sea food, either alone or in combination with chili sauce or ketchup.

1 egg	1½ teaspoons black pepper
½ teaspoon minced garlic (3 or 4 cloves, depending on size)	2 teaspoons sugar
	1½ cups oil
¾ tablespoon salt	½ cup cider vinegar (scant)
1½ teaspoons dry mustard	

In a good-sized mixing bowl, with your electric beater at high speed, beat 1 egg until thick and foamy. Add minced garlic, salt, mustard, pepper and sugar. Add oil very slowly, trickling it in until the emulsion beats up nice and thick. Add vinegar—also slowly—and continue beating a few minutes longer. This will probably take about 10 to 12 minutes from beginning to end, but the electric beater won't get tired. Store in covered jar in refrigerator.

Yield: 3 cups

Creamy Mayonnaise

I had heard so many tales about the complications of making mayonnaise—how it separated and didn't thicken, etc.—that it was with considerable trepidation that I approached the project for the first time. I found to my delight it couldn't be simpler. I don't chill the beater, and I don't chill the bowl as I had been warned I must. The whole business takes about 15 minutes in my electric beater and it comes out perfect each time—creamy, rich, smooth and friendly. In view of all this, I strongly urge you to make your own.

Since mayonnaise is essentially bland, I usually add a little dollop of something to give it interest when I serve it—horse-radish, chopped chives, or dill, chili sauce, curry powder, etc.

1 whole egg
2 tablespoons lemon juice
1 tablespoon vinegar
1 teaspoon salt

1¼ teaspoons sugar
1 teaspoon dry mustard
¼ teaspoon paprika
2 cups oil

In your electric beater at high speed, beat egg with 1 tablespoon lemon juice until frothy. Add sugar, salt, dry mustard and paprika and beat well. Add 1 cup of the oil in a tiny trickle—slowly—until the mixture becomes thick. Don't try to hurry this part, but as soon as the mayonnaise becomes thick, you can add the oil more quickly. When the mixture is very thick, add the remaining tablespoon of lemon juice and the tablespoon of vinegar. Continue adding the remainder of the oil gradually until it is well blended, thick and creamy.

Makes 1⅛ pints

Russian Dressing

1 cup mayonnaise
½ cup chili sauce
2 teaspoons horse-radish
¼ teaspoon dry mustard

1 teaspoon Worcestershire
   sauce
2 teaspoons lemon juice

Stir well and beat with a fork until smooth and completely blended.

Makes 1½ cups

Tartare Sauce

½ cup creamy mayonnaise
1 teaspoon stuffed olives
1 teaspoon capers
1 teaspoon sweet pickle

½ teaspoon chopped parsley
½ teaspoon finely grated onion
1 teaspoon lemon juice

Chop olives, capers, sweet pickle and parsley finely. Add to mayonnaise. Combine with grated onion and lemon juice. Refrigerate in covered jar until ready to use.

Vinaigrette Sauce

Parboiled vegetables, like cauliflowerets, broccoli spears, button mushrooms, or asparagus, make fine salads when marinated in this.

To 1 cup of basic French dressing, add:

1 tablespoon finely chopped onion	2 teaspoons finely chopped tarragon, or ½ teaspoon dried tarragon, finely crumbled
2 teaspoons finely chopped parsley	2 teaspoons finely chopped capers
	1 small sour pickle, finely chopped

Combine all ingredients in a jar and blend well.

Remoulade Sauce

A spicy sauce for cold shrimp. This quantity makes enough for a pound of cooked, cleaned shrimp.

1 teaspoon dry mustard	2 tablespoons scallions, minced
1 teaspoon paprika	2 tablespoons chives, minced
¼ teaspoon salt	2 tablespoons celery, minced
freshly ground pepper	3 tablespoons wine vinegar
4 anchovies, chopped	½ cup (or more) oil

Combine mustard, paprika, salt and pepper in a small bowl. Add the remainder of the ingredients and mix well. (Marinate shrimp at least 1 hour in sauce and serve on slivers of avocado, garnished with watercress.)

Creamy Anchovy Dressing

1 2-ounce can flat anchovies	½ teaspoon salt
½ cup oil	freshly ground pepper
4 tablespoons nonfat milk solids dissolved in ½ cup water	1 clove garlic, split
¼ cup wine vinegar	¼ teaspoon sugar
	2 tablespoons chopped parsley

Drain oil from can of anchovies and discard. Chop anchovies into ½-inch lengths. Place in a pint screw-top jar. Add oil, liquefied skim milk, wine vinegar, salt, pepper, split garlic clove, sugar and parsley. Shake vigorously until dressing is creamy and smooth. Chill until ready to use. Remove split garlic clove before serving.

Yields 1⅞ cup

Basic Recipes for Cream Sauces

THIN	MEDIUM	THICK
1 tablespoon oil	2 tablespoons oil	3 tablespoons oil
1 tablespoon flour	2 tablespoons flour	4 tablespoons flour
1 cup skim milk	1 cup skim milk	1 cup skim milk
½ teaspoon salt	½ teaspoon salt	½ teaspoon salt
dash white pepper	dash white pepper	dash white pepper

The procedure to make any one of these three sauces is the same: heat oil in small saucepan, blend with flour thoroughly over low flame, but don't let it brown. Add seasonings and, over medium heat, while stirring constantly, stir in milk until the mixture thickens and bubbles; reduce heat and cook a minute longer.

You may substitute consommé, meat or fish stock, or wine for part of the milk. If you wish to give the sauce added flavor, the milk you add may be previously scalded with a few thin slices of onion and a few sprigs of parsley, or a bay leaf and clove, according to your taste.

Yield: 1 cup

Shrimp Sauce for Filets

To be served with any kind of baked or broiled fish filets.

2 tablespoons oil	1 pound raw shrimp
2 tablespoons flour	1 teaspoon salt
1 cup skim milk	3 tablespoons sherry

Boil shrimp according to directions on page 149. Shell, devein and split in half lengthwise. Set aside. In a small saucepan, combine oil and flour and stir until smooth. Add milk, slowly, stirring constantly, until thickened and bubbly.

Add shrimp. Add salt. Cook for 5 minutes over low flame. Just before serving, add sherry. Pour over fish fillets and serve.

Serves 6

Lobster Sauce

1 pound frozen lobster tails (or
    ½ pound fresh frozen
    lobster meat)
2 cups skim milk
3 tablespoons oil
1 small onion, chopped

1 teaspoon dry mustard
1 teaspoon salt
3 tablespoons flour
1 tablespoon lemon juice
3 tablespoons sherry

If you are using the frozen lobster tails, thaw by covering them with boiling salted water and cooking 3 minutes longer than the weight in ounces of the largest tail. Drain off hot water, drench with cold, and cut through under-shell with scissors. Remove meat by grasping it firmly with your fingers and pulling it away from the shell. Cube lobster.

In a small saucepan, heat 3 tablespoons of oil. Add chopped onion and cook until limp. Add the combined flour, mustard and salt and stir well. Slowly add milk. Cook, stirring constantly, until thick and smooth. Add lemon juice, sherry and lobster meat and heat through. Taste to correct seasoning. Keep warm over hot water, but do not allow to boil. **This makes enough sauce for 4 to 6 servings**

Jellied Beet Salad

This hearty jellied salad mold is one of our old reliables for buffet suppers. I do it in a ring form and fill the center with either cold mixed vegetables or artichoke hearts which have been marinated in French dressing.

1 package raspberry gelatine
1 1-pound can julienne beets
1 cup beet juice
⅔ cup orange juice
2 tablespoons vinegar
1 teaspoon salt

2 teaspoons grated onion
1 tablespoon prepared horse-radish
    (or more)
½ cup carrot, coarsely shredded
½ cup celery, finely diced

Drain juice from julienne beets. Heat 1 cup of the beet juice to the boiling point, remove from fire and dissolve raspberry gelatine in the hot liquid. Add orange juice, vinegar, salt, grated onion and horse-radish. If the horse-radish is mild, you may need more than 1 tablespoon, but you'll have to decide. The taste should be a bit on the sharp side. Cool the gelatine mixture and refrigerate until thick and syrupy. Add drained julienne beets, carrot and celery. Turn into ring mold which has been rinsed with cold water, and chill until firm. Unmold on round platter (see Note, page 212) and garnish with watercress.

Serves 6 to 8

Cranberry Relish Mold

This has been a family standby at New Year's, Thanksgiving, Christmas—whatever the occasion which calls for a 24-pound turkey or a covey of fowl to feed our ever-loving and ever-growing family.

2 tablespoons (or packages) unflavored gelatine	1 orange
½ cup cold water	1 medium apple
2 cups apple juice	¾ cup sugar
2 cups raw cranberries (½ pound)	¾ cup broken walnut meats

Sprinkle gelatine on cold water and allow to dissolve. Heat 1 cup of apple juice to the boiling point and add to the softened gelatine. Stir until completely dissolved. Add the remaining cup of apple juice and refrigerate until thick and syrupy.

Wash cranberries and drain well. Slice orange, skin and all, and remove all seeds. Peel and core apple. Using medium knife of food grinder, grind together cranberries, orange and apple. Add sugar, stir well and chill. When the gelatine has become syrupy, fold in the chilled fruit mixture. Add nuts, and turn into a 6-cup mold which has been rinsed out with cold water. Refrigerate until firm. Unmold (see Note, page 212) and garnish with preserved kumquats and sprigs of watercress.

Serves 6 to 8

Frozen Pineapple Salad

A hot-weather chicken or sea food salad menu gets a fine boost from this fruited mold.

1 package lime-flavored gelatine
1 cup boiling water
1 20-ounce can crushed
   pineapple

1 cup cottage cheese, whipped
   smoothly
½ cup celery, finely diced
1 tablespoon pimento, chopped
½ cup walnuts, coarsely chopped

Stir gelatine in boiling water until dissolved. Chill until thick and syrupy. When it has reached this state, add undrained crushed pineapple, whipped cottage cheese, celery, pimento and walnuts. Pour into mold or an 8-inch-square cake pan which has been rinsed with cold water. Chill until firm. Unmold (see Note, page 212) and serve on crisp salad greens.

Serves 6

Horse-Radish Ring

This sea-food-filled ring makes an impressive first course.

1 package lime-flavored gelatine
1 cup boiling water
½ cup cold water
1 cup cottage cheese, whipped
   smoothly

2 rounded tablespoons white
   horse-radish (or more)
1 medium cucumber
4 red radishes

In a bowl, dissolve lime gelatine in 1 cup boiling water. When dissolved, add ½ cup cold water. Chill in refrigerator until thick and syrupy.

Beat cottage cheese until smooth and creamy. Peel cucumber and slice very thin. Wash radishes, leaving the red skin on, and slice very thin.

When the gelatine is thickened and syrupy, add beaten cottage cheese, sliced cucumber and radishes, and horse-radish. Mix thoroughly. Taste at this point to see if it wants more horse-radish. The horse-radish should not be so subtle that no one knows it's there —so use your judgment. Rinse 6-cup mold with cold water and pour the gelatine mixture into it. Refrigerate until firm.

Unmold (see Note, page 212) on round platter. Fill center with fish or sea food of your choice seasoned with either Russian or Garlic Cream Dressing.

Serves 4 to 6

Wine Cherry Mold

This is a happy thought with either cold or hot chicken or turkey.

2 packages black cherry gelatine
2 cups boiling water
1 large can (No. 2 or 2½)
   pitted Bing Cherries, drained
1 cup cherry juice

1 navel orange, peeled, seeded
   and diced
½ cup port wine
preserved kumquats
watercress

Dissolve black cherry gelatine in 2 cups of boiling water. Add cherry juice and stir well. (If there is less than a cup of juice, add water to make up the difference.) Add port wine and mix. Rinse out 6-cup mold with cold water and pour the gelatine mixture into it. Cool and refrigerate until it becomes thick and syrupy. When it has reached this state, add cherries and diced orange, distributing them evenly. Chill until firm.

Unmold on round platter, and garnish with watercress and kumquats.

NOTE: To unmold aspics, dip the mold in a bowl of hot water quickly, place the serving plate on top of it, and holding the mold and plate firmly, turn the whole thing over. The mold should slip off easily, leaving the aspic just where it belongs. Another method is to invert the mold on the serving plate and cover it with a cloth which has been wrung out in hot water. Repeat this a few times.

Ambrosia Relish

This is an excellent relish with meat and poultry. It puzzles as much as it pleases, for no one ever seems to be able to identify its main ingredient.

4 cups julienne beets (2
   1-pound cans)
1 orange
3 cups sugar

1 lemon
¼ cup almonds
¼ cup crystallized ginger

Drain beets and soak them overnight in cold water. The following day, drain them thoroughly and place in large, heavy saucepan.

Slice orange very thin and cut into small pieces, leaving the skin on. Add to the beets, along with juice and rind of a lemon. Add sugar and crystallized ginger which has been cut up in small pieces. Cook over low heat for about 2 hours, until the syrup cooks down and the julienne things (I hesitate to call them beets at this point because they have lost this identity) are glazed and a lovely, deep amber color. Add blanched, slivered almonds to mixture and heat through for a minute. When cool, place in covered jar and refrigerate. It will keep for weeks if no one eats it—an unlikely prospect.

Yield: Nearly 1 quart

Frosted Grapes

These make a dainty fruit garnish for cold poultry, molded salads or meats.

clusters of seedless grapes
1 egg white, slightly beaten

superfine granulated sugar
canned peach halves

Dip small clusters of grapes in the slightly beaten egg white. When they are nearly dry, sprinkle with sugar and set in center of the canned peach halves.

Baked Oranges

We trot these out for special dinner parties. They go beautifully with a chicken dish. Covered with a meringue forced through a pastry tube, and then browned in the oven, they'll also do for dessert.

6 large navel oranges
1 No. 3 can crushed pineapple
juice of 1 lemon

sugar to taste
¼ cup sherry
½ cup walnuts, finely ground

Cut oranges into halves and scoop out the pulp. Place this in large saucepan with entire contents of the can of pineapple. Add juice of a lemon and sugar to taste. Cook until it becomes the consistency of a thin marmalade. This may take a few hours over a slow flame, but just let it alone, except for stirring it every once in a while.

While it is cooking, scallop orange shells. I do this with my small embroidery scissors. Two little snips that come together in the middle make a pointed scallop, and very nice they look. It's the kind of idiot work that is welcome on a day you're fussing for guests—it gives you a chance to sit down.

When the orange-pineapple stuff is thick and syrupy enough, add sherry, mix, and refill shells. Sprinkle with chopped nuts. Bake in 350-degree oven for 20 minutes. Do not refrigerate. Serve at room temperature. Garnish main-course platter with the oranges.

Serves 12

Baked Curried Fruit

We serve this hot spicy fruit compote in place of a second vege-table with a beef, veal or chicken dinner. For best results, it should be made a day in advance, refrigerated and reheated.

6 tablespoons oil
¾ cup brown sugar, preferably dark, firmly packed
2 teaspoons curry powder (or more)

1 large can pear halves
1 large can peach halves (or apricots)
1 large can pineapple chunks

Drain fruits and discard juice. Excess liquid remaining on the fruits will make the syrup soupy and thin, so drain them thoroughly. You might even dry them on paper towels.

In a small skillet, heat oil, and add brown sugar and curry powder. Depending on the strength of the curry powder and your family's preference, you may need an additional teaspoonful or more, but taste as you go. Simmer for 3 minutes. The sugar-oil mixture will be very thick, but it will liquefy later.

Oil 2-quart casserole. Combine the drained fruit and sugar mixture in it and mix well. Bake in 325-degree oven for 1 hour, uncovered. Cool and refrigerate, preferably overnight. At serving time, reheat in 350-degree oven, covered, for 20 to 30 minutes, or until the syrup is bubbly. Serve hot with the main course.

Serves 8

15

Lunch and Supper Dishes

IT occurs to me that "lunch and supper dishes" may be more a matter of semantics and household custom than a distinct category of foods, for who is to quibble if we choose to dine off pot roast at noon, or nibble on breakfast waffles at dinner?

For most Americans, however, lunch connotes a light meal—a sandwich, a salad, a bowl of soup. My additional requirement is that it can be assembled from pantry supplies without the necessity for last-minute marketing.

The supper dishes included here are my solution for the easy informality of the occasions when a one-dish meal for the family or to share with friends is indicated. They range from a simple casserole to handsome productions like the spinach-and-chicken-filled cannellone or an impressive paella, all of which can be prepared in advance and require a minimum of last-minute fussing.

Heart of Artichoke and Oyster Casserole

3 dozen oysters
1 10-ounce package frozen
    artichoke hearts
½ cup flour
½ cup oil
2 cups skim milk
⅓ cup nonfat milk solids

1 teaspoon salt
½ teaspoon freshly ground
    pepper
6 tablespoons sherry
1 teaspoon Worcestershire sauce
dash Tabasco sauce (or more,
    according to taste)

Cook frozen artichokes according to directions on package. Drain and clean oysters, discarding the liquid. In a heavy skillet, heat oil.

Add flour and cook and stir until it turns brown. Remove from fire and add milk and nonfat milk solids slowly. Add the drained oysters and return to heat. Over a medium flame, cook and stir constantly until the sauce becomes thick and smooth. Add salt, pepper, Worcestershire sauce, Tabasco and sherry. Lightly oil 2-quart casserole. Line bottom with the drained artichoke hearts and pour the oyster sauce over them. Heat in 350-degree oven for 15 to 20 minutes.

Serves 6

Lobster, New Orleans

The tin of frozen lobster meat you may have in your freezer couldn't be put to better use than in this simply prepared dish.

1 pound cooked lobster meat, fresh or frozen	1 large tomato, peeled and cut into eighths
4 tablespoons oil	½ teaspoon salt
1 medium onion, chopped	freshly ground pepper
1 green pepper, chopped	1 cup tomato sauce
1 clove garlic, minced	1 tablespoon snipped dill
	¼ cup white wine

Cut thawed lobster into small bite-sized pieces.

Heat oil in large, heavy skillet, and sauté onion, green pepper and garlic until tender. Add tomato segments and cook over low flame for 10 or 12 minutes, until the tomato becomes soft. Add salt, pepper, tomato sauce and dill. Add lobster and simmer gently for 10 minutes. Taste and correct seasoning. You may want a bit more salt, depending on the degree of seasoning in the tomato sauce. Add white wine and cook 2 or 3 minutes longer until heated through. Serve with fluffy boiled rice.

Serves 3 or 4

Shrimp Creole

The creole sauce is a perfect base for any kind of sea food or fish. This recipe yields a large quantity of sauce but the leftover may be used for another meal. The flavor improves on standing and it freezes very well. It is particularly good on a thick baked haddock filet.

1½ pounds cooked cleaned
    shrimp
4 tablespoons oil
2 large onions, chopped
1 cup celery, finely cut
1 green pepper, finely cut
1 small clove garlic, crushed
½ pound mushrooms, sliced

2 tablespoons sugar
½ teaspoon salt
freshly ground pepper
½ teaspoon oregano
1 No. 3 can Italian tomatoes
1½ tablespoons cornstarch
¼ cup cold water

In a large saucepan, heat oil. Add onions, celery, crushed garlic and green pepper and cook over low flame for 10 minutes, stirring often. Add sliced mushrooms and cook 2 or 3 minutes longer.

Add salt, pepper, sugar, oregano and Italian tomatoes and simmer 30 minutes, stirring from time to time.

Make a paste of cornstarch and water and stir into the sauce. Bring sauce to the boiling point and boil for 3 or 4 minutes.

Add cooked shrimp and serve with plenty of hot, fluffy rice.

Serves 4

Dried Beef and Tomatoes

This recipe will stretch a can of kidney beans and a small amount of wafer-thin dried beef into a completely adequate meal.

½ pound dried beef
3 tablespoons oil
2 medium sized onions, diced
2 tablespoons flour
2 cups canned tomatoes

1½ cups canned kidney beans
¼ teaspoon oregano
½ teaspoon chili powder (or
    more, according to taste)

Heat oil in heavy skillet. Shred dried beef and cook in the hot oil until the edges curl. Add diced onion and cook 5 minutes more, until the onion becomes transparent.

Stir in flour and blend well with oil in the skillet. Add tomatoes slowly. Cook over low heat, stirring constantly, until thick. Add beans, chili powder and oregano. Taste and add more chili powder if you want it a bit spicier.

Serves 4

Frizzled Dried Beef

2 tablespoons oil
½ pound sliced dried beef,
    shredded
3 tablespoons flour
2 cups skim milk

¼ teaspoon dry mustard
freshly ground pepper
toast triangles
chopped parsley

If the beef is salty (and it generally is), pour boiling water over it, wait 2 or 3 minutes and drain and squeeze dry.

Heat oil in heavy skillet. Add shredded beef and cook for about 5 minutes until it frizzles and gets curly. Sprinkle flour over the beef and stir constantly until the flour turns dark brown—but not burnt. Add dry mustard. Slowly add milk, a little at a time, and stir until the mixture thickens and comes to a boil. Add pepper. If the mixture is thicker than you wish, thin it with an additional ½ cup of skim milk. Serve on toast, sprinkled with a little chopped parsley.

Serves 4

Baked Stuffed Peppers

These are equally good for a family dinner or as part of your offering at a party buffet. They may be prepared in advance and baked at the time you need them.

6 to 8 large green peppers
2 tablespoons oil
1 medium onion, chopped
½ pound lean round steak,
    ground
½ lb. lean chopped veal
1½ cups cooked rice
    (½ cup raw)
1 teaspoon salt
freshly ground pepper

¼ teaspoon thyme
¼ cup chopped walnuts
1 tablespoon chopped parsley
4 tablespoons nonfat milk solids
    dissolved in ½ cup water
2 cups tomato sauce
½ teaspoon basil
1 broth powder dissolved in
    ½ cup hot water

Cut a crosswise slice from the stem end of the peppers and discard. Remove seeds. Cover peppers with boiling water and steep for 5 minutes. Drain and set aside.

In a large heavy skillet, heat oil. Add onion and cook until golden brown. Mix chopped veal and beef together. Add and cook for 5 or 6 minutes longer until it loses its raw look. Remove from heat and add cooked rice, salt, pepper, thyme, chopped walnuts, parsley, liquefied milk. Blend thoroughly with a fork.

Stuff peppers with the meat mixture. Arrange them in a baking dish, close together. Combine tomato sauce, basil, and dissolved broth powder in small saucepan and bring to the boiling point. Pour over and around the stuffed peppers. Cover baking dish with tightly fitting cover, or aluminum foil, and bake in 400-degree oven 40 to 50 minutes, or until the peppers are crisp tender. Remove cover a few times during the baking and baste peppers with sauce.   Serves 6 to 8

Chicken Chow Mein

Even if this Chinese dish is an American invention and completely unknown in China, it's a general favorite and a fine vehicle for leftover chicken or turkey.

2 cups cooked chicken or turkey, cut in large, bite-sized pieces
2 large onions, thinly sliced
2 tablespoons oil
4 large celery stalks, split, cut diagonally in 1-inch pieces
½ cup mushrooms, sliced
½ cup water chestnuts, sliced

1 can bean sprouts, drained
½ cup bamboo shoots
2 tablespoons cornstarch
2 cups chicken broth
1 tablespoon soy sauce (or more)
freshly ground pepper
Chinese noodles
cooked rice

In a large skillet, heat oil and cook onions until slightly soft. Add celery, mushrooms and 1½ cups chicken broth. Cook over low heat for 10 minutes, stirring a few times.

Add water chestnuts, bean sprouts and bamboo shoots. In a small bowl, make a mixture of cornstarch, soy sauce and ½ cup chicken broth and stir until smooth. Add this to the large skillet, along with the chicken or turkey. Add freshly ground pepper and mix well. Simmer for 10 minutes. Taste for seasoning—you may want to add some additional soy sauce.

Serve with hot rice and Chinese fried noodles which have been warmed in the oven.   Serves 6

Chili Con Carne

This classic and popular meat-stretcher may not be an appropriate entrée for a champagne dinner, but it has its uses for an informal family supper.

2 tablespoons oil	1½ teaspoons chili powder
1 large Spanish onion, chopped	½ cup ketchup
1 pound lean round steak, ground	1 cup tomato sauce
	1 teaspoon salt
1 No. 2 can kidney beans	freshly ground pepper

Heat oil in large heavy skillet. Add chopped onions and cook until golden brown. Add chopped meat and brown well, stirring constantly. Add beans, chili powder, ketchup, tomato sauce, salt and pepper and simmer over low heat for 30 to 40 minutes, stirring frequently.

Serves 4

Moussaka
(Greek Eggplant and Veal Casserole)

Unlike Chow Mein in China, the Greeks actually eat moussaka. There are many different versions of it—a confusing situation for an American recipe-hunter in Greece. The nice young lady in charge of the gift shop in our hotel came to my aid, however. Her English was imperfect and my Greek nonexistent, but with the help of sign language and bilingual passers-by we evolved the following formula. If any ingredients were lost in the translation of Greek to English, we haven't noticed them. The native dish is generally made with lamb. We, naturally, will use veal.

1 pound lean veal, ground	½ teaspoon cinnamon
about 1 cup oil	¼ teaspoon nutmeg
1 medium eggplant, peeled and sliced ½ inch thick	½ cup tomato sauce
	2 cups cooked rice
Lawry's seasoned salt	2 tablespoons grated sapsago or Parmesan cheese
2 onions, chopped	
1 teaspoon salt	paprika
freshly ground pepper	

In a large, heavy skillet, heat ⅓ cup oil. Brown eggplant slices 2 or 3 minutes on each side just to give them a brown crust. They'll finish cooking in the oven. Add more oil as you need it for the frying. Drain on paper towels. Dust lightly with Lawry's seasoned salt and set aside.

In the same skillet, heat ⅓ cup oil, add chopped onions and cook until transparent. Add ground veal, salt, pepper, cinnamon and nutmeg. Cook for 10 minutes, stirring often, until the meat is all browned. Add tomato sauce and cook another 3 minutes.

Oil 2-quart casserole. Place a layer of cooked rice on the bottom. Cover with ⅓ of the veal mixture. Cover with a layer of eggplant and continue with layers of rice, meat and eggplant until all are used. End with a layer of rice. Sprinkle with grated cheese and dust with paprika. Bake in 375-degree oven for 35 minutes. Serve hot. This simple meal-in-one-dish needs only the accompaniment of a mixed green salad.

Serves 5 to 6

Salmon Casserole

6 ounces elbow macaroni
1 1-pound can red salmon
2 tablespoons oil
2 tablespoons flour
1 teaspoon salt
freshly ground pepper
¼ teaspoon dry mustard

2 teaspoons Worcestershire sauce
1½ cups skim milk
2 tablespoons lemon juice
¾ cup pitted black olives, sliced
½ cup bread crumbs, browned
    in 2 tablespoons oil

Cook elbow macaroni according to directions on package. Rinse with hot water, drain and set aside.

Drain salmon, reserving the juice. Carefully pick over salmon and remove skin and bones. In medium-sized saucepan, heat oil. Blend with flour thoroughly over a small flame. Add salt, pepper, dry mustard and Worcestershire sauce. Continue to stir and add skim milk and juice from the salmon. Cook until it thickens and bubbles, add lemon juice and cook 1 minute longer. Add macaroni, olives and flaked salmon. Taste for seasoning. Pour into 1½-quart oiled casserole and sprinkle with browned bread crumbs. Bake in 375-degree oven for 30 minutes.

Serves 4 to 6

Salmon Croquettes

1 1-pound can red salmon
2 teaspoons cornstarch
2 tablespoons salmon liquid
½ cup skim milk
1 teaspoon grated onion
1 tablespoon chopped parsley
½ teaspoon salt
freshly ground black pepper
1 teaspoon lemon juice

¼ teaspoon dry mustard
1 tablespoon mayonnaise
⅓ cup corn flake crumbs
1 egg white, stiffly beaten

* * *

1 egg white lightly mixed with
    2 tablespoons cold water
½ cup corn flake crumbs
oil for deep frying

Drain salmon, reserving 2 tablespoons of the liquid. Place salmon in medium-size bowl, remove skin and bones, and flake.

In a small saucepan, blend cornstarch and salmon liquid to a smooth paste. Add skim milk and cook over low flame for 3 or 4 minutes, stirring constantly, until the mixture becomes thick and smooth. Add to the salmon and mix well. Add grated onion, chopped parsley, salt, pepper, lemon juice, mustard, mayonnaise and corn flake crumbs and mix thoroughly. Fold in stiffly beaten egg white. Taste and correct seasoning.

Wet hands in cold water and shape salmon mixture into 6 cylindrical croquettes. Dip croquettes into the egg white and water mixture, and roll in corn flake crumbs. Refrigerate for an hour or longer to give the breading time to dry thoroughly.

Fill deep-fat fryer ⅓ full of oil and heat until the oil reaches 375 degrees, or until a cube of day-old bread browns in 30 to 40 seconds. Fry croquettes until golden brown all around—4 or 5 minutes. Remove with slotted spoon and drain on absorbent paper. Serve with lemon wedges and tartare sauce.

Serves 3

Tuna Tetrazzini

1 large onion, chopped
7 tablespoons oil
4 tablespoons flour
1½ teaspoons salt
3½ cups skim milk
½ pound mushrooms, sliced
2 7-ounce cans tuna fish
½ teaspoon dry mustard

½ cup pitted black olives, sliced
2 tablespoons parsley, chopped
1 tablespoon lemon juice
⅛ teaspoon thyme
½ pound spaghetti
3 tablespoons grated sapsago cheese

Heat 5 tablespoons of the oil in large skillet, add chopped onion and cook until golden. Blend in flour, salt and dry mustard. When smooth, slowly add 3½ cups skim milk, stirring constantly, and cook until thick and bubbly. Add tuna, broken into bite-sized pieces, and olives. In a small skillet, heat remaining 2 tablespoons oil and add sliced mushrooms. Cook for 3 minutes. Add mushrooms and liquid to the tuna mixture, along with parsley, lemon juice and thyme. Taste and correct seasoning.

Cook spaghetti according to directions on package, rinse with hot water and drain well. Mix with the tuna sauce and pour into oiled 3-quart casserole. Sprinkle grated sapsago cheese over top and place under broiler until the top is well browned.

Serves 6 to 8

Tuna Pancakes with Piquante Tomato Sauce

This dish is my ace in the hole on a day when the larder is low and either weather or inclination makes marketing a problem.

2 eggs
¼ teaspoon salt
1 cup plus 2 tablespoons skim milk
2 tablespoons oil
1 cup sifted flour
2 tablespoons chopped pimento

¼ green pepper, chopped fine
1 shallot (or 3 scallions) chopped fine
2 tablespoons oil
2 7-ounce cans tuna fish
½ cup mayonnaise

Piquante Tomato Sauce

1 tablespoon flour	½ teaspoon dry mustard
1 tablespoon sugar	1½ tablespoons oil
¼ teaspoon salt	1½ cups tomato sauce
1½ teaspoons vinegar	chopped parsley

With a rotary beater, beat eggs and salt. Add milk. Add flour gradually, beating constantly. Add 2 tablespoons of oil and mix well. The batter should be the consistency of heavy cream. Let the batter rest while you fix the filling and sauce.

In a medium-sized saucepan, heat 2 tablespoons of oil. Add chopped pimento, green pepper, shallot or scallions and cook for 5 minutes. Add the flaked tuna and mayonnaise and mix thoroughly. Remove from heat.

For the Piquante Tomato Sauce, combine in small saucepan flour, sugar, salt and dry mustard. Over low flame, add oil, stirring constantly. When bubbly, slowly add tomato sauce, stirring constantly, and cook until thickened, about 3 to 5 minutes. Add vinegar and cook 1 minute longer.

With a paper towel which has been dipped in oil, lightly oil 6-inch skillet. Heat over medium flame until a drop of water bounces off like a rubber ball. Pour a thin layer of batter into skillet, tilting it so that the batter covers the bottom evenly, and cook until light brown. Turn the pancake over and cook the other side. Place on towel and repeat until all the batter is used. This should yield 16 pancakes.

Place a mound of the tuna mixture in the middle of each pancake and roll. Lightly oil shallow baking dish and place the rolled pancakes in it, seamy side down. Cover with Piquante Tomato Sauce and bake in 350-degree oven for 15 minutes until heated through. Garnish with chopped parsley and serve hot.

Serves 6 to 8

Skillet Tuna and Corn

⅓ cup green pepper, cut in
    small cubes
1 large onion, chopped
3 tablespoons oil
2 7-ounce cans tuna fish
1½ cups tomato sauce

1 cup whole kernel corn
1 4-ounce can sliced mushrooms
¼ teaspoon salt
1 teaspoon Worcestershire
    sauce
2 cups cooked rice

In a heavy skillet, heat oil. Add cubed green pepper and chopped onion and cook until they are soft. Add tuna fish, which has been broken up into chunks, and tomato sauce, corn, drained sliced mushrooms, salt and Worcestershire sauce. Heat through. Taste and correct seasoning. Serve on a bed of fluffy hot rice.

Serves 4 or 5

Stuffed Zucchini

For this dish, try to get stubby, fat zucchini without any sudden twists or curves, since they'll need to be hollowed out.

A cup of finely minced chicken may be substituted for the tuna fish.

4 plump medium-sized zucchini
2 slices of bread, crusts removed,
    soaked in water and
    squeezed dry
1 tablespoon oil
1 tablespoon chopped parsley
freshly ground pepper
1 7-ounce can tuna fish, finely
    minced

1 tablespoon mayonnaise
¼ teaspoon dry mustard
1 tablespoon oil
1 clove garlic, minced
1 8-ounce can tomato sauce
½ teaspoon salt
freshly ground pepper
½ cup soup stock or consommé

Wash unpeeled zucchini well. Cut off end slices and scoop out center of zucchini with apple corer, being careful not to break outer skin. In a small bowl, combine tuna fish (or chicken), bread, oil, parsley, pepper, mayonnaise and dry mustard. Mix to a smooth paste. Pack zucchini with this mixture.

In a shallow ovenproof baking dish, heat 1 tablespoon of oil over a medium flame and brown minced garlic. Add tomato sauce, salt, pepper and stock or consommé and heat through. Place the stuffed zucchini in the sauce and cook in 375-degree oven for 45 to 50 minutes, or until the zucchini are tender.

Serves 4

Fishburgers

This is a practical lunch solution for the cupful of fish left over from dinner the night before.

4 hamburger rolls, split and
    toasted
1 tablespoon oil
1½ tablespoons green pepper,
    minced
1 tablespoon onion, minced
2 teaspoons flour

½ cup skim milk
½ teaspoon salt
¼ teaspoon dry mustard
1 teaspoon Worcestershire sauce
1 cup cooked fish (halibut, cod,
    salmon), flaked

In a medium-sized saucepan, heat oil. Add green pepper and onion and cook for 5 minutes until soft. Sprinkle flour over all and blend in skim milk, stirring constantly, until the sauce is thick and smooth. Add salt, mustard, Worcestershire sauce and mix well over low heat. Add flaked fish and heat through. Divide the fish mixture among the 4 hamburger rolls, cover with top half, and serve hot.

Serves 4

Hot Veal Salad Sandwich

Every housewife knows the frustration of that little bit of leftover meat—not enough for another meal, and too much to ignore.

1 cup cooked meat (it is generally
    veal), ground
1 tablespoon chopped pickle
1 tablespoon chopped onion
3 tablespoons mayonnaise
2 teaspoons Worcestershire sauce

4 slices of tomato
parsley
1 tablespoon oil
prepared mustard
4 slices of bread

Combine meat, pickle, onion, mayonnaise and Worcestershire sauce. Salt and pepper to taste. Toast bread on one side. Spread a little prepared mustard on the untoasted surface and cover with the meat mixture. Top with a slice of tomato, sprinkle with parsley and dribble a bit of oil over the tomato. Place sandwiches under broiler and broil until the meat and tomato slices brown.　　Serves 4

Shrimp Lasagne

1 pound fresh shrimp.
2 tablespoons oil
1 cup onions, coarsely chopped
2 cloves garlic, minced
1 large can (1 lb. 12 oz.) Italian tomatoes
1 6-ounce can Italian tomato paste
1 teaspoon salt
¼ teaspoon Lawry's seasoned salt
freshly ground pepper

1 teaspoon oregano

1 tablespoon parsley, chopped
1 teaspoon sugar
1 4-ounce can button mushrooms
⅓ cup pitted black olives, sliced (optional)
2 cups cottage cheese
⅓ cup grated sapsago cheese
2 tablespoons grated Parmesan cheese
½ pound lasagne

Boil shrimp according to the directions on page 149. When cool, remove shells and devein.

Heat oil in heavy skillet. Add onions and garlic and cook until limp and transparent. Add tomatoes, tomato paste, salts, pepper, oregano, parsley and sugar. Simmer, uncovered, over low flame for 45 minutes. Add sliced olives and mushrooms and mushroom liquid. Simmer 15 minutes longer, or until the sauce is thick.

Cut shrimp into halves or quarters, depending on their size. The pieces shouldn't be too small, or they will lose their identity. Add cut-up shrimp to the tomato sauce and simmer 5 minutes longer. Taste and correct seasoning.

While the sauce is simmering, cook lasagne according to directions on package. Rinse with hot water and drain well.

Lightly oil shallow casserole—a 9 x 13″ oblong one will do nicely. Place a thin layer of tomato sauce on the bottom, cover with a layer of lasagne, a layer of the tomato-shrimp mixture, a layer of cottage cheese, a light sprinkling of grated cheeses, and repeat until all are used. There should be about 3 layers, ending with cottage cheese sprinkled with grated cheeses. Bake in 350-degree oven for 30 minutes.　　Serves 6

Cannellone

This is our friendly fat version of Sardi's famous dish. It's not as complicated as it seems, since much of the preparation can be done well in advance,

Pancake

2 eggs
2 tablespoons oil
1 cup skim milk

⅔ cup sifted flour
½ teaspoon salt

Beat eggs well with a rotary beater. Add oil and skim milk and continue beating. Add sifted flour and salt and beat until smooth. Let rest for 30 minutes. If the batter is heavier than heavy cream, thin it out with more milk. Heat 6-inch skillet until a drop of water bounces off. With a paper towel dipped in oil, lightly oil pan. Pour as little batter in the pan as you need to cover the bottom. Tilt quickly to distribute evenly. When lightly brown, turn pancake and brown the other side. Place pancake on a towel and repeat process until all the batter is used. Stack the pancakes when cool. Re-oil pan as necessary. This should make 18.

Pancake Filling

For the filling, I usually boil a 2-pound broiler, or 2 large whole chicken breasts, with an onion, a stalk of celery and a carrot, reserving the stock for the sauce. After the chicken is cooked, remove the meat from the bones.

1 to 1½ pounds cooked
    boneless chicken
3 tablespoons chopped, cooked
    spinach
1 tablespoon chopped parsley
½ teaspoon salt

freshly ground pepper
¼ teaspoon rosemary
¼ teaspoon thyme
1 egg white
2 tablespoons white wine

Put chicken through medium blade of food grinder. To the ground-up chicken add chopped spinach, chopped parsley, salt, pepper, rosemary, thyme and egg white. Moisten with wine, a little at a time. Taste for seasoning and correct.

Meat Sauce

½ pound uncooked chopped lean veal
4 large raw mushrooms
1 shallot (or ½ small onion), chopped
1 clove garlic, minced
½ teaspoon salt
freshly ground pepper
1 cup thick tomato purée
½ teaspoon sugar
3 tablespoons oil
3 tablespoons flour
2 cups chicken broth
2 tablespoons grated sapsago or Parmesan cheese

Chop mushrooms very fine and add to veal with finely chopped onion or shallot, minced garlic, salt and pepper. Add tomato purée and sugar. Place in heavy skillet and cook over medium heat for 20 minutes, stirring often.

In a second saucepan, heat oil, blend with flour thoroughly over a small flame, but don't let it brown. Increase heat and add chicken broth, stirring constantly, until the sauce thickens and bubbles. Reduce heat and cook 1 minute longer.

Combine meat sauce with cream sauce. Taste to correct seasoning—the degree of seasoning in the chicken broth is a variable, so you may need more salt and pepper. Keep sauce warm over hot water.

To bake, lightly oil large shallow baking pan—a jelly-roll pan, if you have one, provides a large enough surface. Roll chicken stuffing in the pancakes to form tubes. Lay the tubes alongside each other, but don't stack them. Cover with meat sauce, sprinkle with 2 tablespoons grated sapsago or Parmesan cheese, and place under broiler until the cheese bubbles. Transfer to heated platter and serve hot.

Serves 6

Spaghetti and Chicken Livers

¾ pound lean round steak, ground
2 cloves garlic, crushed
2 medium-sized onions, chopped
3 tablespoons oil
3½ cups tomato purée (or 1 No. 2½ can Italian tomatoes forced through a sieve)
1 7-ounce can Italian tomato paste
1 teaspoon salt
½ pound sliced mushrooms
freshly ground pepper
1 teaspoon dried basil
1 teaspoon oregano
1 tablespoon (or more) sugar
1 pound thin spaghetti
1 pound chicken livers
2 tablespoons oil
salt and pepper

In a heavy skillet or Dutch oven, heat 3 tablespoons of oil. Add chopped onions and cook until transparent. Add meat and garlic. Stir over medium heat until the meat is browned. Add tomato purée, tomato paste, salt, pepper, basil, oregano and sugar. Cook slowly for 2 hours, uncovered, stirring frequently. After the first hour, add sliced mushrooms. If the sauce gets too thick, thin out with a little water, or some canned consommé or Marsala wine. Taste to correct seasoning before serving.

To cook spaghetti, bring salted water to a rolling boil in a large pot. Drop in spaghetti and let it bend its own way into the water. Don't overcook—it should be firm and not mushy. Seven or 8 minutes should do it nicely—you'll have to taste it to make sure. Fine Italian cookery prescribes spaghetti cooked al dente, which means "firm to the bite." When it is done, rinse under hot water to wash out the starch. Drain in colander and return to pan to keep warm.

Cut chicken livers into halves, trimming off the tiny strip of fat that generally adheres to them in the center. Salt and pepper livers. In a skillet, heat 2 tablespoons of oil and add livers a few at a time, so that each can get your undivided attention and be completely seared. When all the livers have been browned, cover skillet and cook for 10 minutes. Add sautéed livers to meat sauce and serve over hot spaghetti.

Serves 4 to 6

Clam Sauce for Spaghetti

½ cup oil
3 cloves garlic, minced
1 teaspoon basil
1 tablespoon green pepper,
    finely chopped

1 15-ounce can chopped clams
    and juice (or tiny whole
    ones)
¼ cup chopped parsley
freshly ground pepper
2 cups clam juice

1 pound spaghetti

In a heavy skillet, heat oil. Add minced garlic, basil and green pepper and cook for 3 minutes. Add drained clams and simmer another 5 minutes. Add parsley, ground pepper and clam juice and simmer over low flame for 50 minutes to an hour, or until the sauce becomes a little thickened. The clam juice is generally seasoned enough not to require additional salt, but taste it to make sure. Cook spaghetti according to directions on page 230. Serve sauce hot over the spaghetti, with the additional sauce in a gravy boat.

Serves 6

Note: If you prefer a red sauce to the white, substitute 1 cup of tomato sauce for 1 cup of the clam juice.

Baked Macaroni

You can make this with elbow macaroni, but for variety try some of the unusual pastas—like the thick stuff that comes in short twisted pieces and looks like a spring. If you prefer a red sauce, add an 8-ounce can of tomato sauce to the cream sauce.

½ pound uncooked macaroni
4 tablespoons oil
½ cup onions, chopped
2 tablespoons celery, finely minced
1 clove garlic
2 tablespoons flour
1½ teaspoons salt
freshly ground pepper
¼ teaspoon oregano

2 cups skim milk
2 cups (1 pound) cottage cheese
2 tablespoons fresh chopped chives (or 1 teaspoon dried chives)
¼ teaspoon paprika
4 tablespoons grated sapsago cheese or ½ cup dry bread crumbs, browned in 2 tablespoons oil

Cook macaroni in boiling salted water until just tender—do not overcook. Place in colander and rinse with hot water. Drain well.

In a heavy skillet, heat oil and cook celery, onion and garlic for 10 minutes, or until soft. Discard garlic. Blend in flour, salt, pepper and oregano. Slowly add milk, stirring constantly, until the sauce is thickened and bubbly. Simmer another minute over low flame. Taste and correct seasoning.

With a rotary beater (or blender), beat cottage cheese until it is fluffy. Add chives and paprika and mix.

Oil 2-quart or 8 x 8″ baking dish. Put a thin layer of sauce on bottom, cover with half the macaroni. Cover with whipped cottage cheese, add the other half of the macaroni and top with the remainder of the cream sauce. Sprinkle with browned bread crumbs or grated cheese. Bake in 350-degree oven for 35 to 40 minutes, or until the top is brown and the sauce bubbles.

Serves 4

Paella
(Chicken and Sea Food Risotto)

This is excellent for a buffet—as a matter of fact, it's difficult to make in small quantities, but the leftover freezes magnificently and can be a great comfort at a later time. There are as many recipes for paella as for curries—but having eaten the dish in restaurants in both Spain and Mexico, I give you this recipe with the assurance that it tastes so authentic that if you have any Madrileños as guests, they will probably start speaking to you in their native tongue after the first taste.

I usually prepare chickens and sea food the day before, since they are sort of a do.

2 2-pound fryers, cut into small serving pieces
1 pound lobster tails (or fresh-frozen lobster meat)
5 cups cold water
1 tablespoon salt
1 pound scallops (cut into small pieces)
½ pound mushrooms, sliced
1 cup Bermuda onion, finely chopped
2 pounds raw shrimp
1 pint mussels (optional)

3 cloves garlic, crushed
2⅔ cups converted rice (Uncle Ben's)
1 No. 1 can (2 cups) Italian tomatoes
1 teaspoon saffron
½ cup chopped parsley
2 teaspoons salt
freshly ground pepper
½ cup oil
1 package frozen green peas
1 small can pimentos

Skin chickens and cut into small portions with poultry scissors, making 10 to 12 pieces from each. Cut out backbones and remove wings. Place backbones, wings, necks and skin in large kettle with 5 cups of cold water. Add 1 tablespoon salt. Simmer slowly for an hour. Skim off whatever film appears on the broth from time to time.

If you are using lobster tails, remove the meat and cut into bite-size pieces. Wash, shell and devein shrimp. Wash scallops. Prepare sliced mushrooms, chopped onion and chopped parsley.

In a large skillet, heat ½ cup oil. Add chicken pieces, seasoned with 1 teaspoon salt and some freshly ground pepper. Brown over high heat for 15 minutes, reduce heat, cover pan and allow to cook another 10 minutes. Turn the pieces a few times, so they will cook evenly. Add chopped onion and minced garlic and cook another 5 minutes or so until the onions are transparent.

Skim and strain chicken broth, return to kettle and bring to a rolling boil. If the broth seems a bit weak, add a bouillon cube or an MBT chicken broth powder. Add shrimp to the boiling broth, cover kettle, and allow to cook for 3 minutes. Add lobster meat and scallops and cook uncovered for 5 minutes. (If you are using the fresh-frozen variety, you may omit this cooking time.) Add saffron and cook a few minutes longer. Add chicken, canned tomatoes, mushrooms, parsley, 1 teaspoon salt and freshly ground pepper, and toss together. If you are doing the paella the day before you need it, this is the point at which you stop and refrigerate the mixture.

To finish the dish, add to chicken and sea food the 2⅔ cups raw rice, the green peas which have been defrosted, mix thoroughly, and transfer to lightly oiled 4- or 5-quart casserole. Bake, covered, in 375-degree oven for 1¼ hours, or until the rice is tender and has absorbed liquid. Stir two or three times during the cooking so that the rice will cook evenly. While this is in the oven, steam mussels in a little water until the shells open. Garnish with strips of pimento and the mussels. Serve hot in casserole.

Serves 12

Cold Veal in Tuna Sauce

In Italy this is known as "Vitello Tonnato." It is a favorite antipasto there but we like it for a cold supper or as a buffet dish.

3 to 4 pounds boneless veal roast	½ teaspoon salt
1 large onion, sliced	freshly ground pepper
2 whole cloves	1 cup dry white wine
1 bay leaf	1 7-ounce can tuna fish
1 clove garlic, minced	10 anchovy filets
2 carrots, sliced	2 tablespoons lemon juice
2 stalks celery, coarsely chopped	½ to ¾ cup oil
4 sprigs parsley	2 tablespoons capers, drained

Have the butcher tie a 3- to 4-pound roast from the leg of veal, without bones or fat, into an evenly shaped roll. Cut 2 anchovy filets into small pieces, pierce the meat here and there with a sharp-pointed knife and insert small pieces of the anchovies into the openings.

Heat 2 tablespoons of oil in heavy kettle or Dutch oven. Brown meat evenly all around. Add sliced onion, cloves, bay leaf, garlic, carrots, celery, parsley, salt, pepper and wine. Bring to a boil slowly, cover kettle, reduce heat and simmer gently until the meat is tender— about 2 hours. Remove meat from kettle, cool and refrigerate.

Continue to simmer contents of the kettle until it is reduced to 2 cups. This may take 30 to 40 minutes. When reduced, pour into a bowl, vegetables and all, and cool and refrigerate. Skim fat when chilled. If the roast was very lean, chances are there won't be much fat, but we're ever watchful.

Purée the skimmed gravy and vegetables. Force tuna fish, remaining anchovies and 1 tablespoon of drained capers through sieve or food mill, beat in lemon juice, and mix together with the puréed gravy, blending well. Beat in the oil, blending well to make a creamy mixture. (All of this may be done in an electric blender, if you have one.) The sauce should be the consistency of very heavy cream. If it is too thick, thin it out with additional lemon juice.

Slice the cold meat thinly, place in large shallow glass or pottery (not metal) dish, and spoon sauce over meat slices. Marinate for a few hours, or overnight. Serve cold, sprinkled with the remaining capers. Garnish with lemon slices and chopped parsley.

Serves 6 to 8

16

Breads, Cakes, Pastries and Desserts

THE limitation on dairy products in our low-fat dietary presents no obstacle to the vast assortment of hot breads, desserts and pastries that can be made. They can be as lavish, eye-filling (and caloric, if you wish) as in the free-wheeling days of unmeasured whipped cream and uncounted egg yolks.

While most commercial bakeshop products, with the exception of bread and rolls, are no longer acceptable, anything is possible in our own kitchens. With a willing spirit, such as the lady of the household at the mixing bowl, no family need yearn in vain for baked goodies.

Quick answers to the dessert question may also be found on your grocer's shelves, which offer a variety of gelatine desserts, canned fruits, apple sauce, etc. Royal custard flavor or vanilla puddings turn into creditable custard sauces when made with double the quantity of skim milk called for. Be on your guard with the toppings and cream substitutes that feature "no dairy fat." In most cases, the vegetable oil listed among the ingredients is coconut oil, making the product more saturated and less suitable for our purposes than the dairy product they seek to replace. For specific information about any of these products, write directly to the manufacturer.

Choice of desserts never seems a problem to me in the spring and summer, when the fruit stores smell like flower shops and look twice as tempting, spilling over with melons, berries, grapes, and other succulent fruits fragrant with natural sweetness. I truly can't think of a better way to top off a hearty dinner than with a mélange of fresh fruits, sparked with some liqueur or brandy perhaps, and attractively served. The lovely Continental custom of serving a bowl or basket of choice fruits at the close of a meal is worthy of emulating, particularly since the value of fresh fruits as a source of essential nutrients in our diet has never been disputed.

Melba Toast

This homemade Melba toast retains its crispness, which makes it particularly nice for table use and cocktail spreads. If you are going to use it for hors d'oeuvres, remove the crusts and cut each slice into 4 quarters. For dinner use, leave the crusts on and divide each slice into 2 triangles.

Place cut slices on a cookie tin and bake in a 300-degree oven for 20 or 25 minutes until they are golden. The time required varies with the freshness of the bread. It isn't necessary to turn the slices—just keep an eye on them so they won't get too brown.

Hot Garlic Bread

Dinner guests never ignore this hot crusty bread, as they often do rolls. Little is ever left. We like our bread quite garlic-y, but the degree of this seasoning is up to you. I keep a covered jar of oil with a few cloves of minced garlic in it in the refrigerator just for this purpose.

Start with a crusty French or Italian loaf. Cut a clove of garlic in half and rub the outside crust lightly with the cut surface of the garlic clove. Slash the loaf into 2-inch wedges, but don't cut all the way through. Stop about ½-inch away from the bottom crust. Add 1 tablespoon of chopped parsley to the garlic oil. With a pastry brush, apply the oil to both sides of each wedge, being careful not to amputate any of them. Place the loaf in the center of a sheet of aluminum foil, close the foil tightly and heat in a 350-degree oven for 20 minutes until the loaf is thoroughly heated. To serve, place the loaf, foil and all, on a long bread platter. Fold the foil down to make a frill around the loaf.

Muffins

Muffins are one of the simplest of all hot breads to prepare. They provide a welcome variety for breakfast or a light lunch.

2 cups sifted all-purpose flour	1 egg
3 tablespoons sugar	1¼ cups skim milk
1 teaspoon salt	4 tablespoons oil
2½ teaspoons baking powder	

Preheat oven to 400 degrees. Oil 12 2-inch muffin cups. Sift flour with sugar, salt and baking powder. Beat egg lightly and combine with milk and oil. Stir into the flour mixture and—this is the secret of perfect muffins—stir *only* enough to moisten the flour. Do *not* beat, or the muffins will have pointed heads and an uneven grain. Spoon into oiled cups, filling them ⅔ full. Bake about 25 minutes, or until brown. Let stand about 5 minutes before removing from pan. Serve warm.

Makes 12 medium-sized muffins

Fruit Cocktail Muffin Variation: For a mixed-fruit-topped muffin, increase the sugar to ⅓ cup, and top each muffin with a spoonful of well-drained fruit cocktail. Mix 1 tablespoon of sugar with ¼ teaspoon of cinnamon and sprinkle on muffins. Bake as directed above.

Buttermilk Marmalade Muffins

The built-in dollop of marmalade makes these an excellent dessert or teatime muffin.

2 cups flour	3 tablespoons oil
⅓ cup sugar	1 egg, separated
1 teaspoon salt	1 cup skim milk buttermilk
¼ teaspoon soda	orange marmalade
2¼ teaspoons baking powder	

Preheat oven to 400 degrees. Oil 12 muffin cups. Sift together flour, sugar, salt, soda and baking powder into mixing bowl. In another bowl, beat egg yolk slightly, add oil and buttermilk. Stir this into the flour mixture, mixing just enough to thoroughly blend. Do not beat. Beat egg white until stiff, but not dry, and fold this into the batter. (If the batter seems a little thick, add 2 tablespoons of cold water to thin it.)

Spoon part of the batter into each muffin cup, filling them ⅓ full. Place ½ teaspoon of orange marmalade on this batter and cover with the remaining batter. Bake for 20 minutes. Let stand in the cup 5 minutes before removing. Serve warm.

Makes 12 muffins

Corn Bread or Muffins

1 cup all-purpose flour	1 teaspoon salt
1 cup yellow corn meal	1 egg
3 teaspoons baking powder	1¼ cups skim milk
2 tablespoons sugar	4 tablespoons oil

Heat oven to 425 degrees. Oil muffin pan or 8x8x2" square pan.

Sift flour and measure. Sift again into medium-sized bowl with corn meal, baking powder, sugar and salt. Beat egg lightly and combine with oil and skim milk. Combine with dry ingredients only until moist, but don't overbeat. Pour into oiled square pan or muffin tins. Fill these ⅔ full. The corn bread will bake in about 30 minutes; the muffins in about 20. They will be golden brown when done.

Yield: 12 squares or
12 to 15 muffins

Baking Powder Biscuits

These taste best when they come directly from the oven to the table, so don't start baking them until you're sure of the dining time.

2 cups all-purpose flour, sifted	⅓ cup oil
3 teaspoons baking powder	⅔ cup skim milk
1 teaspoon salt	

Preheat oven to 450 degrees.

Mix and sift flour, baking powder and salt into medium-sized bowl. Combine oil and skim milk and add to flour. Mix with fork. The dough should be soft but not sticky. Flour your hands lightly and make a round ball of the dough. Place it on a sheet of waxed paper and knead a few times to make it smooth. Pat it out to ½-inch thickness. Cut biscuits with unfloured 2-inch (or smaller) biscuit cutter; and place biscuits, well separated, on ungreased cookie sheet. Bake for 12 to 15 minutes. Serve immediately, piping hot.

Makes 1½ to 2 dozen biscuits

Date-Orange Bread

This fruity, nutty loaf is actually less a bread than a cake. It is a substantial loaf and can substitute for the no-longer-acceptable pound or raisin cakes. Wrapped in aluminum foil, it will keep a long time in the refrigerator or freezer.

The grocery markets carry already chopped dates and powdered orange peel, which simplifies the preparation.

½ cup boiling water	2 teaspoons baking powder
2 tablespoons oil	½ teaspoon salt
1 cup sugar	2 cups sifted all-purpose flour
⅓ cup orange juice	2 tablespoons grated orange rind
1 egg, lightly beaten	1⅓ cups chopped dates
¼ teaspoon baking soda	½ cup coarsely chopped walnuts

Preheat oven to 350 degrees.

Combine boiling water and oil in large mixing bowl. Add sugar. In another bowl beat egg lightly, and stir orange juice into it. Add to sugar mixture.

Add baking powder, baking soda and salt to sifted flour. Sift the flour mixture gradually into the egg and sugar mixture, stirring enough to blend well. (If you are using the packaged chopped dates, soak them in boiling water for 10 minutes and drain well.) Dredge chopped dates lightly with flour, and add them along with the orange rind and nuts to the batter. Stir only enough to distribute them evenly. Turn into lightly oiled 9-inch loaf pan. Bake 50 to 55 minutes, until loaf is browned and pulled away a tiny bit from the edges. Allow to cool in pan for 10 minutes. Loosen with spatula and remove from pan.

Yield: 1 loaf

Popovers

2 eggs, lightly beaten
1 cup skim milk
1 tablespoon oil

½ teaspoon salt
1 cup sifted all-purpose flour

Heat oven to 450 degrees. Oil heavy baking cups lavishly—otherwise the popovers may stick. You can use glass, earthenware, iron or enamel ones. Place oiled cups in the hot oven for 5 minutes.

Beat eggs lightly, add skim milk and oil. Add salt and sifted flour and beat with rotary beater or electric mixer until the batter is completely blended. Don't overbeat—stop when you have a thin, perfectly smooth mixture.

Fill the hot cups half full. Place in oven immediately and bake, undisturbed (no peeking) for 20 minutes. Reduce heat to 350 degrees and bake 20 or 25 minutes longer. If you like them a little moist inside, the 20 minutes should be enough—the additional 5 minutes will make them a little crisper. Remove at once from cups.

Makes 8 to 12

Breakfast Gems

1 cup sifted all-purpose flour
2 teaspoons baking powder
1 egg
1 teaspoon sugar

½ teaspoon salt
1 tablespoon oil
½ cup skim milk

Heat oven to 400 degrees. Generously oil 12 small muffin cups—not more than 2 inches in diameter—and place in hot oven for 5 minutes.

Sift together flour and baking powder. In medium-sized bowl, beat egg vigorously. Add sugar, salt and oil. Add sifted flour and baking powder alternately with milk. You can do this in your electric mixer if you like.

Fill the sizzling-hot muffin cups with the batter and bake for 15 to 20 minutes, or until the gems are slightly brown on top. Remove from cups immediately and serve hot.

Makes 12

Scones

Hot from the oven, or split and toasted, served with raspberry or strawberry preserves, these are a fine idea for breakfast or lunch.

2 cups sifted all-purpose flour	1 tablespoon oil
1½ tablespoons baking powder	1 cup skim milk (or sour
¾ teaspoon salt	skim milk or skim
1 tablespoon sugar	milk buttermilk)

Preheat oven to 300 degrees.

Sift together flour, baking powder, salt and sugar. Add oil and slowly stir in milk.

Turn out on floured board and knead lightly for no more than 30 seconds, adding more flour if the dough is too sticky to handle. Cut dough in half and shape each piece into a ball. Roll 1 ball at a time into a round ½-inch thick. Cut into 6 pie-shaped wedges. Place on very lightly oiled baking sheet and sprinkle lightly with sugar. Bake 30 minutes, or until a cake tester comes out dry. Serve hot.

Makes 12 scones

French Bread

This yields 2 loaves of crusty bread in the true Continental style. It is a heavy dough, requiring about 5 hours for rising, but otherwise small effort.

1 package dry yeast	2 teaspoons sugar
1 cup lukewarm water	3 to 3½ cups sifted all-purpose
1½ teaspoons salt	flour
1 tablespoon oil	

Combine yeast, sugar and salt and pour the lukewarm water over them. Mix well. Add 2 cups of the sifted flour and beat. Add oil. Add more flour until a soft dough forms, leaving sides of bowl. Knead this dough on floured board for 10 minutes or so, or until the dough is smooth and satiny. Place in lightly oiled bowl, cover, and allow to rise for 2 hours in a warm place (80 degrees) until it doubles in bulk. Punch down the dough and let rise again until it doubles in bulk—another hour.

Place on floured board and cover dough and let rest for 10 minutes. Roll out into rectangle 8 by 20 inches and roll tightly, jelly-roll fashion, into long tube. Pinch the edges tightly. Cut into two 10-inch loaves and place on lightly oiled baking sheet. Cut 5 or 6 diagonal slashes in each loaf ¼ inch deep. Brush with cold water and allow loaves to rise again in a warm place for 1½ hours. Preheat oven to 400 degrees and bake for 45 minutes. To make the loaves crusty, brush with cold water every 10 minutes while they are baking.

Onion-Caraway Seed Bread

2¼ to 2½ cups sifted
  all-purpose flour
1 package dry yeast
¼ cup warm water
1 cup cottage cheese
4 teaspoons instant onion

1 tablespoon oil
2 teaspoons caraway seeds
1 teaspoon salt
2 tablespoons sugar
¼ teaspoon soda
1 egg

In a small bowl, soak contents of package of dry yeast in ¼ cup of warm water and stir to dissolve. Heat a cup of cottage cheese in small skillet over low flame until it becomes lukewarm. In a large mixing bowl, combine lukewarm cottage cheese, instant onion, oil, caraway seeds, salt, sugar, soda, egg and yeast mixture. Mix well. Add 1 cup of the sifted flour and beat it well. Stir in gradually the remainder of the flour, using as much as you need to make a stiff dough.

Place dough in greased bowl, turning it once so that the greased side is up. Cover with waxed paper and then with a towel. Allow it to double in bulk in a warm place—this will take 50 or 60 minutes. Punch down the dough and place in well-oiled 2-quart casserole. Cover with a towel and allow it to rise again in a warm place until light and double in bulk—30 to 40 minutes.

Heat oven to 350 degrees. Bake for 40 to 50 minutes, or until nicely brown. Remove from casserole, invert so that the rounded side is up, cut in pie-shaped wedges and serve hot.

Yields 8- or 9-inch round loaf

Swedish Tea Ring

This makes an enormous tea ring adequate to serve 12.

3¾ cups all-purpose flour
1 package dry yeast
¼ cup lukewarm water
¼ cup sugar
1 teaspoon salt
1 teaspoon butter flavoring
⅓ cup nonfat milk solids
1 egg
3 tablespoons oil
¾ cup water

Filling:
⅓ cup sugar
1½ teaspoons cinnamon
¼ cup walnuts, chopped
¼ cup raisins

Vanilla Glaze:
1¾ cups confectioner's sugar, sifted
1½ teaspoons vanilla
1½ tablespoons water

Have prepared on square of waxed paper 3¾ cups of sifted flour.
In small bowl combine 1 package of dry yeast and ¼ cup lukewarm
(not hot) water and stir to dissolve. In large mixing bowl, combine
sugar, salt, butter flavoring, nonfat milk solids, egg, oil, water and
yeast mixture and stir. Add half the flour and mix well. Add the remaining flour gradually and mix with your hands until it forms a ball
of dough. Turn onto lightly floured board and gently pat it out to
flatten. Fold the dough down toward you and with the heels and
palms of your hands press down and away from you (kneading),
using an even rolling motion. Continue this until the dough feels
smooth, satiny and elastic. Put dough in oiled bowl and turn once so
that the oiled side is up. Cover with waxed paper and then with a
towel. Place in a warm spot until it doubles in bulk—about an hour.
Punch down. Cover again with waxed paper and towel and allow to
rise again until nearly double—45 minutes to an hour. Punch down.

Roll dough into a 9 x 15″ rectangle. Brush with 2 teaspoons of oil.
Sprinkle with a mixture of cinnamon, sugar, nuts and raisins. Roll
up tightly, beginning at the wide side. Pinch the edges of the roll
together tightly to seal it. Stretch the roll to make it even. Place the
sealed edge down and form a ring on lightly oiled cookie sheet.
Pinch the two ends together firmly to seal.

For the "dramatic" appearance of the ring, make cuts with scissors around the outside perimeter of the ring, about an inch apart, cutting into the ring about halfway. Turn these slices on their sides, so that the cinnamon and sugar striation shows. This gives a loopy, scalloped effect. Cover ring with towel and let rise until double in bulk—another 45 minutes to an hour. Bake in the center of 375-degree oven until golden brown—25 to 30 minutes. Frost while still a bit warm with vanilla glaze and sprinkle top with ½ cup of broken walnut meats and ⅓ cup of coarsely chopped candied cherries or mixed candied fruits.

Cinnamon Coffee Cake

This requires three risings, but is a beaten, not a kneaded dough.

3½ cups all-purpose flour
2 packages dry yeast
½ cup lukewarm water
⅓ cup sugar
1 teaspoon salt
6 tablespoons nonfat milk solids
½ cup water
1 egg
6 tablespoons oil

For Coating:
5 tablespoons oil
1 teaspoon butter flavoring
¾ cup light brown sugar
1½ teaspoons cinnamon
½ cup walnuts, chopped
¼ cup seedless raisins

Have prepared on a square of waxed paper 3½ cups sifted flour.

In a small bowl combine 2 packages of yeast with ½ cup lukewarm (not hot) water and stir to dissolve. In a large mixing bowl, combine sugar, salt, nonfat milk solids, ½ cup of water and yeast mixture, and stir well. This next may be done in the electric mixer at medium speed. Beat an egg into the yeast mixture and add 2 cups of the flour. Beat well and add 6 tablespoons of oil. Add the remainder of the flour, slowly. It may be necessary to beat in the last of the flour by hand, using a wooden spoon. Beat until the dough is completely smooth. Cover bowl with a sheet of waxed paper and a towel, and place in a warm spot until it doubles in bulk—about an hour. Punch down with a spoon, cover with waxed paper and towel and let it rise again until nearly double in bulk—45 minutes to an hour. Punch down.

In a small bowl combine 5 tablespoons of oil with a teaspoon of butter flavoring. In another bowl, combine brown sugar with cinnamon. Have at hand chopped walnuts and raisins.

Oil an 8- or 9-inch spring form or tube pan, 4 inches high. Scoop out small balls of the dough, about the size of a walnut, dunk lightly in the oil, roll in cinnamon and sugar and place in a layer in bottom of pan, scarcely touching. (If you are using a spring form, leave a space in the middle.) When bottom of pan is covered, sprinkle with half the raisins and nuts. Make a top layer of the remaining dough the same way, sprinkle with the remaining nuts and raisins and dribble whatever oil is left over the top. Cover again with waxed paper and towel and let rise until nearly doubled—45 minutes to an hour. Bake at 350 degrees for 40 to 45 minutes, or until golden brown. Take a look at the cake after 35 minutes and if the top seems to be getting too brown, cover with a piece of aluminum foil. When done, remove the sides of the pan at once and let cake cool on a wire rack.

You can dribble some Vanilla Glaze on this if you want to (see page 243), but we don't feel it needs it.

Yields 1 8- or 9-inch cake
Serves 10 to 12

Butterscotch Cookies

1 cup light brown sugar, firmly packed	½ teaspoon baking soda
	¼ teaspoon cream of tartar
6 tablespoons oil	½ teaspoon vanilla
1 egg, beaten	½ cup chopped walnuts
1¾ cups sifted all-purpose flour	

In a large bowl, combine brown sugar and oil and mix until smooth. Add beaten egg, flour, soda and cream of tartar, and mix well until thoroughly blended. Add vanilla and nuts. Divide dough into 4 parts and, with your hands, fashion them into rolls 1 inch in diameter and about 6 inches long. Wrap them in waxed paper and refrigerate at least 1 hour.

Preheat oven to 375 degrees. Slice cookies about ¼ inch thick and place 1 inch apart on oiled cookie sheet. Flatten them so they will be thin and uniform in size. Bake for 15 minutes. For a crisper cookie, leave them in the oven an additional 4 or 5 minutes.

Yields about 5 dozen

Oatmeal Fruit Cookies

These freeze very well, and you might consider doubling the quantity and tucking some away.

1 cup sifted all-purpose flour
½ cup plus 2 tablespoons sugar
½ teaspoon baking powder
¼ teaspoon soda
½ teaspoon cinnamon
½ teaspoon salt
1½ cups rolled oats (either
   quick or regular)

½ cup raisins or currants
¼ cup candied fruit, cut small
½ cup coarsely chopped walnuts
½ cup oil
1 egg
¼ cup skim milk

Preheat oven to 400 degrees.

Sift together flour, sugar, baking powder, soda, cinnamon and salt. Add rolled oats, raisins or currants, candied fruit and nuts and mix thoroughly. Add oil, egg and milk, in that order. Mix until completely blended. Drop by teaspoonfuls on ungreased baking sheets about 1½ inches apart. Bake 10 to 12 minutes until a bit brown around the edges.

Makes 3 dozen

Apple-Nut Squares

1 beaten egg
¾ cup sugar
½ teaspoon vanilla
½ cup flour
1 teaspoon baking powder

¼ teaspoon salt
2 medium-sized tart apples,
   chopped with skins left on
½ cup broken walnuts

Preheat oven to 350 degrees.

Combine lightly beaten egg, sugar and vanilla. Sift together flour, baking powder and salt. Add this to the egg mixture. Fold in chopped apples and walnuts. This makes a stiff batter. With a spatula spread it evenly in oiled 8 x 8 x 2″ baking dish. Bake for 35 minutes or until a cake tester comes out dry. Cut into 9 squares. Serve warm.

Butterscotch Brownies

1 cup dark brown sugar,
   firmly packed
¼ cup oil
1 egg, unbeaten
1 teaspoon vanilla

½ cup walnuts, coarsely chopped
⅔ cup cake flour, sifted
1 teaspoon baking powder
½ teaspoon salt
confectioner's sugar

Preheat oven to 350 degrees. With a crumpled paper towel dipped in oil, oil an 8 x 8 x 2″ baking pan.

Combine brown sugar and oil. Use the electric mixer if you have one—it will make short shrift of the usually lumpy brown sugar. Add unbeaten egg and mix well. Add nuts and vanilla.

Sift together cake flour, baking powder and salt. Fold into the sugar mixture, stirring only until smooth and well blended.

Spread evenly in oiled baking pan and bake for 25 to 30 minutes. Cut into 16 squares while still warm. Dust lightly with confectioner's sugar when cool.

Fruit-Nut Meringues

These do nicely with a fruit or sherbet dessert at the end of a hearty meal.

2 egg whites
pinch salt
pinch cream of tartar
¼ cup walnuts, finely chopped
¾ cup superfine sugar
½ teaspoon vanilla

3 tablespoons mixed candied
   fruits, cut fine (citron,
   cherries, orange, lemon
   peel, etc.)
⅓ cup dates, finely chopped
1 teaspoon lemon juice

The trick with meringues, if it can be considered a trick, is to add the sugar slowly. You will achieve perfection each time if you add the sugar, a teaspoonful at a time, and beat and beat and beat. Otherwise, the meringue will not be stiff enough, looking more like tired marshmallow.

With this word of caution, beat egg whites with salt and cream of tartar until stiff, but not dry. At this point, the meringue will form peaks which fall to the side. Add sugar, a teaspoonful at a time, beating well between each addition. Beat after all the sugar is used until the mixture will crease and can be cut through with a knife. Add vanilla and lemon juice. Gently fold in nuts, chopped dates and chopped fruits and blend well to distribute. Drop from teaspoon on ungreased cookie sheet. Bake in slow oven, 250 degrees, for 30 to 40 minutes.

You can tint these into a spring bouquet by adding a few drops of vegetable coloring to the meringue before baking.

Yield: 3 to 3½ dozen

Spice Squares

These are one of our cakebox mainstays—rich in taste and fragrant with spices. Also eggless.

1 cup dark brown sugar
1 cup water
1½ cups seeded raisins
⅓ cup oil
1 teaspoon cinnamon
¼ teaspoon each—cloves, salt
    and nutmeg

1 teaspoon soda
1 tablespoon warm water
2 cups sifted flour
½ teaspoon baking powder
½ cup walnuts, coarsely
    chopped
confectioner's sugar

Preheat oven to 350 degrees. In a saucepan, boil together for 3 minutes sugar, water, raisins, oil, cinnamon, cloves, salt and nutmeg. Cool mixture.

Dissolve soda in the warm water and add to boiled mixture. Sift together flour and baking powder and add to mixture in saucepan. Fold in chopped nuts. Spread batter evenly in oiled 8 x 8" baking dish. Bake 30 to 35 minutes, or until cake tester comes out dry. When cool, sprinkle with confectioner's sugar and cut into 16 squares.

Tea Crescents

1½ cups sifted all-purpose flour
¾ cup sugar
2 teaspoons baking powder
½ teaspoon salt
1 egg
3 tablespoons oil
1 teaspoon vanilla

1 tablespoon grated lemon
    rind
½ cup skim milk cottage cheese
½ cup walnuts, finely ground
2 tablespoons sugar
½ teaspoon cinnamon
1 egg white, lightly beaten

In a medium-sized bowl, beat egg, stir in oil, vanilla extract and lemon rind. Sift flour, ¾ cup sugar, salt and baking powder and add to the egg mixture. Whip cottage cheese until fluffy and add. Work the dough together into a soft ball, wrap in waxed paper and chill in refrigerator for an hour.

Combine ground walnuts, 2 tablespoons sugar, and cinnamon in a bowl. Whip an egg white lightly with fork until it is a little frothy. Preheat oven to 375 degrees.

Break off little pieces of dough, roll between your hands and form into small crescents, flattening them out a bit. Brush with egg white, sprinkle with nut mixture and place on oiled cookie sheet. Repeat until all the dough is used. Bake for 15 minutes, or until brown.

Makes 3 to 3½ dozen

Aunt Ella's Lebkuchen

This recipe for Lebkuchen, the traditional German Christmas cake, has been in Aunt Ella's family since the beginning of time. It's simple to make, keeps very well and freezes perfectly.

2 eggs	2 tablespoons lemon juice
1⅓ cups brown sugar	⅞ cup flour
½ tablespoon molasses	1 teaspoon baking powder
½ teaspoon cinnamon	¾ cup candied mixed fruit,
⅛ teaspoon allspice	cut fine
⅛ teaspoon cloves	¾ cup walnuts, coarsely
rind of ½ lemon	chopped

Confectioner's Icing

½ cup sifted confectioner's sugar   2 teaspoons coffee

Preheat oven to 375 degrees.

Beat eggs until light. Add brown sugar and mix well. Add molasses, cinnamon, allspice, cloves, lemon juice and rind, and chopped nuts. In a separate bowl, measure out flour and baking powder, and add candied fruit, coating it lightly. Add the fruit and flour mixture to the sugar and eggs and mix well.

Oil shallow baking dish, 9 by 13 inches. Spread the batter smoothly and bake for 30 minutes, or until a cake tester comes out dry.

Remove from oven. When cooled a bit, cover with confectioner's icing. When completely cool, cut into thin bars which may then be divided in two.   Yield: 20 bars

Molasses Twisted Doughnuts

1 egg
½ cup molasses
1 tablespoon oil
¾ teaspoon baking soda
¼ teaspoon salt
⅛ teaspoon powdered ginger

⅛ teaspoon nutmeg
¼ teaspoon cinnamon
½ cup skim milk buttermilk
2½ to 3 cups sifted flour
oil for deep frying

Beat egg in a large mixing bowl. Add molasses and oil and mix well. In a separate bowl sift salt, baking soda, ginger, nutmeg and cinnamon with 2 cups of flour. Add the flour mixture alternately with the buttermilk to the egg mixture, beating well between each addition. Add more sifted flour to make the dough stiff enough to handle. You will probably need another half cup or so.

Fill your deep-fat fryer ⅓ full of oil and heat over low flame.

Roll out dough to the thickness of ⅜ of an inch on floured board. With sharp-pointed paring knife, cut into strips about ¾ inch wide and 4 inches long. Twist strips, fold the two ends together, twist again, and pinch ends together to make a circle. Fry in 385-degree fat (hot enough to turn a 1-inch cube of bread golden brown in 35 seconds) until brown. I cook 1½ doughnuts at a time—when I'm ready to turn one, I add another. Otherwise, the oil cools too quickly and won't cook properly. Also, make sure you turn the doughnuts only once—when they rise to the top, you can peek at the under portion to see if they're brown enough. Tumbling the doughnuts around in the oil makes them greasy. When done, remove with slotted spoon and drain on paper towels.   Makes 12 or 14

Fruit Cocktail Pudding Cake

1 cup all-purpose flour
1 cup sugar
¼ teaspoon salt
1 teaspoon soda

2 cups canned fruit cocktail
    (1-pound can)
½ cup brown sugar
½ cup coarsely chopped walnuts
juice of ½ lemon

Preheat oven to 350 degrees.

Sift flour, sugar, salt and soda together into a bowl. Add entire contents of 1-pound can of fruit cocktail, including juice, and mix
thoroughly. Oil 9-inch round cake pan, 2 inches deep. Pour batter
into cake pan, sprinkle lemon juice over batter, and cover with brown
sugar and chopped nuts. With the back of a spoon, press topping
gently into batter. Bake in 350-degree oven for 45 minutes. Cool
slightly before serving.

Serves 8

Beignets

These puffy delicate French doughnuts are simply our old friends
the cream puffs, fried in deep fat rather than baked. They may be
served with a fruit or custard sauce, frosted with a thin confectioner's
glaze or lightly dusted with confectioner's sugar. We prefer the latter.

4 tablespoons oil
½ cup boiling water
½ cup sifted all-purpose flour
pinch salt
2 eggs

1½ teaspoons sugar
¼ teaspoon grated orange rind
¼ teaspoon grated lemon rind
oil for deep-fat frying

Pour enough oil into your deep-fat fryer to make it ⅓ full. Slowly
heat oil to 380 degrees, or until a cube of day-old bread browns in
30 seconds.

In a small saucepan, heat water and oil to the boiling point. Add
salt and flour all at once and stir vigorously until the flour is absorbed
and the mixture leaves the sides of the pan. Remove from fire and
add unbeaten eggs, one at a time, beating vigorously after the addition
of each egg. Beat until the mixture is spongy and shiny and forms into
a mound, leaving the sides of the pan. Add sugar and grated orange
and lemon rinds, and mix thoroughly.

Drop by rounded teaspoonfuls into deep hot fat heated to 380
degrees.

An interesting shape for the beignets may be achieved in this manner: cut out 1½-inch squares of brown paper. With a broad-tip pastry
tube, press out dough on each square in the shape of a circle. Drop
papers and dough into the hot fat and detach them as the beignets

cook. Turn the beignets only once. When they rise to the top, you can peek at the under portion to see if it's brown enough. Do just a few at a time so you do not cool the fat. They will cook in about 10 minutes. Remove with slotted spoon and drain on absorbent paper. Sprinkle with confectioner's sugar when cool.

The raspberry sauce on page 280 makes a pleasant sauce for the beignets.   Yields 2 dozen

Angel Cake

The angel cake mix is the only prepared cake mix with the official Nod of Approval from the Friendly Fat League that I know of at this time. I use it and find it highly satisfactory. When using the mix, you can make a coffee-flavored cake either by substituting strong coffee for the water, or by adding 2 tablespoons of instant coffee to the dry mix.

The following recipe is for those who scorn the prepared product. Angel cakes can be tricky so follow the directions precisely.

1 cup sifted cake flour	1¼ teaspoons cream of tartar
1½ cups superfine granulated sugar	¼ teaspoon salt
	1 teaspoon vanilla
1¼ cups egg whites (10 to 12)	¼ teaspoon almond extract

Have egg whites at room temperature before you start. They won't achieve maximum volume if they're too cold. Preheat oven to 325 degrees.

Sift flour with ½ cup of the sugar 3 times, and set aside.

In a large bowl, and using either a wire whip, a rotary beater or an electric mixer, beat egg whites until foamy throughout. Add cream of tartar and salt and beat only until soft moist peaks form when the beater is lifted out of the meringue.

Add the remaining sugar, 2 tablespoons at a time, beating about 10 seconds after each addition. Add vanilla and almond flavoring.

Place sifted flour and sugar in the sifter and sift about 3 tablespoons over the surface of the meringue. Do not stir or beat the flour into the meringue—this will diminish the amount of air you've just pumped into it. Instead, cut and fold the flour-sugar mixture gently into the meringue. Use large spoon or wire whip to do this; cut down through the center of the mixture, lift a spoonful, and turn over, turning the bowl a quarter of a turn with each stroke. Cut and fold only until the flour disappears—not more than 10 strokes. Repeat this process until all the flour and sugar are added, and completely blended.

Push this batter, which will be very thick, into ungreased 10-inch tube pan (4 inches high), trying not to stir it in the moving process. With a knife, carefully cut through the batter, 5 or 6 times, to make sure there aren't any large air bubbles. Level the batter so it is even.

Bake 55 to 60 minutes in 325-degree oven. It is done when the top springs back when lightly touched.

Don't worry if deep cracks appear in the top of this cake. That's *comme il faut* with angel cakes.

As soon as you remove cake from oven, invert the pan on a bottle or the neck of a funnel and let it hang until it is cold.

To remove cake from pan, loosen from sides and tube with a spatula. Turn pan over and hit the edge sharply to loosen.

Two-Egg Sponge Cake

Like a basic black dress, this airy, delicate cake can do yeoman's service for practically any occasion. Baked in two 8- or 9-inch layers, filled with icing, custard or fruit preserves, and generously masked with a fluffy frosting, it can be a fine party affair.

You may also bake it in a single layer in a 2-inch-deep 9 x 13″ pan. It will yield many cuttings that can be dressed up with fruit, any of the uncooked toppings on pages 270-1, or served plain with a sprinkling of confectioner's sugar. I generally freeze half for future use when I bake it in this single layer. Like all cakes and breads, it can be frozen, thawed and refrozen, and be none the worse for it.

2 eggs
1½ cups sugar
2¼ cups cake flour, sifted (or
    2 cups all-purpose flour,
    sifted 3 times)
3 teaspoons baking powder

1 teaspoon salt
⅓ cup oil
1 cup skim milk
1 teaspoon vanilla
1 teaspoon grated lemon rind

Preheat oven to 350 degrees. Have eggs at room temperature. Separate eggs, and beat whites until frothy. Add ½ cup of sugar, a little at a time, beating well between each addition, and continue beating until the meringue becomes shiny and stiff and stands in peaks.

Sift the rest of the sugar with flour, baking powder and salt into a large mixing bowl. Add oil, half the skim milk, vanilla and lemon rind and beat in electric mixer at medium speed for one minute (or 150 strokes by hand). Scrape bottom and sides of bowl constantly. Add the rest of the milk, the egg yolks, and beat a minute longer, continuing to scrape sides of the bowl.

Fold the stiffly beaten meringue gently into the batter. Turn bowl often as you cut meringue down through batter, across the bottom, and up and over.

Pour batter into 2 oiled and lightly floured 8- or 9-inch cake tins, or a 9 x 13″ oblong.

Layers will need 30 to 35 minutes' baking time, oblong 40 to 45 minutes. Bake until a cake tester comes out dry and the tops are nicely browned.

Cool and frost with Sea Foam Frosting or cut into squares. The oblong will yield 32 to 40 portions.

Sea Foam Frosting

2 egg whites, unbeaten
1½ cups brown sugar, firmly
    packed
pinch of salt

¼ teaspoon cream of tartar
⅓ cup water
1 teaspoon vanilla

(In order to make a smoother frosting and to prevent the sugar from crystallizing, wipe down the sides of the pan with a fork wrapped in a damp cloth before and during cooking and beating.)

Combine egg whites, brown sugar, salt, water and cream of tartar in top of double boiler. Beat with rotary beater one minute until thoroughly mixed. Place over boiling water and beat constantly for 7 minutes, or until the frosting stands in stiff peaks. Scrape frosting up from sides and bottom of pan with rubber spatula a few times.

Remove from boiling water and add vanilla. Beat a minute longer, or until thick enough to spread. This will generously frost tops and sides of 2 9-inch layers.

Applesauce Cake

This makes a moist, fruity, nutty, spicy loaf that keeps very well.

1 cup applesauce	1 teaspoon baking soda
¾ cup sugar	3 tablespoons hot water
¼ teaspoon salt	1¾ cups all-purpose flour, sifted
⅓ cup oil	2 tablespoons sherry or rum
1 teaspoon cinnamon	½ cup walnuts, coarsely chopped
¼ teaspoon ground cloves	1 cup seedless raisins

Preheat oven to 350 degrees.

If you are using unsweetened applesauce, you may require an additional ¼ cup of sugar, but taste it to make sure.

In a good-sized mixing bowl, combine sugar, salt, applesauce and oil. Beat well. Add cinnamon and cloves. Dissolve baking soda in hot water and add, mixing well. Moisten raisins with sherry or rum and sprinkle them lightly with a few tablespoons of the flour to coat them. Beat in the rest of the flour to the applesauce mixture. Add nuts and floured raisins and thoroughly mix. Pour into oiled 9 x 5" loaf pan and bake for 45 to 55 minutes, or until a cake tester comes out dry. When cool, remove from pan and dust top lightly with confectioner's sugar.

Yield: 1 loaf

Quick Coffee Cake

¼ cup oil	1 egg
⅓ cup sugar	about ½ cup skim milk
1 cup plus 2 tablespoons unsifted Presto cake flour	

Topping

1 tablespoon oil	½ cup chopped walnuts
2 tablespoons sugar	1 tablespoon skim milk
cinnamon to taste	

Preheat oven to 350 degrees.

Pour ¼ cup oil into 8-inch round cake pan. Stir in sugar thoroughly with fork. Put unsifted Presto flour on top of the sugar mixture. Break an egg into measuring cup and add enough skim milk to make ¾ of a cup. Pour into cake pan and stir until all the flour disappears. Bake in 350-degree oven 25 minutes. Dribble 1 tablespoon oil over top of cake, sprinkle with cinnamon, sugar and chopped nuts, and pour 1 tablespoon skim milk over topping. Return to oven for 5 minutes. Serve warm.

Serves 8

Apricot Cake

1 cup sugar	½ teaspoon salt
2 eggs	2½ teaspoons baking powder
1 teaspoon vanilla	⅓ cup oil
1¾ cups cake flour	½ cup skim milk

Preheat oven to 375 degrees.

Mix sugar with 2 well-beaten eggs and beat until light. Sift together cake flour, salt and baking powder. In a measuring cup, stir oil and skim milk to a froth. Add alternately with the flour to the sugar and egg mixture, beating well after each addition. If you have an electric mixer, so much the better. Beat in vanilla.

With a crumpled paper towel dipped in oil, oil 2 8- or 9-inch cake tins. Divide the batter between the two tins. Bake in preheated 375-degree oven for 25 to 30 minutes. Let stand 5 minutes. Turn out and cool on racks.

It is easier to split cake layers after they've stood for a few hours, so make the layers first thing in the morning or even the day before.

Apricot Filling and Meringue

2 cups dried apricots	1 teaspoon grated lemon rind
1½ cups water	2 egg whites, stiffly beaten
1 cup sugar	2 tablespoons sugar
¼ teaspoon salt	1 teaspoon lemon juice

Wash apricots. Place in saucepan with water, cover and simmer for about 30 minutes until tender. Put through sieve or Foley food mill, juice and all. Add 1 cup sugar, salt and lemon rind to the apricot purée. Cook slowly until thick, stirring constantly.

Split the cake layers. Save ⅔ of the apricot mixture for the meringue and spread the rest between the 3 bottom layers.

Beat 2 egg whites until foamy. Gradually add 2 tablespoons sugar and beat well. Fold in remaining ⅔ cup of the apricot purée and lemon juice. Frost top and sides of the cake with the apricot meringue, giving it additional eye appeal with twirls and swirls.

Serves 10 to 12

Custard Cream Chiffon Cake

This custard-filled, confectioner's glazed cake is always our choice for the HAPPY BIRTHDAY greeting etched with raspberry meringue.

2¼ cups cake flour, sifted	1¼ cups water
3½ teaspoons baking powder	2 teaspoons vanilla
1 teaspoon salt	4 egg whites
⅔ cup oil	¼ teaspoon cream of tartar
4 tablespoons nonfat milk solids	1½ cups sugar

Preheat oven to 350 degrees.

Sift together flour, baking powder and salt. Add oil, nonfat milk solids, water and vanilla and beat at medium speed on your mixer, scraping sides and bottom of the bowl frequently. Beat until the batter becomes perfectly smooth—2 or 3 minutes.

In another bowl, beat egg whites until frothy. Add cream of tartar, and gradually add sugar, a little at a time, beating continually until the meringue is very stiff and glossy.

Gently fold the meringue mixture into the batter with the angel cake technique of the down-up-and-over motion, blending well. Divide batter into 2 9-inch waxed-paper-lined cake tins and bake for 35 to 40 minutes, or until the tops are delicately brown and a cake tester comes out dry.

When the layers are cooled, remove from pans and peel off waxed paper. Put the layers together with Vanilla Cream Filling, top with Confectioner's Glaze and garnish with raspberry meringue piped through a pastry tube. Refrigerate until ready to serve.

Serves 10 to 12

Vanilla Cream Filling

1 package prepared vanilla pudding
1¾ cups skim milk

Prepare a package of vanilla pudding according to directions on package, using only 1¾ cups skim milk. When cool, cover and chill in refrigerator. When firm and chilled, beat with rotary beater until the pudding is smooth and fluffy.

Confectioner's Glaze

1 cup confectioner's sugar, sifted   1½ teaspoons light corn syrup
1 tablespoon warm water   ¼ teaspoon vanilla

Mix the above ingredients together and stir until smooth. Spread glaze over top of cake, leaving an outside border of cake a scant inch wide.

Raspberry Meringue Garnish

1 egg white   2 heaping tablespoons raspberry
2 tablespoons sugar   preserves

Beat egg white until frothy. Add sugar, a teaspoonful at a time, beating constantly until the meringue is stiff and glossy. Blend in raspberry preserves, mixing well. With a pastry tube, border the cake with the raspberry meringue and make a few fancy swirls as your artistic streak dictates.

Rum Cake Supreme

This single-layer cake is a not-too-heavy dessert for even a hearty dinner.

2 eggs   1 tablespoon oil
¼ teaspoon salt   1 cup sifted cake flour
1 cup sugar   1 teaspoon baking powder
1 teaspoon rum flavoring   apricot preserves
½ cup skim milk

Preheat oven to 350 degrees. Beat eggs until thick and light in your electric mixer. Beat in salt, sugar and rum flavoring. Heat skim milk and oil to boiling point in small saucepan. Beat this into the egg mixture. Sift flour and baking powder and add to mixture, beating only until smooth—no longer.

With a crumpled paper towel dipped in oil, oil a cake pan, 9 inches by 2 inches deep. Turn batter into pan and bake for 35 to 40 minutes, or until cake tester comes out dry.

While the cake is baking in the oven, make this Rum Coffee Syrup:

Rum Coffee Syrup

⅔ cup sugar
⅔ cup strong coffee
¼ cup (or more) rum

Combine sugar and coffee in small saucepan. Stir over low heat until the sugar dissolves. Boil 3 minutes and cool. Add rum.

When the cake is finished, remove from oven and allow to cool in pan for 10 minutes. Turn the cake layer out of the pan on a round platter and spoon Rum Coffee Syrup slowly over the entire surface of the warm cake.

Let a few hours, at least, pass before you split this layer. Overnight is even better. It's always easier to split a cake which has had a chance to firm up a bit after leaving the oven. Split the layer equally into two parts. (I always stick a few toothpicks around the outside perimeter of the cake as a guide.) Fill with rum cream and replace top.

Rum-Cream Filling

1 package prepared vanilla pudding
1¾ cups skim milk
1½ teaspoons rum flavoring

Prepare a package of vanilla pudding according to directions on package, using only 1¾ cups skim milk. Add rum flavoring and mix well. Pour into small bowl and cover with waxed paper or foil. When cool, chill in refrigerator. When thoroughly chilled, beat with rotary beater until the pudding is light and fluffy.

Cover top of cake with a thin coating of apricot preserves—just enough to glaze it. Edge cake with the apricot meringue run through a pastry tube.

Apricot Meringue

1 egg white
¼ teaspoon cream of tartar
pinch of salt

¼ teaspoon vanilla
2 tablespoons sugar
2 tablespoons apricot preserves

Beat egg white with cream of tartar and salt until it becomes frothy. Add sugar slowly, a teaspoon at a time, and continue beating until stiff and glossy. Fold in apricot preserves, using the clear part without the fruit, so it won't clog the pastry tube, and blend well. Add vanilla.

Berry Torte

Blueberries or raspberries, shiny with a glaze, are equally effective on this torte. It must stand at least eight hours, so plan to make it first thing in the morning or even the day before you use it.

Torte:
3 egg whites
1 cup sugar
1 teaspoon vanilla
1 teaspoon baking powder
¾ cup cracker crumbs (20 Ritz crackers, rolled fine)
½ cup walnuts, finely chopped

Glazed Berries:
1 pint blueberries or raspberries
1 cup currant jelly
2 teaspoons cornstarch
1 tablespoon lemon juice

(Twenty Ritz crackers, rolled fine, will yield exactly the required ¾ cup of crumbs. To crush them, place them between the folds of a tea towel and use a rolling pin over them a few times until properly pulverized.)

Preheat oven to 350 degrees. Oil 9-inch spring form.

In a medium-sized bowl, beat egg whites until foamy. Gradually add sugar, a little at a time, beating well between each addition, until the meringue is stiff and shiny and stands in firm peaks. Beat in baking powder and vanilla. Carefully fold in cracker crumbs and finely chopped walnuts. Pour into spring form and bake for 20 to 30 minutes, or until the top is lightly brown and well set. Remove from oven and let cool. When completely cool, remove sides from spring form. Let stand at least 8 hours before serving.

An hour or so before you are ready to serve it, cover with the glazed berries and refrigerate.

Serves 8 to 10

Glazed Berries: In a small saucepan over low flame, heat a cup of currant jelly until it melts. Add cornstarch and lemon juice and cook, stirring until it bubbles and becomes clear—3 or 4 minutes. Remove from stove and let cool. When cooled, add berries, mix lightly to coat berries and arrange over top of torte.

Lemon Meringue Torte

This torte comes out of the oven with its topping already baked on.

1¼ cups cake flour, sifted
¾ cup sugar
2 teaspoons baking powder
¾ teaspoon salt
¼ cup oil

½ cup water
1 egg yolk
3 egg whites, stiffly beaten
1 teaspoon vanilla
⅛ teaspoon cream of tartar

Meringue Topping

3 egg whites
¾ cup sugar
½ teaspoon vanilla
¾ cup walnuts, finely chopped

Lemon Filling

1 package lemon-flavored instant
   pudding (Jello brand)
1⅔ cups skim milk
1 tablespoon fresh lemon juice

Preheat oven to 375 degrees.

Sift together into large bowl cake flour, sugar, baking powder and salt. In the order mentioned, add to the flour mixture oil, water and egg yolk, beating well between each addition until the batter is perfectly smooth. You may do this in the electric mixer at medium speed, if you wish.

In a separate bowl, beat the 3 egg whites and cream of tartar until stiff but not dry. Add vanilla. Fold beaten egg whites into the batter carefully. Divide batter into 2 ungreased 8-inch cake tins.

MERINGUE TOPPING: Beat egg whites until frothy. Slowly add ¾ cup of sugar, a few tablespoons at a time, and continue beating until the meringue is stiff and glossy. Beat in vanilla.

Cover batter in each pan with half the meringue. The batter is a thin one, so spread the meringue with a light hand to keep it on the surface. Don't worry if you find it difficult to spread the meringue to the very edge of the pan. Get it as close as you can and it will spread itself as it bakes and cover the entire surface. Sprinkle chopped nuts evenly over meringue. Bake for 25 to 30 minutes, or until cake tester comes out dry and meringue is golden and puffy. Remove from oven and let cool in pan.

LEMON FILLING: Prepare instant lemon pudding according to directions on package, using only 1⅔ cups skim milk. Add fresh lemon juice. After pudding is set, beat it with a fork to make it fluffy.

Remove one cooled layer from cake tin and place meringue side down on a cake platter. Cover the layer with the fluffy lemon filling. Cover with the other layer, meringue side up. Refrigerate until ready to serve.

Serves 8 to 10

Glazed Cheesecake

The fruit toppings can be varied according to your mood and the ingredients available in your pantry. I have described a few below.

For the cheesecake, use a springform eight or nine inches in diameter.

Graham Cracker Crust

1¼ cups graham cracker crumbs
¼ cup sugar
⅓ cup oil

Blend crumbs, sugar and oil together in oiled baking pan. Pack mixture firmly on bottom and sides of pan, bringing crumbs up evenly to the rim. Bake in 350-degree oven for 7 minutes. Cool and chill while you prepare the filling.

1½ pounds cottage cheese
½ cup sugar (or more)
3 tablespoons flour
2 eggs
1 scant cup water

7 tablespoons nonfat milk solids
¼ teaspoon salt
½ teaspoon vanilla
2 tablespoons lemon juice

Preheat oven to 350 degrees.

With your electric mixer, using the large bowl, beat cottage cheese at high speed until very smooth—5 to 10 minutes. Blend in sugar, add flour gradually, and continue beating until thoroughly mixed.

Add eggs one at a time, and beat well after each addition. Reduce speed to medium and add water, nonfat milk solids, salt, lemon juice and vanilla. The mixture will be quite thin. Taste for sweetness—you may want to add more sugar. Ladle it carefully into chilled graham cracker crust. Bake 50 minutes, or until set. It will firm as it cools— don't overbake it. Let cool at least ½ hour before removing sides of springform and adding the glaze.

Bing Cherry Glaze

1 1-pound can pitted black Bing cherries	cornstarch juice of one lemon

Drain juice from cherries. Arrange cherries on top of the cake.

Measure cherry juice and mix with cornstarch to the proportion of 1 tablespoon cornstarch to 1 cup of liquid. Place in small saucepan and add juice of a lemon. Cook over medium heat, stirring constantly, 2 or 3 minutes, or until the syrup thickens and becomes shiny. When cool, spread evenly over the cherries. Refrigerate cake.

Fresh Strawberry Glaze

1 pint fresh strawberries ½ cup sugar	2 teaspoons cornstarch 1 tablespoon sugar

Slice washed berries and place in small bowl with ½ cup sugar. Mix slightly and allow to stand about 2 hours, until the sugar draws ½ cup of juice from the berries.

Drain off juice and put in small saucepan with cornstarch and 1 tablespoon sugar. Stir until smooth. If the juice looks too light, add a drop or two of red food coloring. Cook over medium heat until mixture is thickened and shiny, 2 or 3 minutes. Place sliced berries on top of cake and spread glaze evenly over the berries.

A glaze from frozen strawberries or raspberries may also be used, following the directions for Bing Cherry Glaze, after the berries are defrosted. Taste for sweetness, however—the frozen berries are usually not sweet enough.

Apricot Glaze

½ cup sugar
2 tablespoons cornstarch
¼ cup undiluted frozen orange
   juice, thawed

1 tablespoon lemon juice
1⅓ cups cooked or canned
   apricots, thoroughly drained

In a small saucepan, combine sugar and cornstarch and stir in juices. Put apricots through sieve or blender and add this purée to the mixture. Cook over medium heat, stirring constantly, until it comes to a boil and becomes thick and clear—2 or 3 minutes. When cool, spread over cheesecake.

Plain Cheesecake

Using the basic cheesecake recipe, on page 262, increase the vanilla to 1 teaspoon and add ½ teaspoon of cinnamon. Reserve ⅓ cup of crumbs from crust mixture and spread over top of cake before baking.

Basic Pie Dough

It seems we've come full circle, for I remember my grandmother always used to make her pie crusts with oil. My mother told me she used oil because it was cheaper—but whatever the reason, Grandma had the right idea. Oil makes a fine, flaky crust that can hold its own in any contest.

Double crust for an 8- or 9-inch pie:

2 cups sifted all-purpose flour
1 teaspoon salt

½ cup oil
5 tablespoons cold skim milk

Sift together flour and salt. Combine oil and cold skim milk in measuring cup. Beat with fork until thickened and creamy and pour all at once over the flour mixture. Press into a smooth ball and cut in half.

Place one half of the dough between 2 sheets of waxed paper, 12 inches square. If you wipe the table with a damp cloth, the paper will not slip. Roll out until the dough forms a circle, to the edges of the paper. Remove top sheet of waxed paper, invert dough over pie plate, ease and fit into pie plate, and peel off paper. Trim dough even with rim of pan. Add filling. Roll other half of dough as above and place over filling. Roll edges under the bottom crust. Seal by pressing gently with fork or fluting edges. Cut small gashes in top crust for steam to escape. Bake at temperature required for filling used.

Make this crust at the time you use it. Do not store in refrigerator.

Single crust for 8- or 9-inch pie:

Use exactly half the ingredients required for the 2-crust pie. Fit into the pie plate as described above and trim ¼ inch beyond the rim of the pan. Fold edge under even with rim of pan and flute. For a baked pastry shell, prick entire surface of the crust and bake for 10 to 12 minutes in hot oven, 475 degrees.

Apple Pie

Out of deference to the American tradition of two-crust apple and blueberry pies, I offer the following recipes, but with a nagging sense of reluctance. If you have a weight problem at all, eat only one crust and concentrate on the filling.

basic pie pastry for crust,
    9-inch pie (page 264)
3 pounds tart apples (about 8),
    peeled, cored and sliced
    about ⅜ inch thick
1 cup dark brown sugar

¼ teaspoon nutmeg
¼ teaspoon cinnamon
¼ teaspoon salt
2 tablespoons lemon juice
1 tablespoon grated lemon rind
1 tablespoon oil

Preheat oven to 450 degrees. Line 9-inch pie plate with half the pie dough. Combine sugar, nutmeg, cinnamon, salt and lemon rind. Place apples in layers in pie plate and sprinkle each layer lightly with sugar and lemon juice, leaving enough for the top layer. When all the apples are used, dribble the tablespoon of oil over all, cover with the top crust, seal tightly and flute the edges. Brush with a little lightly beaten egg white and sprinkle with sugar. Cut a few decorative slits in the top crust. Bake for 15 minutes in 450-degree oven, reduce to 350 degrees and bake another 20 to 30 minutes, or until the apples are soft and the crust is nicely browned.

Serves 8

Blueberry Pie

1 recipe basic pie dough
  (page 264)
1 quart fresh blueberries (or
  frozen, if out of season)
2 tablespoons flour

½ cup sugar
dash salt
juice of ½ lemon
⅔ cup brown sugar
1 tablespoon oil

Preheat oven to 400 degrees. Line 9-inch pie plate with half the pie dough.

Place blueberries in bowl. Add flour, sugar, salt and lemon juice and stir. When all dissolved, turn into the pie shell. Sprinkle the brown sugar and dribble oil over the filling.

Roll out top crust and place over berries. Seal well and flute edges. Cut gashes in the crust to allow the steam to escape.

Brush the top of the pie with slightly beaten egg white and a sprinkling of granulated sugar. Bake for 40 to 50 minutes, until the crust is brown and the juice bubbles out of the slits in the crust.

Serves 8

Apple Butterscotch Tart

Single crust for pie (page 264)
1 1-pound 4-ounce can pie-sliced
  apples
2 tablespoons cornstarch or
  minute tapioca
⅓ cup light brown sugar
½ teaspoon salt

1 teaspoon cinnamon
½ cup corn syrup, light or dark
⅔ cup liquid (water plus juice
  drained from apples)
2 tablespoons oil
2 tablespoons lemon juice
½ cup chopped walnuts

Preheat oven to 400 degrees.

Line 8- or 9-inch pie plate with dough. Drain the apple slices and reserve the juice. In medium-sized saucepan, combine the cornstarch (or tapioca), sugar, salt and cinnamon. Stir in corn syrup and the drained apple syrup, to which you have added enough water to make ⅔ cup of liquid. Add oil and lemon juice. Cook over medium heat until mixture is thick, stirring constantly. When thickened, remove from heat. Fold in apple slices.

Fill crust with the apple mixture. Sprinkle chopped walnuts over top.

Bake in 400-degree oven for 15 minutes. Reduce heat to 350 degrees and bake until the crust is brown. This will take about 30 minutes longer.

Serves 8

Apricot Velvet Pie

This can be made with a conventional piecrust or a graham cracker crust.

Meringue Crust

3 egg whites
¾ cup sugar

¾ cup finely chopped walnuts
1 teaspoon orange extract

Beat egg whites until frothy. Add sugar, a tablespoon at a time beating between each addition of sugar, until the meringue is stiff and shiny. Fold in chopped walnuts and orange extract. Spread evenly in oiled 10-inch pie pan and bake in cool oven 250 to 275 degrees for 50 minutes to 1 hour. Cool thoroughly before filling.

Filling

1 pint dried apricots
1 cup water
1 cup sugar
dash cinnamon
3 tablespoons lemon juice
½ cup orange juice
1 teaspoon almond extract
1 tablespoon unflavored
    gelatine
1½ cups cold water

2 egg whites
2 tablespoons sugar
⅓ cup nonfat milk solids
⅓ cup chilled apricot nectar
2 tablespoons lemon juice
3 tablespoons sugar

For garnish: slivered, toasted almonds or chopped walnuts, red and green cherries, sliced

In a medium-sized saucepan, combine water, sugar, lemon and orange juices and cinnamon. Add apricots and simmer until they are tender and the liquid is syrupy—20 to 30 minutes, stirring occasionally. While they are cooking, stir gelatine into 1½ cups cold water and heat until thoroughly dissolved, stirring constantly.

Force the cooked apricots and syrup through food mill. Add almond extract. Combine this purée with the gelatine mixture and chill until thick and beginning to set. When it reaches this stage, beat well with rotary beater.

Beat 2 egg whites until frothy. Add 2 tablespoons of sugar, a little at a time, until the meringue is stiff and shiny.

Measure ⅓ cup of chilled apricot nectar into medium-sized bowl. Add ⅓ cup nonfat milk solids. Whip 3 or 4 minutes until soft peaks form. Add 2 tablespoons lemon juice and continue whipping 3 or 4 minutes longer, while gradually adding 3 tablespoons sugar. Whip until stiff peaks form.

Gently fold beaten egg whites and whipped skim milk into the apricot mixture. Pour well-blended mixture into baked meringue or pie shell. Garnish with toasted slivered almonds or chopped walnuts and trim with slices of green and red maraschino cherries. Chill until firm.

Serves 8

Lime Chiffon Pie

Crust

1¼ cups corn flake crumbs
⅓ cup oil
2 tablespoons sugar (optional)
1 tablespoon grated lemon rind

Preheat oven to 350 degrees.

Mix together in 9-inch pie plate the crumbs, oil, sugar and lemon rind until crumbs are dampened. Spread evenly, pressing firmly against bottom and sides of plate. Bake for 7 minutes and cool.

Filling

1 package lime Jello
¾ cup boiling water
grated rind of a lemon
4 tablespoons sugar (or equivalent artificial sweetener)
½ cup nonfat milk solids
½ cup ice water
2 tablespoons lemon juice
4 tablespoons sugar

Dissolve a package of lime Jello in ¾ cup of boiling water. Add sugar or sweetener and stir well. Add grated lemon rin.. Cool until syrupy—30 to 40 minutes.

Measure ½ cup of nonfat milk solids into mixing bowl. Add ½ cup ice water. Beat 3 or 4 minutes until soft peaks form. Add lemon juice and continue beating. Add sugar gradually, beating all the while until the mixture is stiff.

Fold stiffly beaten milk into the syrupy Jello mixture and combine thoroughly. Turn into the crumb crust and spread evenly. Chill until firm. Garnish with slivers of red and green cherries.

Serves 8

Fruit Pie with Cottage Cheese Lattice

2½ cups pitted sour red cherries (No. 2 can)
1 10-ounce package sliced frozen strawberries, thawed
1 cup sugar
¼ teaspoon salt
2 tablespoons cornstarch
2 tablespoons quick-cooking tapioca
juice of ½ lemon
10 ounces skim milk cottage cheese
2 teaspoons sugar
½ teaspoon vanilla
1 teaspoon lemon juice
½ basic pie dough crust

Make ½ recipe of the basic pie dough (page 264) and line 9-inch pie plate. Set aside.

Drain cherries and thawed strawberries and reserve juice. In a small saucepan, mix together 1 cup sugar, salt, tapioca, and cornstarch. Add the two fruit juices and cook over low heat, stirring constantly, until thick and clear. This will take 7 or 8 minutes. Remove from heat and add cherries and strawberries. Add lemon juice. Allow to cool a little before pouring into unbaked pie shell. Bake in 425-degree oven for 25 or 30 minutes.

Beat cottage cheese until smooth and fluffy. Add 2 teaspoons sugar, vanilla and 1 teaspoon lemon juice. When the pie is baked and completely cooled, decorate it, lattice fashion, with the cottage cheese forced through a pastry tube.

Serves 8

Bea's Pumpkin Pie

1 unbaked 9-inch pie shell
   (page 264)
1 1-pound 13-ounce can
   pumpkin
1 egg
1 teaspoon salt
1 teaspoon cinnamon

¼ teaspoon ground cloves
¼ teaspoon nutmeg
½ cup light brown sugar
½ cup granulated sugar
¾ cup nonfat milk solids
¾ cup water
8 walnut halves

Preheat oven to 350 degrees.

Beat egg with rotary beater until light and foamy. In a large bowl, combine pumpkin with salt, cinnamon, ground cloves, nutmeg, sugars and beaten egg. Make a smooth mixture of nonfat milk solids and water and add to pumpkin, blending well. Turn into unbaked pie shell, garnish with walnut halves and bake for 50 minutes, or until a silver knife inserted in the middle comes out dry.

Serves 8

Uncooked Toppings for Cake

Strawberry Whip

1 package frozen strawberries or
   raspberries, thawed
¾ cup sugar

2 egg whites
1 teaspoon lemon juice
dash salt

Drain half the juice from berries and reserve. You can add a little for tinting after it is stiffly whipped. Combine berries, sugar, lemon juice, salt and egg whites and beat in electric beater until thick and fluffy.

Banana Fluff

2 or 3 medium-ripe bananas
½ cup sugar
1 egg white
1 teaspoon lemon juice

dash salt
few drops yellow coloring
   (optional)
1 tablespoon rum (optional)

Slice bananas and mix with sugar, egg white, lemon juice and salt. Beat in electric beater until thick and fluffy. Add coloring and rum if desired.

Red Currant Fluff

1 cup red currant jelly (or
    any other tart jelly)
1 egg white

1 teaspoon lemon juice
few drops red food coloring
    (optional)

In the electric beater, whip together jelly, egg white and lemon juice—and red coloring, if desired.

Macédoine of Fruits

Whatever is fresh and available at your fruit market can go into this. Figure about 6 cups of fruit for 6 servings.

I always include fresh, sectioned oranges which provide a juicy base, but you could also use a 10-ounce package of frozen, mixed fruits, which when thawed, will give you enough liquid.

To section an orange (or a grapefruit), peel it and remove every bit of the white membrane that lines the skin. Hold the orange in one hand over a bowl to catch all the juice, and with a sharp-pointed knife cut between the membrane that separates the sections. Peel out the orange section, cut at next membrane, remove the section, etc., until all the segments are removed. After you've once mastered the technique—and it takes a bit of practice—you'll find it goes quickly and the segments are appetizingly firm and whole.

These are some of the fruits that may go into the macédoine. Use at least 4 or 5.

peaches
apricots
pears
apples
oranges
grapefruits
melon balls

bananas
grapes (seedless or pitted)
strawberries
cherries
pineapple
raspberries

lemon juice
6 tablespoons liqueur (kirsch,
    Cointreau, maraschino,
    brandy)

sugar to taste (or artificial
    sweetener)

Wash, peel, core, drain and cut fruit into 1-inch pieces. Sprinkle with lemon juice to prevent discoloration. Sweeten according to taste with superfine granulated sugar or confectioner's sugar. Add liqueur and stir. Refrigerate at least 4 hours and stir occasionally so that all the flavors will blend. To serve, transfer to a glass serving bowl and serve at the table.

Melon Medley

3 cantaloupes	6 tablespoons kirsch or
1 cup raspberries	grenadine
1 small pineapple, cored, peeled	2 tablespoons lime juice
and diced in ½-inch cubes	sugar (or artificial sweetener)

Divide cantaloupes into halves and scoop out tiny melon balls. Even out insides of melons with a teaspoon so they will have a smooth, unruffled surface. Combine the melon balls with raspberries, diced pineapple, liqueur and lime juice. Taste to see if it needs sweetening. Refrigerate fruit for a few hours. Scallop cantaloupe shells. When ready to serve, fill shells with the chilled fruits.

Serves 6

Strawberries Supreme

1 quart fresh strawberries	1 package frozen strawberries,
sugar	thawed
2 tablespoons Cointreau	1 egg white
(optional)	½ cup sugar
	1 tablespoon lemon juice

Hull and wash strawberries. Sugar them to taste. Combine with Cointreau and refrigerate until ready to serve.

Drain thawed berries, reserving juice. In the electric mixer, beat egg white, sugar, lemon juice, drained strawberries and half the juice until stiff. Place whole berries in individual dessert bowls, top with whip and serve at once.

Serves 4

Fresh Fruit Platter

This fresh-fruit arrangement has taken the place of the more conventional fruit bowl for our after-dinner serving. The individual chunks of melons and pineapple generally find favor with guests who might hesitate to attempt a large piece of fruit.

1 medium-sized pineapple	1 cantaloupe
strawberries	1 honeydew melon or portion of
seedless grapes	a watermelon (or both)

Divide pineapple lengthwise into four quarters, cutting right through the leaves so that each quarter will have its own plume. With a sharp knife, separate pineapple from the shells in one piece. Trim away core, place the pineapple triangles back in the shells and cut into half-inch wedges. Sugar lightly if the pineapple is not very sweet. Place an unhulled strawberry on each pineapple wedge and secure with a toothpick. Arrange pineapple quarters on flat serving tray. Cut cantaloupe, honeydew and/or watermelon into strips or crescents half an inch thick. Surround the pineapple shells with a mound of green grapes cut into small bunches, a section of cantaloupe strips, a section of honeydew melon strips, etc., until all are used. Provide picks for the melon pieces.

The pineapple shells alone do nicely as a dessert. If the fruit is a bit large, you may want to cut it in sixths rather than quarters.

Serves 6 to 8

Apple Snow

2½ cups applesauce	2 teaspoons gelatine
⅓ cup nonfat milk solids	2 tablespoons cold water
⅓ cup chilled apple juice	1 teaspoon grated lemon rind
3 tablespoons sugar	dash cinnamon
2 tablespoons lemon juice	dash nutmeg

Soak gelatine in 2 tablespoons cold water. Stir over hot water until completely dissolved.

Whip nonfat milk solids with chilled apple juice for 3 or 4 minutes, until it stands in soft peaks. Add lemon juice and continue to beat until completely stiff. Gradually beat in sugar.

Add dissolved gelatine to applesauce and mix in lemon rind, cinnamon and nutmeg. Fold in whipped milk and combine thoroughly. Mound in dessert saucers or sherbet glasses and chill until set.

Serves 6

Fruit Whip

The supplies of baby food which I now keep on hand against unexpected visits from our grandson serve two purposes—they keep the small one nourished and make excellent quick fruit whip desserts.

6 ounces puréed fruit (prune, apricot, peach, plum, etc.)
2 egg whites

¼ teaspoon salt
3 tablespoons sugar
1 tablespoon lemon juice

Grated raw apple or applesauce may also be used.

Beat egg whites and salt until frothy. Gradually add sugar, a little at a time, beating until stiff and shiny. Fold in puréed fruit and lemon juice and blend well. Mound in 4 sherbet glasses and chill.

Serves 4

Fruit-Flavor Whipped Topping

This whipped cream substitute is low in calories, completely fatless, and answers a need for those who think a bowl of Jello or a piece of cake looks a bit naked without some adornment. You can use it on whatever your fancy dictates: Jello, pies, pudding, fruit, etc. It hasn't the staying power of what it's pretending to be, so whip it as near to the time when you'll be using it as you can. It requires vigorous beating, but it's a breeze in an electric mixer.

You may use any fruit juice—grape, apricot, cranberry, grapefruit, orange, pineapple or apple. Just make sure it is well chilled.

½ cup chilled fruit juice (or ice water)
½ cup nonfat milk solids

2 tablespoons lemon juice
¼ cup sugar

Measure fruit juice or water into large mixing bowl. Add nonfat milk solids. Whip for 3 or 4 minutes until soft peaks form. Add lemon juice and continue whipping 3 or 4 minutes longer while gradually adding the sugar. Continue beating until stiff peaks form.

Makes 2½ to 3 cups topping

Baked Red Apples

A state of perfection for baked apples is not achieved, ironically, by baking them. This cooking procedure makes them brown and wrinkled. For best results, the apples should be steamed first to make them tender, then glazed under the broiler. Start with the largest and best baking apples you can find—like firm Rome Beauties or Northern Spies.

6 fine baking apples	⅔ cup water
¾ cup sugar	1 teaspoon red cinnamon candies,
½ teaspoon cinnamon	or a few drops of red
3 slices of orange (unpeeled)	vegetable coloring
3 slices of lemon (unpeeled)	

Wash and core apples, leaving skin intact at the very bottom. Peel apples about a third of the way down.

Mix sugar and cinnamon together. Place in bottom of covered large heavy skillet deep enough to hold the apples. Add orange and lemon slices. Place apples, peeled side down, on the layer of sugar. Tint the ⅔ cup of water red either by heating it with the cinnamon candies until they melt, or by adding the red coloring. Pour water over apples. Cover skillet tightly and steam on top of stove for 15 minutes over low flame. Remove cover and carefully turn apples over, replace cover and continue to steam until apples are fork-tender. This may take anywhere from 15 to 40 minutes longer, depending on the type of apple you're dealing with. Watch them carefully and don't overcook. It is the necessity for judgments like this that makes cooking an art and not a science.

When the apples have reached the proper degree of done-ness, soft enough to let a spoon pierce them easily, yet firm enough to maintain their bulges, remove lid from skillet, sprinkle a bit of sugar over apples and place under broiler for about 10 minutes. Constantly baste apples with the syrup while under the broiler so that the tops will be glazed, crisp and bubbly.

Serves 6

Apple Crisp

This is really the insides of an apple pie without the crusts.

4 or 5 large tart apples
1 teaspoon cinnamon
½ cup white sugar
⅓ cup water

2 tablespoons lemon juice
½ cup flour
½ cup brown sugar
3 tablespoons oil

Core, peel and slice apples. Oil 1½-quart casserole and place sliced apples in it. Combine sugar and cinnamon and add to apples. Add lemon juice and water and mix lightly. In a small mixing bowl, blend flour, brown sugar and oil until crumbly. Sprinkle this over apples. Bake in 350-degree oven for 50 minutes, or until browned and the apples tender. Serve warm.

Serves 4 or 5

Peach Cobbler

1 1-pound 4-ounce can sliced
    peaches
1 tablespoon cornstarch
½ cup sugar
1 tablespoon lemon juice
½ teaspoon cinnamon

1 cup sifted all-purpose flour
1 tablespoon sugar
½ teaspoon salt
1½ teaspoons baking powder
½ cup skim milk
3 tablespoons oil

Preheat oven to 400 degrees.

In a saucepan, combine sugar and cornstarch. Add peaches and syrup and lemon juice. Bring to a boil, stirring constantly, and boil for 1 minute. Pour into 1½-quart casserole and sprinkle with cinnamon. Place in oven while you prepare the biscuit topping.

Sift together flour, sugar, salt and baking powder in small mixing bowl. Add oil and milk and stir. Drop by spoonfuls on the hot fruit. Bake 25 to 30 minutes until golden brown. Serve warm.

Serves 6 to 8

Aunt Rosa's Apple Fritters

Aunt Rosa made the batter with beer and so I did too. But then one day I ran out of beer and discovered that water worked just fine.

3 large tart apples, peeled
  and cored
2 teaspoons sugar
1 teaspoon grated lemon rind
⅓ cup brandy
1 tablespoon lemon juice
6 tablespoons flour

6 tablespoons tepid beer or
  water
1 generous tablespoon oil
pinch of salt
2 egg whites, stiffly beaten
oil for frying

Slice peeled and cored apples crosswise into ⅜-inch slices. Each apple should yield 4 slices. Combine brandy with lemon rind, lemon juice and sugar. Marinate apple slices in this for at least ½ hour.

Batter: Place flour in small bowl. Gradually add beer or water, stirring until you get a smooth batter of a thick pasty consistency. Add a pinch of salt and the tablespoon of oil, beating well. Let this rest at room temperature for at least ½ hour. I usually prepare both apples and batter in the late afternoon, well in advance of dinner.

When you're ready to make the fritters, beat whites of 2 eggs until stiff but not dry and fold gently into the batter mixture. The batter should have the consistency of heavy cream.

Pour oil into heavy skillet to the depth of ½ inch. Heat for 4 minutes over medium flame.

Dip drained apple slices in batter and fry in hot oil until crisp and golden, turning once. Remove from pan with slotted spoon, drain on absorbent paper and sprinkle both sides with superfine granulated sugar. These may be kept warm in a slow oven until dessert time.

Serves 6

BANANA DESSERTS

This fine fruit is too often neglected at dessert time. From the standpoint of flavor, nutrients, flexibility, economy and availability, bananas are outstanding. We fry them, bake them, broil them and even flame them.

Banana Fritters

Split 4 or 5 bananas lengthwise and then in half. Mix together ⅓ cup lemon juice with 2 teaspoons sugar and pour over banana quarters.

Follow procedure as outlined in Apple Fritter recipe.

Baked Bananas

Heat oven to 375 degrees. Split bananas lengthwise, leaving them in their skins, and place in baking dish. Sprinkle a little lemon juice and brown sugar over them and bake in 375-degree oven for 25 to 30 minutes, or until they are soft and browned. Serve hot, 2 halves per portion.

Bananas Baked in Orange Juice

6 medium-sized bananas, slightly green
1 orange, peeled and cut in pieces
2 tablespoons orange juice
2 tablespoons lemon juice
⅓ cup brown sugar
pinch nutmeg and cinnamon
⅓ cup crystallized ginger, chopped (optional)

Lightly oil shallow 9 x 11" inch baking dish. Peel bananas, split lengthwise and arrange in dish. Sprinkle lemon juice, orange juice and orange chunks over fruit. Mix cinnamon and nutmeg with sugar, and top the bananas with this. Sprinkle with chopped ginger. Bake 25 to 30 minutes in 325-degree oven, or until the bananas are brown and tender. Baste a few times while baking. Serve 2 halves per portion.

Meringue Baked Bananas: For a dress-up version, cover bananas with a meringue made of 3 egg whites, 3 tablespoons sugar, ⅛ teaspoon cream of tartar and ½ teaspoon vanilla, and bake as directed above.

Baked Banana Compote

5 bananas
½ cup unpared diced red apple
⅓ cup orange juice
3 tablespoons lemon juice
¼ cup strained honey
½ cup walnuts, coarsely chopped
1 cup mandarin orange sections

Peel bananas and cut crosswise slices ½ inch thick. Place banana slices mixed with diced apple in lightly oiled 1-quart casserole.
Combine orange juice, lemon juice and honey and pour over fruit. Bake in 400-degree oven for 20 minutes, or until soft. A few min-

utes before the casserole comes out of the oven, sprinkle with nuts. Garnish with orange sections. Serve hot.

Serves 6

Flaming Bananas

4 medium-sized bananas
3 tablespoons oil
1 tablespoon lemon juice
¼ cup brown sugar
½ cup orange juice

¼ teaspoon ground cinnamon
¼ teaspoon ground nutmeg
¼ cup sherry
⅓ cup rum

Preheat oven to 350 degrees.

Peel bananas and roll in oil to coat well. Sprinkle with lemon juice and place in oiled shallow baking dish.

Combine brown sugar, orange juice, cinnamon, nutmeg and sherry. Heat for a moment and pour over fruit. Bake for 20 to 25 minutes until bananas are tender, basting a few times with the syrup. Transfer to chafing dish, pour warmed rum over them and ignite. (See note on burning brandy, page 287.)

Serves 4

Baked Fruit Compote

1 can peach halves
1 can apricot halves
1 can Bing cherries, pitted
juice of 2 oranges
2 tablespoons lemon juice

¼ cup thinly sliced orange rind
¼ cup thinly sliced lemon rind
4 tablespoons brown sugar
2 ounces kirsch (optional)
½ cup coarsely chopped walnuts

Drain all fruits, discarding juice. In a small saucepan, combine orange juice, lemon juice, brown sugar, orange and lemon rinds and simmer over low flame for 5 minutes.

Place drained peach and apricot halves in glass baking dish. Cover with syrup and bake in 325-degree oven for 30 minutes, stirring frequently. Ten minutes before serving, add the drained cherries, kirsch and chopped nuts.

Each portion should consist of 1 peach half, 1 apricot half and cherries. Serve hot.

Pineapple and Bing Cherries Flambé

1 ripe, medium-sized pineapple
1 large can pitted Bing
  cherries, drained
¼ cup sugar
½ cup sherry

½ cup water
2 tablespoons lemon juice
1 12-ounce jar currant jelly
½ cup kirsch or brandy

Peel pineapple and split in half lengthwise. Remove core and slice each half into paper-thin slices.

In medium-size skillet, combine sugar, sherry, water and lemon juice and heat to the boiling point. Lower heat and add pineapple slices. Poach for 5 or 6 minutes, or until they become the least bit tender. Remove slices and syrup from skillet and set aside.

In the same skillet, melt currant jelly over low heat. Add drained pineapple slices and simmer for 3 minutes. Add syrup slowly and blend well. Add drained cherries and heat for 5 minutes. Transfer to chafing dish, add warmed kirsch or brandy and ignite. When flame dies out, serve in individual dessert bowls.

Serves 6

Peaches Victoria

6 fresh large peaches
1 cup water
½ cup sugar
1 1-inch vanilla bean
3 tablespoons lemon juice

Raspberry Sauce:
1 package frozen raspberries,
  defrosted
1 tablespoon sugar
1 teaspoon cornstarch
2 tablespoons cold water
3 tablespoons kirsch (optional)
¼ cup blanched slivered
  almonds

In a saucepan large enough to hold the peaches so they won't be crowded, make a syrup of sugar, water, lemon juice and vanilla bean. Peel peaches carefully and poach in the syrup until done. This may take 15 or 20 minutes—perhaps longer if the peaches are very firm. Cook them until they are fork-tender but not mushy. When they are soft enough, remove from syrup and keep warm.

Raspberry Sauce: In a small saucepan, combine raspberries with sugar. Mix cornstarch with water and combine with raspberries. Simmer for 3 minutes, until bubbly and clear, and mash through sieve or food mill. Return to saucepan and heat just enough to warm through. Add kirsch and mix. Spoon sauce over peaches and sprinkle with almonds.

Heavenly Hash

A credit line to the pretty young lady named Annette who ate this and remarked, "What heavenly hash." Which is what it's been ever since.

1 No. 2 can pineapple tidbits	juice of 1 lemon
1 cup marshmallows, diced	½ cup walnuts, coarsely
1 medium banana, diced	chopped
3 tablespoons confectioner's sugar	2 tablespoons rum

Please make sure you use the pineapple tidbits—not the crushed, or the chunks. The first is too fine, the second too large. The tidbits are just right. Drain pineapple and reserve juice. In a glass bowl, combine pineapple, marshmallows, banana, sugar, lemon juice and nuts. Use marshmallow miniatures if you can get them. They'll save you the sticky procedure of making little ones out of big ones. Add enough of the juice to thoroughly moisten the whole business. You'll probably use about ⅓ cup. Add the rum and chill in the refrigerator at least 3 hours.

Serves 6

Raspberry Sponge with Custard Sauce

1 pint red raspberries	2 tablespoons cornstarch
5 tablespoons sugar	4 egg whites
pinch salt	

Allow egg whites to stand at room temperature. In a small saucepan, crush raspberries and bring to a boil. Mix together sugar, salt and cornstarch and add slowly to the berries. Cook until thickened, stirring constantly. Cool.

Beat egg whites until stiff, but not dry. Fold the cooled raspberry mixture into the stiffly beaten egg whites. Pour into lightly oiled 1½-quart casserole which has been dusted with sugar. Set in pan of hot water and bake in 325-degree oven for 35 to 40 minutes. Cool. Serve with custard sauce—see recipe at bottom of page.

Serves 4 to 5

Pears in Port Wine

6 large pears
1 cup port wine
2 tablespoons lemon juice
½ cup water

½ cup sugar
few pieces lemon rind
1 1-inch piece cinnamon stick

Peel whole pears carefully, leaving stems intact.

In a skillet large enough to hold the pears without crowding, combine wine, lemon juice, water, sugar, lemon rind and cinnamon stick and bring to a boil. Add pears, cover skillet, reduce heat and simmer slowly until the pears are tender, but not mushy. Cooking time depends on the species and ripeness of the fruit, so watch them carefully. When they reach the point of being soft enough not to offer resistance to a spoon, but not cooked to a fare-thee-well, remove them from syrup with a slotted spoon, set aside, and simmer syrup until it is reduced to 1 cup. Discard cinnamon stick and lemon rind. Cover pears with syrup and refrigerate when cooled.

Serves 6

Poached Pears with Sherry Custard Sauce

The Royal custard flavor prepared pudding mix makes a highly satisfactory custard sauce—without an egg in sight.

4 large firm pears
juice of 1 lemon
¼ cup sugar
red vegetable coloring

Custard Sauce:
½ package Royal custard flavor
    pudding mix
1¾ cups skim milk
2 ounces sherry

Choose large, firm Bosc, Bartlett or Anjou pears. Peel carefully, leaving stems. Put in saucepan with juice of 1 lemon, sugar and enough water to cover. Don't crowd the pears or they won't cook

through evenly. It is impossible to tell you how long they must cook
—I've had Bartlett pears reach the right degree of tenderness in 25
minutes—and some Anjous that didn't capitulate until they had sim-
mered well over an hour. You'll have to watch them and use your
own judgment as to when they're ready—they should be in perfect
shape, not the least mushy, but fork-tender. If you want them
sweeter, you may either add more sugar or some artificial sweetener.
When they are done, lift them carefully with a slotted spoon to a
flat dish, tint a few tablespoons of the syrup red with the vegetable
coloring, and dribble a teaspoonful of the coloring on each pear. This
will bring a rosy flush to their, by now, pale cheeks and make them
look pretty. Refrigerate when cool.

For the sauce, cook ½ package of the Royal custard pudding mix
with 1¾ cups skim milk according to directions on package. Cool
and refrigerate. If the pudding has congealed when ready to serve,
beat it with a rotary beater. Add sherry. Serve the pears in your nicest
dessert bowls and pass the sauce separately.

Serves 4

Sometimes we serve the pears with the Raspberry Sauce on page
280. On such an occasion, omit the red dye on the pears' cheeks—
they'll blush anyway.

Apple and Rice Pudding

5 large apples, peeled, cored and thinly sliced
2½ cups skim milk
¾ cup rice
2 egg whites, stiffly beaten

2 teaspoons grated lemon rind
2 teaspoons grated orange rind
6 tablespoons sugar
¼ teaspoon nutmeg

In a heavy saucepan, combine sliced apples with 1 tablespoon
sugar. Cook over low flame until apples are limp—8 to 10 minutes.
Set apples aside. Rinse saucepan with cold water, but do not dry,
and pour milk into it. Bring to a boil over low flame and add rice
and orange and lemon rinds. Increase flame and cook for 20 minutes, stirring from time to time. Lightly oil 1½-quart casserole. Place
a layer of apples and a layer of rice and liquid in casserole, alternating

until all are used. Sprinkle the remaining 5 tablespoons of sugar and nutmeg over the mixture. Beat egg whites until stiff, but not dry, and gently fold into the casserole. Bake in 350-degree oven for 30 minutes, or until brown on top. Serve hot.

Serves 6 to 8

Creamy Refrigerator Rice Pudding

No cooking at all—except for the rice, of course. The rice, marshmallow and pineapple can be mixed together early in the day—but the whipped milk mixture should be prepared and added just before you're ready to eat it.

1½ cups cold cooked rice
1 cup diced marshmallows
½ cup drained crushed canned pineapple
8 maraschino cherries, chopped

½ cup walnuts, coarsely chopped
½ cup nonfat milk solids
½ cup pineapple juice, chilled
2 tablespoons lemon juice
¼ cup sugar

Combine cooked rice, marshmallows, pineapple, cherries and nuts in good-sized bowl. Measure pineapple juice into large mixing bowl. If there is less than ½ cup, make up the amount needed with cold water. Add nonfat milk solids. Whip for 3 or 4 minutes until soft peaks form. Add lemon juice and continue whipping 3 or 4 minutes longer, while gradually adding sugar. Continue beating until stiff peaks form.

Fold whipped milk into rice mixture. Heap into serving dishes and serve as soon as possible.

Serves 6

Poor Man's Rice Pudding

This pudding probably earned its name because of the paucity of its ingredients—which makes it fine for us.

½ cup uncooked Uncle Ben's rice
⅓ cup sugar
⅛ teaspoon salt
⅛ teaspoon cinnamon

½ teaspoon vanilla
pinch nutmeg
3 cups fortified skim milk
1 tablespoon oil
⅓ cup seedless raisins

Oil 1-quart casserole. Add rice, sugar, salt, cinnamon, nutmeg, raisins, vanilla and skim milk. Place in 325-degree oven and bake for 2 hours. Stir it from time to time. After the first hour, add oil and mix well. Allow the pudding to bake undisturbed for the last ½ hour, but watch it carefully so it doesn't dry out. We want it soft and creamy.

Serves 4

Apricot Soufflé

As you know, soufflés are an impatient lot and don't like to wait. This is no exception, so pop it into the oven just thirty minutes ahead of dessert time.

6 ounces dried apricots	¼ cup sifted dark brown
1 cup water	sugar
5 egg whites	dash salt
¼ cup granulated sugar	½ teaspoon vanilla

Simmer apricots in 1 cup of water until mushy. Purée through food mill or buzz in blender, retaining the syrup.

Oil 1½-quart soufflé dish and sprinkle lightly with sugar.

Preheat oven to 350 degrees.

Beat egg whites until stiff but not dry. Add granulated sugar, a tablespoon at a time, and beat between additions. Add brown sugar and beat lightly again until well mixed. Fold in the apricot purée slowly and gently. Add salt and vanilla. Pour mixture into prepared dish. Sprinkle a little more sugar on top. Place dish in shallow pan of hot water and bake 30 minutes. Serve at once.

Serves 4

Apricot Crepes

These are a favorite party dessert. The crepes may be made the day before, which leaves the last-minute fixing a simple matter. Don't worry about refrigerating the crepes overnight. I've done it successfully many times.

Crepes:

3 eggs
1 teaspoon salt
1½ teaspoons sugar
2 tablespoons brandy
1 scant cup flour
1⅔ cups skim milk
2 tablespoons oil
apricot preserves

Sauce:

1 12-ounce can apricot nectar
1 No. 2 can apricot halves
grated rind of 1 orange
juice of 1 lemon
jigger of Cointreau
2 ounces brandy

To make the crepes, beat 3 whole eggs until light. Use your electric mixer. Add salt, sugar and brandy. Beating constantly, add alternately flour, milk and oil. The batter should be the consistency of heavy cream. Let the batter rest at room temperature for 1 hour. I suppose there's a perfectly logical reason for this, but I don't know what it is. I only know that if you don't, the crepes won't do properly in the frying pan, so straighten out your dish closets, clean the silver or read a book, and come back later.

To cook the crepes, lightly oil 6-inch skillet with crumpled paper towel dipped in oil. (Keep a small bowl of oil at hand for re-oiling the skillet when necessary. You won't need much.) Heat skillet over medium heat until a drop of water sizzles and bounces off. Use as little batter as will cover the bottom of the pan because we want the crepes thin and delicate. After the first few, you will learn to judge how much you need for each one. I find a soup ladle convenient for pouring the batter. Tilt pan quickly so that entire bottom is covered. Cook over medium heat until underside of crepe is delicately browned. Turn crepe over with spatula, brown other side and transfer to a towel. Repeat until all batter is used, stacking crepes on top of each other when cooled. This should yield between 20 and 24. Wrap them in aluminum foil and store in refrigerator if you're planning to use them the next day.

For the sauce, drain apricots and put fruit aside. In a saucepan, combine apricot nectar with the syrup from the can, orange rind and lemon juice, and cook uncovered for 15 minutes. Just before serving, add apricots to sauce and heat through. Add Cointreau.

Spread each crepe with apricot preserves, roll into a cylinder and place in lightly oiled shallow pan. Don't stack them—lay them side by side. A jelly-roll pan is useful for this. Spoon some of the sauce over them to keep them moist. Cover with aluminum foil. While the main part of the meal is being eaten, put them into 400-degree oven so they will be piping hot. At dessert time, transfer them to your chafing dish. Sprinkle some fine sugar over them, cover with sauce and fruit. Pour warm brandy over crepes and ignite. When flame burns out, serve on warm plates, 2 crepes to a serving, with plenty of sauce and fruit on each.

Serves 10 to 12

Crepes Normandie

24 crepes	¾ teaspoon cinnamon
5 medium-sized apples, peeled and thinly sliced	3 tablespoons brown sugar
	1 tablespoon oil
6 tablespoons sugar	½ cup apple brandy

Make crepes as for Apricot Crepes, page 285. In a heavy saucepan, combine sliced apples, sugar and cinnamon. Cook over low heat until the apples wilt, 8 to 10 minutes, stirring frequently. Cool for 15 minutes.

Place a tablespoon of the apple mixture on each crepe and roll carefully. Arrange rolled crepes in large flat baking pan which has been lightly oiled. Moisten brown sugar with oil and sprinkle over the crepes. Bake in 375-degree oven for 15 minutes. Transfer to chafing dish. Pour warmed brandy over the top and ignite.

Serves 10 to 12

On Burning Brandy

For a long time I waged a losing fight with what my family jibingly called Operation B.B. (burning the brandy). I warmed it, just as the books advise, and poured it lovingly and hopefully over the contents of the chafing dish. I lit matches until the air was thick with phosphorus fumes, and all I'd have to show for my trouble was an ashtray full of burnt-out matches. Sometimes, if I were lucky, a feeble blue light would flicker for a fraction of a moment. If you closed your eyes, you'd miss the whole show. And all that good brandy wasted!

I watched enviously when the dignitaries in posh restaurants, with a flick of the bottle, would set off a flame that practically licked the ceiling. (I'm still convinced there's some kind of hanky-panky involved—they probably conceal a bottle of kerosene in their sleeves.) At any rate, came the dawn at long last. Now I warm the brandy in the kitchen, tote it into the dining room, and light it just as I pour it into the chafing dish. The dish comes alive with dancing blue flames that would make the headwaiter at "21" green with envy. When I tell people about this monumental discovery, I'm invariably greeted with a "I always knew that—why didn't you ask me?" kind of answer. For goodness' sake—why didn't somebody *tell* me?

Baked Caramel Custard

A prepared custard pudding called FLAN, available in many markets, is satisfactory but not as good as this one that you'll make yourself. Since the 3 eggs in this recipe will yield 6 portions, the half egg in each custard keeps it within limits.

1 cup sugar	1 thin slice lemon peel
¼ cup boiling water	3 eggs, slightly beaten
3 cups fortified skim milk	½ teaspoon vanilla
¼ teaspoon salt	

Measure ¼ cup of sugar into small heavy skillet. Melt sugar over low flame, stirring constantly. Add another ¼ cup of sugar and continue to heat, stirring constantly, until it melts. Add ¼ cup boiling water and cook and stir until a smooth sauce is formed. Remove from heat and cool. Lightly oil 6 custard cups and spoon a little of the caramelized sugar into each.

Preheat oven to 325 degrees. Pour 3 cups of skim milk into top half of double boiler. (If you rinse the pan with cold water, but do not dry, the milk won't stick to the pan.) Add the remaining ½ cup of sugar, salt and lemon peel. Cover and cook over boiling water until tiny bubbles begin to appear around the edges (otherwise known as scalding). Remove lemon peel.

Beat eggs lightly in small bowl and slowly stir in half the scalded milk. Return this egg mixture slowly to the scalded milk in the pan, stirring constantly. Add vanilla and cook, stirring all the time, until the mixture thickens and coats spoon—about 12 to 15 minutes. Turn into the caramel-lined custard cups. Set in pan of hot water to the depth of 1½ inches and bake for 40 to 50 minutes, or until a silver knife inserted in the middle comes out clean. Remove from water, cool and refrigerate. Unmold just before serving.

Serves 6

Cream Puffs with Butterscotch Sauce

½ cup boiling water
¼ cup oil
½ teaspoon salt
½ cup flour
2 eggs

Filling:
1 package Royal Custard or
    Vanilla pudding
2 cups skim milk
2 teaspoons powdered coffee
    (optional)

Preheat oven to 400 degrees.

In a medium-sized saucepan, heat oil and water to the boiling point. Add salt and flour all at once and stir until the flour is absorbed and the mixture forms a ball. Remove from fire and add unbeaten eggs, one at a time, beating vigorously after the addition of each egg. The mixture will become spongy and shiny and leave the sides of the pan, forming a mound. This whole business needn't take more than 10 minutes, from beginning to end.

Oil cookie tin. Drop batter by large tablespoons into 6 mounds. Heap batter high in the middle and make the puffs as round as possible. Allow a couple inches between each.

Bake for 25 minutes in 400-degree oven. Reduce heat to 350 degrees and bake 15 minutes longer, or until the puffs are golden and very well-done looking on the outside. Take one from oven for a test: if it does not fall, consider them done. When cool, slit an opening on one side and fill.

Cream Filling: Add contents of 1 package of pudding mix to 2 cups of skim milk and cook according to directions on package. (If you wish a coffee-flavored filling, add 2 teaspoons of powdered coffee to the pudding mix and proceed as directed.) Cool and refrigerate the pudding. Shortly before serving, fill cream puffs and replace in refrigerator until you're ready for them.

Serve on individual dessert plates. Cover each puff with about 2 tablespoons of hot butterscotch sauce.

Serves 6

Butterscotch Sauce

1 cup light brown sugar	½ teaspoon butter flavoring
2 tablespoons light corn syrup	4 tablespoons nonfat milk solids
1½ tablespoons oil	dissolved in 5 tablespoons water

In a small saucepan, combine sugar, corn syrup, oil, butter flavoring and dissolved nonfat milk solids. Cook over low flame, stirring constantly, for 7 or 8 minutes, or until it reaches the "soft ball" stage. (Determine this by dropping a tiny bit of the syrup in cold water. If the water remains clear and the syrup forms a soft ball and just keeps its shape when rolled between the fingers, it is done.) Remove from direct heat at once. Keep sauce warm over simmering water.

Yields about ¾ cup sauce

Lemon Pudding

A good dessert choice after a substantial dinner.

1 cup sugar	1 egg yolk
3 tablespoons flour	2 egg whites, beaten stiff
juice and grated rind of 1 lemon	1 cup skim milk
pinch salt	1 tablespoon oil

Stir sugar, flour, salt and juice and rind of 1 lemon in 1½-quart oiled ovenproof casserole. Add beaten egg yolk and 1 cup skim milk to the mixture. In another bowl, beat egg whites until stiff, but not dry, and gently fold into the mixture. Add 1 tablespoon of oil and mix. Place in pan of hot water and bake in 350-degree oven for about 45 minutes. The sponge will rise to the top, leaving a delicate lemon-y sauce to spoon over each portion. Serve warm.

Serves 4

Low-Calorie Pineapple Fluff

1¾ cups unsweetened pineapple juice
½ grain tablet saccharin

1 tablespoon unflavored gelatine
4 tablespoons sugar
pinch salt

In a small saucepan, heat pineapple juice to the boiling point.

Combine gelatine, sugar and salt and add to pineapple juice. Cook for a minute or two, stirring until gelatine is dissolved. Add saccharin. Place in bowl and chill until it becomes a little thicker than unbeaten egg white.

Beat with rotary beater until the mixture becomes frothy and doubles in volume.

Pour into 4 sherbet or parfait glasses and chill until set.

Serves 4

Coffee Sponge

1⅔ cups strong coffee
1 tablespoon unflavored gelatine

⅓ cup sugar
1 teaspoon vanilla
⅛ teaspoon cinnamon

In a small saucepan, combine gelatine, sugar and ½ cup coffee. Cook over low heat, stirring constantly, until the gelatine is dissolved. Remove from heat and add the remainder of the coffee, vanilla, and cinnamon. Refrigerate until it becomes a little thicker than the consistency of unbeaten egg white. This will take about an hour.

Beat with rotary beater until it doubles in bulk, becomes fluffy and light, and holds its shape.

Mound in dessert dishes and chill.

Serves 6

Prune Compote

A jar of these prunes in your refrigerator can serve as a breakfast fruit or dessert for dinner. The coffee loses its identifying flavor and enhances the taste of the prunes, while making a rich, dark syrup.

1 pound large sweet prunes
1 cup strong coffee

1 cup canned crushed pineapple
2 tablespoons lemon juice

Wash prunes and place in saucepan with a cup of strong coffee. Add lemon juice and enough water to cover the prunes. Cover and simmer gently for 25 minutes over low flame. Add drained crushed pineapple and bring to boil. Pour into a Pyrex bowl and cover tightly with a lid or dish. The hot syrup will continue to tenderize the prunes and make them expand. When cool, refrigerate. Serve 3 to 5 prunes (depending on the size) per portion, with the pineapple and sauce generously spooned over them.

Strawberry Mousse

This mousse does equally well in a parfait glass or generously heaped on sliced angel cake.

2 10-ounce packages frozen, sliced strawberries, thawed and drained
½ cup nonfat milk solids

½ cup chilled juice from strawberries
1 egg white stiffly beaten
2 tablespoons lemon juice
4 tablespoons sugar

In your electric mixer, beat nonfat milk solids with strawberry juice. Add ice water to juice if you have less than ½ cup. Beat until soft peaks form (3 to 4 minutes). Add 2 tablespoons lemon juice and continue beating until firm peaks form (3 to 4 minutes longer). Gradually add 2 tablespoons of sugar. In another bowl, mash strawberries with remaining 2 tablespoons sugar to a smooth pulp. Beat egg white stiffly. Fold together whipped milk, mashed strawberries and egg white. Freeze in tray in freezing compartment of refrigerator for 3 hours.

Serves 6

Cranberry Sherbet

½ pound fresh whole
   cranberries (about 2⅓ cups)
1¼ cups cold water
1 cup plus 2 tablespoons sugar
½ envelope (1½ teaspoons)
   unflavored gelatine dissolved
   in 2 tablespoons water

¼ teaspoon grated lemon rind
4 tablespoons lemon juice
pinch salt
2 egg whites

In a covered saucepan, cook cranberries in 1¼ cups cold water for about 10 minutes, or until the skins pop. Force both the berries and the liquid through food mill. Add sugar to this purée and mix thoroughly. Add dissolved gelatine to cranberry mixture and stir well. Add lemon juice and rind.

Pour into freezer tray, replace in freezer compartment and freeze until mushy. This seems to get stiff very quickly, but don't worry about it if you find it has become quite hard. Just turn it into a mixing bowl and soften it with a fork. Beat in electric mixer or with rotary beater until it becomes fluffy and increases in volume. Beat egg whites with salt until they form soft peaks, but are not dry. Fold beaten whites into cranberry mixture and return to freezer. Freeze until firm.

Serves 5 to 6

Creamy Apricot Sherbet

For a party look, we serve this in crystal dessert dishes and flank the scoop of sherbet with two or three large apricot halves which have been marinated in apricot liqueur.

1 tablespoon gelatine
2 cups skim milk
½ cup nonfat milk solids
¼ cup sugar

1 1-pound can apricots, drained
   and puréed
2 tablespoons lemon juice

In a small saucepan, soak gelatine in ½ cup of the skim milk until it becomes softened. Heat over low flame until gelatine is dissolved, stirring constantly. Place in large mixing bowl, add remaining milk, nonfat milk solids, sugar, puréed apricots and lemon juice. Either in your electric mixer or with a rotary beater (preferably the first), beat for 3 or 4 minutes, until the mixture thickens a bit. It won't get real thick, so don't try. Place this mixture in a tray (this amount fills a 5½ x 10″) in freezing compartment of refrigerator and freeze until partially firm. Remove and transfer to bowl. If it seems quite hard, just attack it with a fork and your beater and beat until smooth, but not melted. Replace in freezer. Beat once more in 30 minutes and chill until firm.

Serves 4 to 6

Mint Sherbet

Dribble some crème de menthe over a scoop of this and serve in your prettiest parfait or sherbet glasses for an imposing dessert.

1 tablespoon gelatine
1½ cups cold water
¾ cup boiling water
1 cup sugar
juice of 3 lemons

1½ tablespoons fresh mint leaves, finely chopped, or 1½ tablespoons crème de menthe or ½ teaspoon essence of peppermint
1 egg white, stiffly beaten
few drops of green vegetable coloring (optional)

Soak gelatine in ½ cup of the cold water. Add boiling water and stir until dissolved. Add sugar, the remaining cup of cold water and lemon juice. Beat well with rotary beater. Pour mixture into freezing tray and place in freezer compartment of refrigerator.

When this has become frozen around the edges, transfer mixture to large chilled bowl and beat vigorously until creamy and foamy. Stir in the mint or creme de menthe or essence of peppermint. Fold in stiffly beaten egg white. Add coloring, if desired. Replace in tray and freeze.

Serves 6

Spiced Walnuts

Try these with your coffee after a fruit dessert.

1½ cups walnut halves	½ teaspoon nutmeg
1 cup fine sugar	¼ teaspoon powdered cloves
1 teaspoon powdered ginger	1 egg white
1 teaspoon salt	1 tablespoon cold water

In 350-degree oven, heat walnuts for 5 or 10 minutes—just to make them fresh and crisp.

After you remove the nuts from the oven, reduce heat to 275 degrees.

Sift together sugar, ginger, salt, nutmeg and cloves, and place in shallow bowl. Add the cold water to the egg white and beat until it becomes frothy. Stop before it becomes too stiff and mounds.

Dip nuts in egg white and then roll in sugar-spice mixture. Sprinkle half of the remaining sugar-spice mixture over bottom of baking sheet and arrange nuts on it, keeping them separate. Sprinkle the rest of the sugar-spice over the top. Bake in 275-degree oven for about 1 hour. Remove from baking sheet at once. Shake off excess sugar.

Yield: 1½ cups

Yogurt

The commercial yogurt is made partly from whole milk. While the printing on the cartons tells us that part of the butterfat is removed, it fails to make mention of the portion of butterfat that remains.

Making your own yogurt from skim milk is a simple procedure. All you need besides the skim milk is a quart-sized glass jar with a top and 1 tablespoon of yogurt, or preferably, yogurt culture, which is available in some places. After that, it is self-perpetuating. You will need a tablespoon of fresh culture about once a month.

Five easy steps does it:

1. Put 1 tablespoon yogurt in a thoroughly clean glass jar.
2. Bring 1 quart of skim milk to a boil and remove from heat.

3. Allow milk to cool until it is lukewarm, stirring frequently. This will take about 1 hour.

4. Pour lukewarm milk over the yogurt, stir well, cover jar, and put in a warm spot for 6 hours. Or you may place the jar covered with a towel over the pilot light on your gas stove overnight.

5. Refrigerate. When the yogurt is almost used up, save a tablespoon of it and begin all over again as in Step 1.

This yogurt is less firm than the commercially prepared one. It is unflavored and bland. For interest and variety, add sugar or artificial sweetener, vanilla, cinnamon or any flavor of jam or fruit purée, such as mashed bananas, prunes, apricots or berries.

17

Company Coming?

GOOD FOOD and good talk with good friends can add up to a delightful evening for the hosts, provided the hostess hasn't worn herself limp preparing for it. Happily, the day when course followed course until the assemblage was stuffed into a state of semi-consciousness has passed. Few people today have either the time or the kitchen staffs needed for such gastronomic excesses. We know better, anyway. Three courses, imaginatively planned, well prepared and appetizingly served, are completely adequate for a blissful meal.

We have made a practice, with six or more to dinner, of serving the first course in the living room with the pre-dinner drinks. This simplifies table service considerably, eliminating one whole round of plate changing, and cuts down the need for a succession of hors d'oeuvres—an added bonus in these calorie-conscious days. Foods that must be kept hot are served from a chafing dish or an electric hot tray—two items I find indispensable.

Some fine culinary reputations have been established even with a limited repertoire, so if you make an outstanding dish that your guests rave over, let it be your *spécialité de la maison*, and don't hesitate to repeat it. (This doesn't hold for families—they generally thrive on variety.) Hostesses often work madly to avoid a minor kitchen triumph which they have served before to the same guests, only to hear them groan with disappointment at not having it.

Following are some of the party menus we serve. They were planned to distribute the work load evenly between the oven, the broiler, the top of the stove, and the cook. With proper organization—silverware cleaned, marketing, baking and as much of the food preparation as possible taken care of the day before—you should be able to greet your guests looking almost as fresh and rested as they do.

Horse-radish Ring Filled with Boiled Shrimp or Crab Meat
(Russian or Garlic Cream Dressing)

Chicken Breasts in Wine and Tomato Sauce
Poppy Seed-Noodle Casserole   String Beans, Amandine

Canned Button Mushrooms, Vinaigrette
with Romaine or Chicory

Apricot Cake

Scampi

Baked Steak
Baked Stuffed Potatoes   Zucchini and Tomato Sauté

Raw Mushroom Salad

Apple Butterscotch Tart

Coquille St. Jacques

Breaded Veal Cutlet with Artichoke Hearts and Tomatoes
Mushroom Rice DeLuxe   Broccoli Sauté

Pickled Beet and Endive Salad

Macédoine of Fruits
Spice Squares

Crab l'Aiglon

Glazed Duck with Bing Cherry Sauce
Wild Rice and Almond Casserole   Stuffed Mushrooms

Tossed Green Salad

Apricot Velvet Pie

Shrimp and Avocado Cocktail

Cornish Hens with Wild Rice Stuffing

Asparagus Polonaise   Curried Baked Fruit

Mixed Green Salad in Creamy
Anchovy Dressing

Rum Cake Supreme

Southern Crab Cakes with Mustard Sauce

Chicken Kiev

Rice and Noodle Pilaf   Broccoli Sauté

Baked Oranges

Belgian Endive in Vinaigrette Sauce

Lime Chiffon Pie

Cream of Tomato Soup

Filet of Sole, Shelly, with Lobster Sauce

Parsleyed New Potatoes   Fried Cucumbers

Asparagus and Watercress Salad

Apricot Crepes

Salmon Mousse with Cucumber Sauce

Roast of Veal

New Potatoes with Caraway Seed   String Beans, Roman Style

Tossed Greens and Grapefruit Salad

Meringue Torte

Onion Soup

Veal Rolls, Marsala

Baked Rice   Peas, Country Kitchen

Pickled Beets

Peaches Victoria
Spiced Walnuts

Gazpacho

Cold Sea Food Platter:
Lobster Mayonnaise (½ lobster per serving)
Fresh lump crab meat in lettuce cup with
French or Russian dressing

Sliced Tomatoes   Cold Zucchini Piquante

Hot Garlic Bread

Mint Sherbet

Watercress Pea Soup

Grilled Shrimp

Pan-Crisped Potatoes   Cauliflower Sauté

Cucumber Salad with Cottage Cheese Dressing

Cream Puffs with Hot Butterscotch Sauce

Mushrooms Trifolati

Curried Sea Food

Boiled Fluffy Rice   Spiced Onions

String Bean Salad

Poached Pears in Sherry Custard Sauce
Fruit-Nut Meringues

18

Herbs and Spices

THE subtle, elusive flavors that judicious use of herbs brings to foods are no secret to most people who cook in these sophisticated days. The renaissance of interest in herb cookery which has taken place over the last few years is evidenced in food markets, where large sections of shelves are devoted to a vast variety. The best way to learn to use herbs effectively is, of course, to experiment with them.

Both herbs and spices should be stored in airtight containers away from heat and direct light. Whole spices like cinnamon sticks and whole cloves will last indefinitely when kept in this manner. Ground spices retain their vitality and aroma for about six months; herbs tend to dry out and lose their flavor after about four months. Consequently, both of these should be purchased in small quantities.

Herbs should always be used with a light hand so that only an expert could tell which are present. As an extremely general guide for amounts, figure about a quarter of a teaspoon of a spice or dried herb (triple that amount when using fresh herbs) per six servings. You can go on from there, adding more as you need it. Once you've overseasoned, there isn't much you can do about it, so proceed with caution. Heating herbs with the fat heightens and extends their flavor.

The dried herb leaves such as tarragon and rosemary should be crumbled finely with the fingers or pulverized with a mortar and pestle when used.

Some herbs have an affinity for almost any food, while others are more limited in their scope. Here is a brief list of some harmonious combinations:

ALLSPICE: Stews, fricassee chicken, pot roasts, fish stews, poached fish or shrimp, and soups.

ANISE SEED: Sweet rolls and breads, French dressing, sweet pickles, cookies, cakes, candy.

BASIL: Any tomato dish, salads, fish and shellfish, aspics.

BAY LEAF: Roast meats or poultry, baked fish, sauces, stews and soups. Use sparingly.

CARAWAY SEED: Cottage cheese spreads, noodles, cole slaw, sauerkraut, potato salad, cookies.

CARDAMOM SEED: Pastries, buns, demitasse, curries.

CELERY SEED: Veal roast and stew, cheese, salads, French dressing, mayonnaise, sea food and meat sauces, cabbage, potatoes.

CHERVIL: Good in blend with other herbs; cottage cheese, any beef dish, roast lamb, cream of tomato sauces, soups and vegetables.

CHIVES: Good in blend with other herbs; cottage cheese, fish, salads, vegetables, cream soups, potatoes.

CINNAMON: Baked custards, bread and rice puddings, cakes, cookies, fruits, sweet potatoes, yellow squash.

CLOVE: Hot cider or tea, cooked fruit dishes, meat and fish sauces, beets, tomatoes, yellow squash.

CORIANDER SEED: Cottage cheese, ground up for buns and biscuits, French dressing, meat stock.

CUMIN SEED: Cottage cheese, rice dishes, codfish, chili con carne, bean and cabbage dishes. (Use with caution)

DILL: When fresh dill is unobtainable, use dill seed or dried dill weed. Good in blend with other herbs; cheese, fish and meat dishes, marinades, fish sauces, potatoes, cabbage, cole slaw, cucumber, green and seafood salads, poultry stuffings.

FENNEL SEED: Breads and biscuits, boiled fish, beef stew, salad dressings, carrots, zucchini and squash.

GINGER: Stewed apples and pears, spiced fruits, curries, chicken, cakes, cookies, veal pot roast, shrimp.

MACE: Any form of beef, fruit salad dressing, creamed crab meat or oysters, carrot, onion or celery dishes.

MARJORAM: Fish, meats, stuffings, poultry, cream soups, vegetables, salads.

MUSTARD SEED: Pickled or marinated meats, potato and tossed green salads, beets, cabbage.

NUTMEG: Beef stew, apple and pear desserts, puddings and sauces, spinach and sweet potatoes.

OREGANO: Tomato dishes, fish, veal stew, roasts, stuffing, green salad, spaghetti sauces.

PARSLEY: Good in blend with other herbs; soups, salads, sauces, stews, vegetables; excellent garnish.

BLACK PEPPER: Freshly ground pepper is excellent as seasoning on all savory dishes and sauces.

POPPY SEED: Sprinkle on almost any canapé spread, cottage cheese, noodles, cole slaw, in sauce with green vegetables and cauliflower, steamed cabbage, potatoes.

ROSEMARY: Any fish, meat, poultry dish, stuffing, vegetables.

SAFFRON: Bouillabaisse and other fish stews, rice pilafs, risottos, chicken, bread and rolls.

SAGE: Cottage cheese, fish chowder, veal roast and stew, soups, vegetables, tomatoes.

SAVORY: Sea food, chicken and meat dishes, cottage cheese, French dressing, tomato salad, vegetables. bean. lentil and split pea soups.

SESAME SEED: Toasted, add to unbaked bread, rolls and pastries, sandwich spreads and cottage cheese, fish stuffing and sauces, chicken salad, asparagus, cabbage, tomatoes and mixed-green salads.

TARRAGON: Tomato juice, fish, shellfish and poultry, mayonnaise, salads, French dressing, sauces, potato and tomato soups, vegetables.

THYME: Cottage cheese spreads, all tomato dishes, roasts, stews, salads, poultry stuffing, fish sauces and stews, onion soup, vegetables.

TURMERIC: Fish, meat and cream sauces, French dressing, curries.

SUMMARY FOR LOW-FAT DIETERS

	USE	AVOID
MEATS *	BEEF: Eye, top and bottom round Lean ground round LAMB: Leg PORK: Lean loin Well-trimmed ham steak Canadian bacon VEAL: Scaloppine Lean loin chops Rump or shoulder Leg of veal Eye roast	All beef richly marbled with fat All visible fat All visible fat Spareribs Fat bacon Sausages All visible fat
POULTRY	Young chickens often, white meat preferred Young turkey (white meat) Duck (no skin)	Fat poultry including skin
FISH AND SEA FOOD	All fish, fresh, dried, frozen, smoked, canned in vegetable oil Shellfish (occasionally)	Canned fish packed in vegetable or cottonseed oil is preferable to that packed in olive oil

* Limit meat portions to 4 to 6 ounces uncooked. Beef, lamb, mutton, pork: no more than 4 times a week.

	USE	AVOID
EGGS	Egg whites, unlimited Up to 4 egg yolks per week	More than 4 egg yolks per week
DAIRY PRODUCTS	Skim milk buttermilk Skim milk (dry and liquid) Skim milk cottage cheese Farmer cheese and hoop cheese Skim evaporated milk Sapsago cheese	Sweet cream Sour cream Whole milk Butter Whole milk cheeses
FATS AND OILS	Safflower, corn, cottonseed Soybean, sunflower oils Homemade mayonnaise and salad dressings Special margarines (see page 307)	Ordinary margarines Hydrogenated vegetable shortenings Lard Coconut oil
SOUPS	Fat-free soups Homemade cream soups (see recipes) Consommé	Canned cream soups Canned soups made with butter or hydrogenated oils Cream soups of unknown ingredients
FRUITS AND VEGETABLES	All fruits All vegetables cooked with polyunsaturated oils	Vegetables prepared in sauces of unknown ingredients
CEREALS AND BAKERY PRODUCTS	All cereals Whole-grain breads, rye bread Breads made without added fats Italian and French bread Hard rolls Homemade cakes, pastries, waffles and pancakes Angel cake Rice Barley Spaghetti, macaroni	Prepared cake mixes made with whole milk or hydrogenated fats All commercially prepared baked goods unless you are sure they do not contain butter, margarine, hard fats, whole milk, cream, etc.

	USE	AVOID
DESSERTS AND SWEETS	Gelatine desserts Imitation ice cream * Jams, jellies, sugar, honey Most pudding mixes when made with skim milk Water ices or sherbets Fresh fruit Canned or frozen fruit Marshmallows, gumdrops Walnuts (desirable) Pecans Almonds Peanuts	Chocolate in all forms Ice cream Puddings made with whole milk Milk sherbets Coconut Cashews Filberts Macadamia nuts
SEASONINGS AND HERBS	All herbs, condiments and spices	

* No butterfat content: available in some states

APPROXIMATE COMPOSITION OF COMMON FOOD FATS

	Cholesterol (Milligrams)	% Polyun-saturates	% Mono-saturates	% Saturates
OILS: Coconut	0	0	8	92
Cocoa Butter	0	5	34	61
Corn	0	58	31	11
Cottonseed	0	59	16	25
Olive	0	7	81	12
Peanut	0	31	46	23
Safflower	0	78	12	10
Sesame	0	43	43	14
Soybean	0	63	21	16
Hydrog. Soybean	0	37	49	14
Sunflower	0	53	15	12
FATS: Butter (1 tablespoon)	30	4	37	59
Lard (1 tablespoon)	13	10	52	38
Crisco	0	26	49	25
Regular hydrogenated shortening	0	7	70	23
SPECIAL MARGARINES:				
Chiffon	0	55	31	14
Sheed's Safflower	0	43	42	15
Saffola	0	43	39	18
Fleischmann's	0	33	48	19
Mazola	0	34	46	20

CHOLESTEROL CONTENTS OF SOME FOODS

Food*	Amount†	Cholesterol (Milligrams)
Brains	2 ounces	1,700
Butter fat	3½ ounces	280
Cheese, cheddar	1 ounce	30
Cream (half-and-half)	¼ cup (4 ounces)	30
Crab meat	3½ ounces	125
Egg yolk	1	236
Fish	3½ ounces	70
Ice cream	½ cup	30
Kidney	2 ounces	250
Liver	3½ ounces	300
Lobster	3½ ounces	200
Meat (lean)	3½ ounces	90
Meat in general	3½ ounces	100
Milk, skim	1 cup	7
Milk, whole	1 cup	30
Oysters	3½ ounces	200
Poultry	3½ ounces	75
Shrimps	3½ ounces	125

*All meats, poultry and fish are cooked weight.
†3½ ounces is approximately 100 grams.

TABLE OF WEIGHTS AND MEASURES

60 drops = 1 teaspoon
3 teaspoons = 1 tablespoon
2 tablespoons = 1 liquid ounce or ⅛ cup
4 tablespoons = ¼ cup
8 tablespoons = ½ cup
16 tablespoons = 1 cup
1 cup = ½ pint (8 ounces)
2 cups = 1 pint
4 cups flour = 1 pound
2 cups granulated sugar = 1 pound
2⅔ cups confectioner's sugar = 1 pound
2⅔ cups brown sugar = 1 pound
4 tablespoons flour = 1 ounce
1 pound walnuts or pecans in shell = ½ pound, shelled
1 cup shelled walnuts or almonds = ¼ pound
1 cup shelled pecans = ⅓ pound
⅓ cup blanched almonds = 1 ounce

TABLE OF CALORIES *

FOODS	PORTIONS	CALORIES
BEVERAGES		
Beer	12 ounces	175
Buttermilk	1 cup	85
Carbonated (cola type)	1 cup	105
Chocolate malted milk	8 ounces	500
Ginger Ale	8 ounces	80
Heavy cream	1 tablespoon	50
Coffee	1 cup	—
Buttermilk (skim milk type)	1 cup	85
Skim milk	1 cup	85
Dry skim milk	1 tablespoon	30
Whole milk	1 cup	165
Mixed drink	1 cocktail glass	155
Whiskey, rye or scotch	1 ounce	75
BREADS, CEREALS, GRAIN PRODUCTS		
French or Vienna	1 slice, average	55
Raisin, plain	1 slice	65
Rye	1 slice	55
White, enriched	1 slice, ½" thick	65
Whole wheat	1 slice, ½" thick	55
BREADS (OTHERS)		
Baking powder biscuit	1 average (2" diameter)	110
Cinnamon bun	1 average	160
Coffee cake (iced)	1 small 4½" square	195
Crackers (saltines, graham)	1 average	15-25
Danish pastry	1 small	140
Doughnut, plain	1 average	135
Flour	1 tablespoon	30
Muffin, corn meal	1 medium	130
Muffin, plain	1 average	120
Pancake	1, 4"	60
Pretzels	5 small sticks	20
Roll, hard white	1 average	95-120
Roll, sweet	1 average	180
Waffle	1 average	215
CEREALS		
Bran flakes	¾ cup	95
Corn flakes	1 ounce (1½ cups)	110
Farina	1 cup cooked	105
Hominy or grits	⅔ cup, cooked	80
Puffed rice	1 cup	55
Oatmeal	1 cup, cooked	150

* Compiled from American Institute of Baking, and H. J. Heinz Co.

FOODS	PORTIONS	CALORIES
Macaroni	1 cup, cooked	210
Noodles	1 cup, cooked	105
Rice (converted)	1 cup, cooked	205
Spaghetti	1 cup, cooked	220

CHEESE

Cheddar	1" cube (1 ounce)	115
Cottage (skim milk)	1 ounce	25
Cream cheese	1 ounce	105
Swiss cheese	1 ounce	105

DESSERTS

Brownies	1 portion, 2x2x¾"	140
Cake		
Angel	⅟₁₂ of 8" cake	110
Chocolate cupcake	1 medium, fudge icing	280
Fruit cake, dark	2x2x½"	105
Plain cake, iced	1 square, 2x2x1"	130
Sponge	⅟₁₂ of 8" cake	115
Cookies	1, 3"	110
Vanilla wafer	1 small	20
Custard, baked	4 oz. (made with skim milk)	105
Gelatine dessert	1 serving (⅔ cup)	110
Eclair, chocolate icing	1 average	315
Ice cream		
Chocolate	¼ pint	240
Peach	¼ pint	280
Vanilla	¼ pint	200
Pie		
Apple (regular)	average serving	375
Cherry (regular)	average serving	360
Custard (regular)	average serving	265
Lemon chiffon (regular)	average serving	210
Pumpkin (regular)	average serving	330
Sherbet	½ cup	200

EGGS

Egg yolk, 60; white, 15	1 medium	75

FATS, OILS AND SALAD DRESSINGS

Butter or margarine	1 tablespoon	115
Cooking fats (vegetable)	1 tablespoon	110
Mayonnaise (commercial)	1 tablespoon	90
French (commercial)	1 tablespoon	60

FRUITS

Apples, raw	1, 2½"	75
Applesauce, sweetened, commercial	1 cup	185

FOODS	PORTIONS	CALORIES
Apricots		
Fresh	3	55
Canned	4 halves and 2 tbsp. syrup	95
Dried, cooked, unsweetened	1 cup	240
Canned, water pack	4 halves, 2 tbsp. juice	30
Avocados, fresh	½	280
Banana, fresh	1 medium (6x1½")	90
Blackberries, fresh	1 cup	85
Cantaloupe, fresh	½ melon, 5"	35
Cherries		
Sweet	25 small, 15 large	60
Canned, red, sour	1 cup	120
Dates, dried or fresh	3-4 pitted	85
Figs, dried	1 large	55
Grapefruit, fresh	½ medium, 4½"	70
Grapes		
Green seedless	1 bunch, about 60 grapes	65
Tokay or Malaga	1 bunch, about 23 grapes	65
Honeydew melon	¼ small, 5"	30
Lemon, fresh	1 medium	30
Orange, fresh	1 medium, 3"	70
Peaches		
Fresh	1 medium (2½x2")	45
Canned, regular	2 halves, 1 tbsp. syrup	70
Canned, water pack	2 halves, 1-2 tbsp. juice	25
Frozen	½ cup, sliced scant	80
Dried, cooked, unsweetened	1 cup	225
Pears		
Fresh	1 medium (3x2½")	95
Canned, regular	2 halves and 2 tbsp. syrup	80
Canned, water pack	2 halves, 1 tbsp. juice	30
Pineapple		
Fresh, diced	1 cup	75
Canned	1 large slice and 2 tbsp. syrup	95
Plums, fresh	1, 2"	30
Prunes, cooked (no sugar)	4-5 medium	105
Raisins (dried)	1 tablespoon	25
	1 cup	430
Raspberries, red	1 cup	70
Rhubarb, cooked	½ cup, sweetened	135
Strawberries, fresh	1 cup	55
Tangerine	1 medium, 2½"	35
Watermelon	½ slice, 1½" thick, 6" diameter	45

FRUIT JUICES

Apple juice	4 ounces	65
Grape juice	3½ ounces	70
Grapefruit juice, unsweetened	3½ ounces	40
Lemon juice	1 tablespoon	4

FOODS	PORTIONS	CALORIES
Orange juice		
Fresh or frozen	3½ ounces	45
Canned, sweetened	4 ounces	75
Pineapple juice, unsweetened	4 ounces	60
Prune juice (bottled)	4 ounces	85
Tomato juice	4 ounces	25

MEAT, POULTRY

FOODS	PORTIONS	CALORIES
Bacon, medium fat	2 strips	95
Beef, cooked, boneless		
Chuck	3 ounces	265
Hamburger	3 ounces	315
Sirloin	3 ounces	255
Dried	2 ounces	115
Corned (canned)	3 ounces	180
Rib (cooked)	2 slices, 3x2¼x¼″	190
Liver, fried	2 ounces	120
Porterhouse, broiled with gravy	5 ounces	515
Tongue	3 slices, 3x2x¼″	160
Heart, beef, uncooked	3 ounces	90
Leg of Lamb, cooked	3 ounces	230
Pork, loin or chops, cooked	3 ounces	285
Pork, cured ham	3 ounces	340
Bologna sausage	2 slices, ¼″ thick, 4½″ diameter	130
Salami sausage	2 slices, ¼″ thick, 3½″ diameter	260
Veal, scaloppine, cooked	3 ounces	185
Chicken, stewed	1 thigh or ½ breast	205
Turkey	2 slices, 3½x2½x¼″	160

FISH

FOODS	PORTIONS	CALORIES
Cod, dried	1 ounce	105
Crabmeat, canned	3 ounces	90
Flounder, uncooked	4 ounces	80
Haddock, baked	3x3x½″	80
Lobster		
baked or broiled	1, ¾ lb.	110
canned	¾ cup	100
fresh	½ cup	84
Oysters, raw	5-8, medium	85
Scallops	6 large	100
Salmon, red, canned	3 ounces	120
Shrimp	5 large	100
Trout, brook, broiled	4-5 ounces	215
Tuna fish, canned, drained	3 ounces	170

SUGARS AND CANDIES

FOODS	PORTIONS	CALORIES
Caramels, plain	1 medium	40
Fudge, plain	1 ounce (1¼″ square)	120

FOODS	PORTIONS	CALORIES
Jams and marmalades	1 tablespoon	55
Jellies	1 tablespoon	50
Sugar, all varieties	1 tablespoon	50
Honey, strained	1 tablespoon	60
Marshmallows	1 ounce	90
Sweet milk chocolate	1 ounce	145

BEANS, PEAS AND NUTS

Almonds, salted	12	100
Beans, red kidney (canned)	1 cup	230
Beans, lima, fresh or canned	½ cup	100
Peanuts	20-24	100
Peanut butter	1 tablespoon	90
Peas, dried, cooked	½ cup	175
Pecans	5 halves	75
Walnuts, English	4 to 8 nut meats	50

VEGETABLES

Asparagus, cooked	6 medium stalks	20
Beans, lima, cooked	1 cup	150
Beans, snap, cooked	1 cup	25
Beets, cooked	1 cup	70
Broccoli, cooked	1 cup	45
Brussels sprouts, cooked	1 cup	60
Cabbage		
Raw, shredded	1 cup	25
Cooked	1 cup	40
Carrots, raw or cooked	1 cup	45
Cauliflower, cooked	1 cup	30
Celery, raw or cooked	1 cup	22
Corn	1, 5" ear	85
Canned, creamed	1 cup	170
Cucumber, uncooked	6 slices, ⅛" thick	5
Eggplant, 4" by ½" thick	3 slices	50
Endive, uncooked	1 pound	90
Kale, cooked	1 cup	45
Lettuce	¼ head	15
	2 to 4 leaves	5
Mushrooms	10 small, 4 large	15
2½"-diameter onion, uncooked	1	45
Scallions	6	25
Parsnips, cooked	1 cup	95
Peas, green, cooked	1 cup	110
Peppers, green, uncooked	1	15
Potatoes		
Baked	1 medium, 2½"	95
Boiled in skin	1 medium	120
French fried	8 pieces	155
Radishes	4 small	5
Sauerkraut, canned	1 cup	30

• COFFEE CREAM •

FOODS	PORTIONS	CALORIES
Spinach, cooked	1 cup	45
Squash		
Summer, cooked	1 cup	35
Winter, baked	1 cup	95
Sweet potatoes		
Baked	5x2"	185
Boiled	5x2½"	250
Tomatoes		
Raw	1 medium, 2x2½"	30
Canned or cooked	1 cup	45
Juice, canned	1 cup	50
Turnips, cooked	1 cup	40
Potato chips	10 pieces, 2"	110

PALATABLE VEGETABLE-OIL MILK *

Dr. Theodore W. Houk of Seattle devised this vegetable-oil mixture for patients who are restricted to skim milk and have been instructed to implement their diet with polyunsaturated oil.

5½ cups cold water
2 cups nonfat milk solids

2⅓ ounces oil
from 4 to 13 drops butter flavor, according to taste

Place all ingredients in 2-quart blender. Blend at high speed for 7 minutes. Store in covered jar in refrigerator. After several hours, most of the foam will have settled. In pouring milk, hold back remaining foam with a spoon. If a little creamlike mixture rises to the top, shake jar to disperse it.

COFFEE CREAM

1 cup cold water
⅓ cup nonfat milk solids

2 ounces oil
4 to 12 drops butter flavor (according to taste)

Combine ingredients and blend for 2 minutes at high speed. Store in pint jar in refrigerator.

* J.A.M.A., Vol. 172, No. 13

GLOSSARY OF COOKING TERMS

BAKE: To cook by dry oven heat.

BARBECUE: To broil or roast on a spit over charcoal. To cook with a special (and usually spicy) barbecue sauce.

BASTE: To moisten food while it is roasting by spooning over it fat, liquid, or pan drippings.

BLANCH: From French *blancher*—to whiten. To make skins of fruits or nuts easily removable by steeping them in boiling water for a few minutes.

BLEND: To mix ingredients together until thoroughly mixed and smooth.

BOIL: To cook in liquid at boiling temperature reached when bubbles rise continually and break on the surface, 212 degrees F. at sea level. At high altitudes, food takes longer to cook.

BRAISE: To brown in fat and cook gently in a little liquid, covered, on top of the stove or in the oven.

BROIL: To cook uncovered on a rack placed under or over direct heat, as in barbecuing or grilling.

BROWN: To cook in little fat at high heat until seared, to seal in juices.

CREAM: To mash or mix one or more foods together until consistency is soft and creamy.

DEEP FRY: To cook in deep hot fat until crisp and brown.

DRIPPINGS: Fat which has drained out of meat and fowl during cooking, becoming liquid (completely expendable).

FRICASEE: To braise individual servings of meat and poultry in sauce or stock.

FRY: To cook in hot fat or oil, uncovered, on top of the stove.

GRILL:	See "Broil."
GRIND:	To reduce to small particles either through a food grinder or with a mortar and pestle.
JULIENNE:	Food cut in long thin strips.
KNEAD:	To work a mixture with the hands, pressing, stretching, and folding to make it smooth.
MACEDOINE:	A mixture of cut-up fruits or vegetables.
MARINATE:	To soak foods in a seasoned, liquid mixture usually containing oil with vinegar, wine or lemon juice to add flavor or to make more tender.
MINCE:	To put through a press or mincer, or to chop finely.
PAN BROIL:	To cook uncovered in a heated skillet with little or no fat, pouring off fat melted from the food.
PAN FRY:	To cook in a skillet on top of the stove with a small amount of fat.
PARBOIL:	To boil until partly cooked.
PARE:	To remove the skin of fruit or vegetables with a knife.
POACH:	To simmer in liquid just below boiling point.
PINCH:	Less than ⅛ teaspoon.
POT ROAST:	To cook a meat roast slowly in a covered pan on top of the stove with added liquid.
PREHEAT:	To heat oven to selected temperature before using.
RICE:	To force food through a fine sieve to make it light and fluffy.
ROAST:	To cook uncovered without water in the oven.
ROUX:	A mixture of oil and flour cooked to a smooth paste in a saucepan and used as thickening. A white roux is cooked long enough to remove

the raw taste of the flour; a brown roux until the mixture turns light brown.

SAUTE: To brown quickly in a little oil on top of the stove.

SCALD: To heat liquid, usually milk, to just below the boiling point, when tiny bubbles start to form and break around the edge. Also, to pour boiling water over food.

SEAR: To brown the surface of the meat at high temperature in a heated skillet either in the oven or on top of the stove to seal in the juices.

SIMMER: To cook in liquid just below the boiling point. Bubbles form slowly and break below the surface. (Temperature 185 degrees F. to 210 degrees F.)

SLIVER: Cut into tiny shreds.

STEAM: To cook food in steam, with or without pressure. Food may be steamed on a rack or in a perforated pan over boiling water, or in a covered container.

STEW: To cook in liquid at simmering temperature.

STOCK: The liquid strained from fish, meat, vegetables, etc.

TENDERIZE: To break down tough connective tissues in meat either by pounding with a cleaver, marinating, or applying a commercial meat tenderizer.

TRIM: To cut away unwanted and unsuitable parts of food either before or after cooking.

TRUSS: To tie wings and legs of a bird to the body with string or skewers so that it holds its shape during cooking.

REFERENCES

1. Ahrens, E. H., Hirsch, J., Insull, W., Tsaltas, T. T., Blomstrand, R., and Peterson, M. L.: Dietary control of serum lipids in relation to atherosclerosis. *J.A.M.A.* 165:1905, 1957.
2. Ahrens, E. H., Tsaltas, T. T., Hirsch, J., and Insull, W.: Effects of dietary fats on the serum lipids of human subjects. *J. Clin. Invest.* 34:918, 1955.
3. American Heart Association: Report by Central Committee for Medical and Community Program. Dietary fat and its relation to heart attacks and strokes. *J.A.M.A.* 175:389, 1961.
4. Bronte-Stewart, B.: Effect of dietary fats on the blood lipids and their relation to ischemic heart disease. *Brit. M. Bull.* 14:243, 1958.
5. Bronte-Stewart, B., Antonis, A., Eales, L., and Brock, J. F.: Effects of feeding different fats on serum cholesterol level. *Lancet* 1:521, 1956.
6. Flipse, N. Jay: Pathogenesis of Coronary Artery Disease. *J.A.M.A.*, Vol. 172, No. 11, p. 1130, Mar. 12, 1960.
7. Hilditch, T. P.: *Chemical Composition of Natural Fats* (3rd Ed.), Chapman and Hall, London, 1956.
8. Houk, T. W.: Palatable vegetable oil milk. *J.A.M.A.*, 172:1387, 1960.
9. Jolliffe, N.: *Reduce and Stay Reduced*. (rev. ed.) Simon and Schuster, New York, 1957.
10. Jolliffe, N.: Fats, cholesterol and coronary heart disease. *New York J. Med.*, 57:2684, 1957.
11. Jolliffe, N., Rinzler, S. H.: Practical dietary control of serum cholesterol in free-living American men aged 50 to 59. *Postgraduate Medicine*, Vol. 29, No. 6, June, 1961.
12. Keys, A.: Diet and the development of coronary heart disease. *J. Chron. Dis.* 4:364, 1956.
13. Keys, Ancel and Margaret: *Eat Well and Stay Well*. Doubleday.
14. Kinsell, L. W., Michaels, G. C., Friskey, R. W., and Splitter, S.: Essential fatty acids, lipid metabolisms and atherosclerosis. *Lancet* 1:334, 1958.
15. Kinsell, L. W., Partridge, J., Boling, L., Margen, S., and Michaels, G.: Dietary modification of serum cholesterol and phospholipid levels. *J. Clin. Endocrinol.* 12:909, 1952.
16. Malmros, H. and Wigand, G.: Atherosclerosis and deficiency of essential fatty acids. *Lancet* II:749, 1959.
17. Page, I. H.: Dietary Fat and its relation to heart attacks and strokes. *Circulation* 23, 133 (1961).
18. Page, I. H.: The pathogenesis of atherosclerosis as of January 1961.

N. Y. Heart Association Conference on Atherosclerosis, Jan. 24, 1961.

19. Pollack, H.: Linoleic acid contents of fats and oils. *J.A.M.A.* 172: 1165, 1960.

20. Rinzler, S. H. *et al.*: The Anti-Coronary Club, A Dietary Approach to the Prevention of Coronary Heart Disease: A Seven-Year Report. American Journal of Public Health, February, 1966.

21. Council on Foods and Nutrition of the American Medical Association. The Regulation of Dietary Fat. J.A.M.A., August 4, 1962.

22. Stamler, J. *et al.*: Coronary Artery Disease. Archives of Environmental Health. September, 1966.

23. White, P. D.: *Atheroma and Thrombosis: Major Threats to our Health Today.* Lyman Duff Memorial Lecture, Council on Arteriosclerosis, American Heart Association, American Society for the Study of Arteriosclerosis, Nov. 8, 1959, 21:65, 1960.

Index

GENERAL INDEX

RECIPE INDEX